Ethics of Citizenship

William A. Barbieri Jr.

Ethics of Citizenship

Immigration and Group Rights in Germany

Duke University Press   Durham and London   1998

© 1998 Duke University Press
All rights reserved
Printed in the United States of
America on acid-free paper ∞
Typeset in Carter and Cone Galliard
by Keystone Typesetting, Inc.
Library of Congress Cataloging-in-
Publication Data appear on the last
printed page of this book.

Because of Gabriele

Contents

I t is now a commonplace that in the wake of the Cold War the new world order has become increasingly shaped by the politics of ethnic, national, and racial identity. Yet, all too little reflection has been devoted to the lineaments of the political and moral challenges presented by this development. There is a pressing need to increase our understanding of the ethical dimensions of the diversity that has come to characterize contemporary societies. Indispensable to this effort are sustained exercises in applied ethics focused on specific cases. Such is the role envisioned for this book.

No study of the ethics of diversity can ignore the central significance of modern citizenship. Although this institution may be evolving, its division of the world's population according to membership in states continues to constitute the basic political and legal reality within which the rights and wrongs of interactions among collectivities are formulated and contested. Equally important, citizenship itself serves as a primary basis of identity, one that has become imbued with its own corresponding set of moral meanings. For these reasons, citizenship forms one of the poles of analysis for my inquiry.

The other pole is the notion of group rights. In a certain sense, group rights are inseparable from the basic idea enshrined in citizenship—especially nation-state citizenship—of the self-determination of peoples. More germane to present-day debates, however, is the understanding of group rights embodied in multiculturalism—the belief that ethnic or cultural plurality should be respected and, where appropriate, legally and politically protected. Group rights in this sense appear to cut against citizenship in two ways: From the point of view of the citizenry as a whole, they seem to imply factionalism, while from the point of view of the individual citizen, they may smack of collectivism. This apparent conflict, however, is belied, or at least ameliorated, by an underlying commitment to equality and human rights that unites the ideals of democratic citizenship and group rights. That, at any rate, is part of the argument of this book.

The setting for the ethical analysis presented here is the Germany of today. In its very public struggle over how to deal with "guestworkers" and other migrant groups, in its rapidly growing diversity, and in its pronounced preoccupation with problems of national identity, Germany provides an instructive case for exploring the ethics of citizenship and diversity. This is not to say, however, that the German case simply provides a concrete context for the presentation of an abstract thesis or for the examination of a problem generic in its outlines. Applied ethics takes its shape as much from the particulars of its subject matter as it does from the theoretical concerns that guide it. As a result, not only the structure of this study but to some extent its conclusions emerge from the specific features of the discourse surrounding the area of collective activity I designate as German membership policy.

All the same, there remains an overarching concern that guides the inquiry presented here: How, ethically speaking, do communities constitute themselves? On one level, this question calls for social analysis of the sort that is requisite for any serious work in applied ethics. To this end this study attempts to trace the mechanisms and history of the formation of communal boundaries in German society. At a deeper level, however, this question requires reflection on a constellation of normative issues having to do with what I would call *constitutive justice* (as opposed to the commutative, distributive, and retributive varieties). Who is entitled to belong to a political—or moral—community? In what ways? On what basis? Achieving a measure of clarity in how we think about such matters is, in the rapidly changing world of the present, a task of no little moment. If the account I present of human rights, equality, and the morality of membership contributes in some small way to this goal, this book will have more than fulfilled its purpose.

In the process of writing, I have incurred debts to many people in several countries. Heading the list of those I would like to thank for their guidance, advice, and assistance are Margaret Farley and Ian Shapiro, who, in their distinctive ways, gave challenging support to the project in its first incarnation as a dissertation in Yale University's ethics program. Prof. Dr. Jürgen Fijalkowski of the Free University of Berlin very graciously served as an additional advisor and critic for the parts of the study dealing with the German case. Helpful comments on sections dealing with their areas of expertise were provided by Helmut Walser Smith and Steffen Angenendt. I also profited from conversations with Yasemin Soysal, Ertekin Özcan, Liselotte Funcke, Barbara John, Almuth Berger, Jim Grossklag, and Michael Walzer, as well as from discussions with members of the Political Science Department at the Hebrew University of Jerusalem and the Council for Research in Values and Philosophy at the Catholic University of America, where some of the ideas of the book were presented. Finally, I benefited from the suggestions of Valerie Millholland at Duke University Press and several anonymous reviewers.

For financial and logistical support, I am grateful to several organizations. A Mellon Fellowship from the Institution for Social and Policy Studies at Yale University and a stay at the Free University of Berlin's Otto Suhr Institute sponsored by the Friedrich Ebert Foundation enabled me to carry out my initial program of research. Additional phases of the project were made possible through grants from Yale's Council on West European Studies and the Orville Schell Center for Human Rights, as well as a Yale Dissertation Year Fellowship. I received invaluable help from the staffs of various archives and libraries in Berlin, Bonn, and Zirndorf. The production of the manuscript was facilitated by a research grant-in-aid from Catholic University.

Lastly I wish to thank the club Türkspor-Berlin for the opportunity to have extended my soccer career in the context of my work.

"Guestworkers" and the Ethics

of Political Membership

Our citizenship—official membership in a particular political community—constitutes a part of our identity that we seldom have cause to question. It is true that the passport we possess determines a great deal: whether we may enter and leave a country at our will, live and work there, own and inherit property, vote and serve in political office; whether, where, and when we may be asked to stake our lives in military service. Citizenship, too, greatly affects our economic prospects, for the right to live in one of the world's wealthy societies is a valuable commodity indeed. Yet because it is something that we usually acquire at birth, we tend to think of our citizenship as a given, objective aspect of our existence, much like our gender or religion or ethnic character. This assumption is made as often by the politicians who shape the conditions of our society as it is by the philosophers who theorize about them. In actuality, however, political membership is a human creation, a status we grant to ourselves, and given its importance we might reasonably ask why it is given to some and not to others. The question is posed particularly sharply in the challenge to modern nation-state citizenship presented by transnational migration and its effects.

In the past few decades, many states have witnessed the formation of new minorities of long-term resident aliens who live without some of the basic rights associated with citizenship. These minorities consist primarily of migrant laborers—"guestworkers"—and their family members, although more and more they have come to include illegal immigrants and refugees fleeing perils of various sorts: focused government persecution, wars, natural and man-made disasters, and the debilitating effects of poverty and other forms of structural disadvantage. The migrants have settled — often permanently — and participate in the daily life of all the leading democratic societies of the West; nonetheless, in most cases they have not found full acceptance as *members* of these societies.

This is not to say that they exist wholly without rights in their host countries. These "denizens"[1] often enjoy an assortment of civil, social, economic, and cultural rights comparable to those of their neighbors. Still, in one deeply important sense they remain apart: Because they do not possess citizenship and, indeed, often find it effectively denied them, they are blocked from political membership — the possession of the basic civil and political rights that make up the core of belonging in a political community.[2] They are consigned instead to a sort of political limbo, a perpetual state of partial membership and disenfranchisement in which their powerlessness to promote their interests magnifies any inequalities or discrimination they may face in other spheres.[3] In this sense these migrants are akin to other groups in recent history, such as the blacks under apartheid in South Africa and the Palestinians in the Israeli-occupied territories, that have been assigned a subordinate membership status in the political and social ordering of the society in which they live.

Why long-term resident aliens are included in many spheres yet remain barred from political membership is in one sense a historical question,[4] and in another sense a political question.[5] At the same time, it is an ethical question,[6] for the subordination of this population prompts us to ask: Is a status of permanent partial membership *justifiable* for these (to some extent uninvited) groups? On what *normative* basis may they be denied political membership? Answers to these characteristically moral questions depend in turn on more fundamental considerations: What *rational* grounds do states have for excluding people? Who is *entitled* to full membership (i.e., citizenship) in a political community, and on what terms?

Because migration is, at root, a global phenomenon, most of the problems it poses may ultimately be addressed only by concerted efforts on the part of the international community aimed at establishing peace, promoting development, and protecting human rights. In the current world system, however, the political exclusion of migrants constitutes an exception to this rule. *Who* receives political membership and *how* are issues governed by the citizenship, immigration, and naturalization policies of individual states, which jealously guard a sphere of authority they regard as touching on the very core of their right to self-determination.

Within states, the persons entrusted with the formation and revision of these policies may not regard their task as an ethical one; instead, they may see questions of citizenship as problems to be resolved with reference to objective legal standards or according to "natural" criteria dealing with ethnic or national identity. Whether they recognize it or not, however, policymakers faced with questions regarding political membership are always required to make judgments on a basic set of moral and political issues: Who should be allowed to enter the country? Should political membership be based on nationality or residence? Is assimilation to the dominant culture an acceptable precondition for the extension of political rights? What is a fair price for citizenship? Moreover, arguments and concrete proposals regarding such issues necessarily presuppose views about the nature and proper scope of political organization, the character that membership should assume, and the appropriate normative basis for distributing this membership. And these views in turn reflect fundamental assumptions about the nature of human beings. The premise of my treatment is that it is with reference to these underlying moral commitments that competing political claims concerning membership are best compared and criticized.

This book thus aims to provide an ethical analysis of modern citizenship. Citizenship, of course, has two basic senses that in the present day remain only tangentially connected. First, it refers to a status employed to classify people, a form of membership, a legal and political identity we often refer to as nationality. Second, it indicates an ideal or virtue or type of responsibility involving public-spiritedness or patriotism. Our concern is with the formal rather than the explicitly ethical dimension of citizenship.[7] But this is hardly to say that the status of citizenship is devoid of moral content. It is rather to note that the focus of our inquiry is on the group of moral issues relevant to — and indeed inextricable from — citizenship viewed as a question of social structure, as opposed to a question of individual morality.

Among these issues, the matter of rights is certainly a prominent one. As a powerful instrument for drawing boundaries and shaping interactions within and among contemporary societies, citizenship leaves a deep imprint not only on moral identity but also on the web of structured interpersonal relationships most commonly described today in terms of rights and duties. Because citizenship mediates in this manner among the concerns of persons, social groups, and entire political communities, it addresses the rights not only of individuals but also of various collectivities. Beyond this, the issue of the basis of citizenship is intimately bound up with questions regarding the relations between moral and legal rights and the very foundations of law. For these reasons an ethical examination of citizenship is also an examination of rights — civil and human, of individuals and groups.

It is likewise an examination of the nature and basis of equality, for central to the notion of citizenship is the idea of relations among equals. Citizenship policy, augmented by the workings of the international economy, provides the primary means for the social construction of equal and less-than-equal relations among persons and groups in the modern world, most evident in the wide gaps in socioeconomic and political conditions that exist among states. At the same time, the negative connotation of "second-class citizenship" in contemporary political discourse illustrates a broad acceptance, at least in democratic milieux, of equality of citizenship as a norm of justice. Equal citizenship takes into its compass not only suffrage but also civil rights and a basic quality of life for all groups within a state. Its treatment of equality and rights distinguishes this book as a study in the ethics of political community.[8]

My exploration of the ethical issues posed by long-term resident aliens focuses on a particular case, that of the migrant worker minority in the Federal Republic of Germany. The German case provides a particularly clear example of the problems of citizenship, rights, and equality raised by the political exclusion of foreign residents. Of the roughly five million members of Germany's migrant worker minority (following reunification, about 6 percent of the population), nearly all are permanent residents. Due largely to the restrictive nature of Germany's political membership policies, however, a negligible few have become German citizens. As a result, these residents are locked into a subordinate role in German society, in which they are greatly hindered in their efforts to combat the various forms of inequality and discrimination they face. The general consensus among German policymakers is that this situation is not tenable in the long run. Disagreement prevails, however, as to what an appropriate solution might be. Through my discussion of German debates on such topics as voting rights, cultural homogeneity, and dual citizenship, I seek to provide an empirical grounding for my analysis of the ethical aspects of political membership.

Based on my treatment of these debates, I provide a typology of influential normative orientations toward political membership in modern states, ranging from an extremely exclusive view to an extremely inclusive one. In explicating and criticizing these competing views, I attempt to show that they are based on incomplete political anthropologies. I then set about developing a normative theory of political membership that incorporates a more balanced understanding of the significance of human communality, individuality, and universality for political life.

The theory I present is in some respects based on Michael Walzer's account of the just distribution of membership in *Spheres of Justice* (1983). Unlike Walzer, however, I argue that decisions about political membership should be governed by considerations of *human rights*. This follows from the peculiar nature of membership in modern states. After providing an account of human rights grounded in a prohibition against domination, I argue that established residents of states have a right to citizenship and moreover, in democratic states at least, a right to *equal* citizenship.

Equality in this context, I further contend, should be understood to apply to groups as well as to individuals; for this reason, equal citizenship for new minorities will often entail not only political inclusion on an individual basis but also the provision of various sorts of group rights. This perspective carries with it some fairly concrete implications for directions in which a more just political membership policy in Germany might be sought.

The book is divided into five chapters. Chapter 1 is devoted to an account of the historical context informing contemporary discussions of political membership in Germany. In it I provide a set of historical theses regarding German membership, followed by a description of how the migrant worker minority became established and an examination of the ways in which this minority is subordinated. Chapter 2 consists of a characterization of the policymaking process in Germany coupled with an analysis of a number of specific "membership debates" concerning Germany's migrant minority. Based on this analysis I distinguish five basic normative orientations toward political membership. In Chapter 3, after a brief methodological discussion regarding political anthropologies, I criticize these orientations with reference to their empirical suppositions, internal consistency, and assumptions about the political nature of human beings. Chapter 4 contains a proposed alternative account, provided in two parts, of just criteria for the attribution of political membership: first, a critical exposition of Michael Walzer's theory of membership and second, a constructive argument about modern political membership, human rights, domination, equality, and consent. In Chapter 5 I spell out the understanding of equal citizenship and group rights that follows from this argument and offer some reflections on the implications of my theory for the German case. The migrants, I propose, not only should be extended the individual political rights accompanying formal citizenship but also should be granted certain group rights in the economic and cultural spheres. Along with my suggestions, I offer some observations on the limits of the view I have presented and on the future of political membership. I conclude that despite the ongoing evolution of political structures, the institution of citizenship in independent and sovereign states is likely to maintain its central importance to us for some time. For this reason, it is all the more important that we persist in subjecting the attribution of citizenship to rigorous ethical scrutiny.

Chapter One

The Making of Boundaries

Although they are as a rule born and raised in Germany and fluent in the language, the children of migrant workers are in many ways less than the equals of their classmates. A class field trip to Switzerland, for example, may be out of bounds for them for reasons having to do with citizenship, residence permits, and visas. Their history and cultural heritage receive little or no attention in textbooks that chronicle the accomplishments of the German *Volk*. Their chances of eventually finding an apprenticeship or winning a spot at a university, statistics show, are slim. Beyond the classroom, the subtle and not-so-subtle forms of discrimination, the poor social and economic possibilities, and the administrative hurdles and legal barriers do not cease. In the only world they know, these children remain outsiders, their existence marked indelibly by the marginalized status of the foreign resident.

Any attempt to understand how and why this marginalization has occurred must begin in a historical vein. The boundaries that have come to separate migrant worker families from other German residents have emerged through the conjuncture of two processes: the complex definition over the past several centuries of what it means to be German, and the more recent formation of the migrant worker minority in German society. Through an analytical treatment of these two processes and the forms of human agency they have involved, we may gain a picture of the norms and structures that have enabled the establishment of a subordinate status for Germany's foreign residents.

Toward a History of German Membership

An analysis of the historical process through which membership in the German context has been defined necessarily begins with the question, What is German membership? In answering this question, the first step must be to establish the meaning of its terms. Logically, the notion of membership suggests an entity in which membership is held by a group of persons satisfying a given set of criteria. Much depends, therefore, on which entity one specifies and on which criteria, as well as on who does the judging. Membership may be ascriptive or voluntary; it may also be a matter of degree. The case of German membership provides an excellent illustration of these inherent complexities. Is a German one who speaks German as his or her native language? One who has German forebears? One who was born on German territory? One who lives in a German society? One who identifies him or herself as German? One who possesses German citizenship?

Each of these criteria plays an important role in the context of this study, for each points to a crucial aspect of what we might call German belongingness — the normative basis for the distribution and denial of those goods and burdens associated with being German. Historically, who has counted as German has been shaped by a number of diverse factors, among them the development of an ethnic and eventually a national German consciousness,[1] the formation of a succession of distinct German political entities, the economic transformations and migrations associated with the transition to industrial capitalism, religious conflicts,[2] the establishment of compulsory education and the standardization of a German national culture, the growth of a German citizenship with an accompanying administrative apparatus, the presence at times of other ethnic minorities in German states, and the construction of a modern welfare system. A full account of the complex interplay of these factors, in short, *a history of German membership,* would take us far afield. Nonetheless, some such account is essential for an inquiry into the nature of membership in Germany today. What follows is an outline of a set of historical theses regarding German membership and then, to illustrate the theses, a selective overview of developments bearing on membership in the last two hundred years of German history.

1. *German membership is best understood for political purposes in terms of*

three overlapping but distinguishable communities: the German ethnic group or Kulturnation, *the German state society,*[3] *and the German citizenry.* These three strands of German membership have informed one another considerably and at the same time have remained distinct. Their distinctness is perhaps best captured with reference to one of the distinguishing aspects of the concept of membership itself: Membership implies both inclusion and exclusion, and we may always ask, of whom and on what basis?

– The first membership group, the ethnocultural nation, differentiates among persons on the basis of ethnicity. Although ethnic identity is a notoriously intractable topic,[4] we may say provisionally that this group includes those who speak German, have a German heritage, are of German stock, and are identified by others and by themselves as Germans. Excluded as a rule are those of other ethnic or national groups: the French, Russians, Turks, Native Americans, Kurds.

– The second membership group, the state society, differentiates on a structural basis. Its members are included in various ways and to different degrees, but in general they participate in society, enjoy rights, and receive benefits, all in economic, social, and political ways.[5] State societies are administratively and territorially distinct from other states and may deny admission and residence to members of other states.

– Membership in the German citizenry is defined in terms of both ascriptive identity and common political commitment. The community of German citizens has the character of a club open only to persons belonging to both the ethnocultural nation and the state. Eligible are those who take part in the life of the state society, who belong to the German cultural group, and who are prepared to assume the responsibility of political control and to sacrifice their lives if necessary for the defense of the German state. This group excludes German ethnics in other countries and members of German society who lack the requisite German ethnocultural membership. The definition of German citizens is, as we shall see, in some ways an unhappy compromise between the other two groups.

2. *Historically, these three groups have been formed through interrelated yet analytically distinct processes.* The context in which these groups interact is the modern system of nation-state capitalism, and it follows that their nature and scope have been decisively shaped by the political, social, and

economic processes through which our present global society of sovereign nations has emerged. The rise of nation-states has been the topic of a considerable body of scholarship, which may be drawn from to show how each of the three German membership groups has undergone its own process of development — for the first group, a process of nation-building, for the second group, of state-building, and for the third group, of what I call *"civitas*-building" — the construction of a distinct community of citizens.

– Nation-building in Germany has thus involved, independent of a fixed political basis, the origins and growth of a sense of ethnic community and shared culture, as well as the definition of enemies and perceived threats to a unified German identity.

– German state-building has been characterized by the gradual but thoroughgoing establishment of centralized control over a territory and populace, through military and other coercive means, the construction of a unified market and a highly industrialized economy, the ambitious pursuit of state and ethnonational interests in foreign policy, and the eventual construction of a comprehensive welfare systems.

– The central dynamic in the German process of *civitas*-building has been the development of a distinction between natives and aliens (*Inländer* and *Ausländer*) and the evolution of an accompanying set of privileges and controls.

These three processes have of course been closely intertwined. For example, the case of nation-building has been aided decisively by the administrative homogeneity and compulsory education required for effective state-building. Cultivation of the German language has been of central significance to all three groups. Each, however, has exhibited individual features that it is important to identify in order to grasp the tensions inherent in German membership policy today.

Nation-Building
When people speak of Germans, it is usually taken for granted that the word refers to a concrete, identifiable group, be it a kinship organization, a community of native speakers, or a group of initiates into a cohesive cultural entity. Particularly when employed in contrast to other comparable groups — Turks, for instance — references to Germans seem to have a relatively clear meaning and fixed referent. At the same time,

the problems associated with concepts such as culture, identity, race, and ethnic groups are well known.[6] And although the attribute "German" may seem to indicate an objective, ahistorical category, the elusive nature of this concept becomes clear as soon as borderline cases, such as black Germans or German-Soviet Jews, are examined.[7] The German ethnic classification has not always been distinct, but is rather a historical product that even now encompasses a highly diverse group. The degree of homogeneity and unity responsible for the coherence of the term "German" is the outcome of a long process of cultural and political inclusion and exclusion, of identification and differentiation — of, in a phrase, ethnic boundary making. Such boundary making, problematic though it may be, is a universal phenomenon. The hallmark of the German process is that its cultural and political aspects have been largely independent of one another.

Thus, the sense of ethnic identity and community among Germans considerably predates the existence of the modern German state. On the one hand, we can identify a cultural entity based on a common language, certain general traditions, and the occupation of a specific territory in central Europe. The collective consciousness of this group has been to a great extent created by intellectuals. On the other hand, this territory was marked by a number of different types of political organizations, and it was only relatively late, after comparable developments had occurred in France and England, that a modern nation-building process characterized by a widespread attempt to create a homogeneous national culture was launched. The characteristic goal of nation-building is to "increase the loyalty, commitment and acquiescence" of the people in order to strengthen community bonds for purposes of both defense and political control (Tilly 1975b, 78–79) and is pursued through the standardization of language, religion, and education, as well as through the writing of history. This state-initiated process has gone quite far in Germany, but it has not wholly replaced the ethnic basis of identity, evidenced by the continuing recognition of German minorities left out of the nation-building process but nonetheless identified as German.

While the term "German" referred originally to a speech group distinguished from Latin speakers, most accounts locate the cradle of German national consciousness in the Holy Roman Empire of the German Nation founded by Charlemagne. The political consciousness that developed at this early point was, however, as Werner Conze argues, decidedly not a national consciousness in the modern sense of nation-states (1985, 27). Rather, the political framework in which German consciousness found expression was that of an empire within which Germans as a people were distinct from other component groups. More-over, the sense of identity as German was not particularly strong in relation to other memberships. The climate of the times did not rein-force this sense, for as Charles Tilly notes, the Europe of the fifteenth century was in the degree and scope of its homogeneity comparable only to imperial China, while the primary memberships and bases of loyalty were overwhelmingly local and religious (1975a, 18). Following the Renaissance and the Reformation, a gradual increase in ethnonational German consciousness occurred (Conze 1985, 28–30), yet by the mid-dle of the eighteenth century the notion of a distinct German nation had become centuries removed from any organizational reality.

At this point, however, two important developments in German iden-tity occurred, largely in response to developments in France.[8] While the spread of the universal values of the Enlightenment culminated in a revolution in France that heralded the birth of a modern political con-ception of "nation," early critical reflection on the notion of "nation" in the German principalities tended to emphasize the cultural aspects of nationhood, as reflected for example in Herder's definition of *"Volk"* or Schiller's notion of an *"inneres Reich."* The prevailing intellectual en-vironment, which to that point was exemplified by the benign cosmo-politanism of Goethe, began increasingly to celebrate the particularity, the nobility, of being *German*. This growing national consciousness was abruptly politicized following Napoleon's conquest of Prussia in 1806. A surge of patriotic sentiment in reaction to the French occupation glori-fied German cultural particularity and portrayed it as being suppressed by the alien, universalist ideas of the French regime. A seminal role was played in this process by Fichte's *Reden an die deutsche Nation,* which, in its evocation of a suppressed German spirit ("To have character and to be German are clearly synonymous"; cited in L. Hoffmann 1990, 77 [my translation]), helped mobilize resistance to the French, culminating in the War of Liberation from 1813 to 1815.[9]

In the wake of liberation, the prior individual German states were restored. This restoration, however, did not prevent the newly invigorated sense of collective purpose from developing further through movements in philosophy and literature. Romantic writers, in their emphasis on feeling over rationality, on the significance of "thick" tradition and cultural unity over hollow, soulless universalism, at once crystallized and valorized a new German identity. Thinkers such as Friedrich von Savigny, Leopold von Ranke, and G. W. F. Hegel[10] contributed to a conception of the German nation as an individualized organic entity, a *Volksgeist* expressed in a unique language and set of customs.[11] The state was required as the *expression* of the organic spirit of the people, its logical outcome; but the people were prior. While the military, political, and geographic realities of central Europe worked against the formation of a comprehensive German state, as the fate of the 1848 revolution illustrated,[12] Romantic notions of the ethnocultural unity of the German people formed an ideology that eventually served as a legitimating basis in the formation of the German nation-state.

With the founding of the German *Reich* following a second victory over France, a new era of nation-building as a concerted effort to homogenize the population and culture began. In the new Prussian-dominated state, German national feeling was harnessed in an effort to build a unified and loyal populace (Kocka 1985). As a result, Germanness was intimately linked to the military buildup and foreign policy adventures of the late nineteenth century. The presence of minorities in German territory, in particular the Poles,[13] was exploited to sharpen the sense of being German and to fuel a need for ethnic unity. This was reflected in the energetic prosecution of the *Kulturkampf* against the Catholic influence in Germany, as well as in the alarmed identification of an *Überfremdungsgefahr* (the danger of too strong a foreign presence) and the widespread implementation of Germanization policies directed against ethnic minorities (Hagen 1980, 120–50; Herbert 1986, 24–25; Woydt 1987, 17–18). At this point, the prevailing notion of Germanness was not simply a matter of language, birthright, tradition, or place of residence, although each of these played a role. Rather, the ideas of intellectuals describing the German *Volk* as a sort of cohesive reality unto itself, or at least a prospective reality that was to be gradually implemented through the cultural consolidation of a German polity, had begun to take root. Being German was a question of quality, and other ethnic or national groups in German society were often distinguished as lesser or inferior (Lepsius 1985, 51). In effect, following the creation of the German *Kaiserreich,* a cultural group was continuously constructed in which Germans were not simply members but also components of a higher ontological unit, the people (Bauer 1975). The sense of people-hood led at the turn of the century to a volatile Pan-German movement as well as to calls for the assumption of sovereignty over Austria. The actual basis of belonging to the German ethnocultural group remained intangible. Yet as Lutz Hoffmann argues, even if no German "people" existed prior to political consolidation in fact, once the ideology of an age-old, living *Volk* became internalized politically, such a national group became a social reality (1990, 86).

Although social-democratic ideas long provided a counterpoint to this ideology and began to exert a greater influence following the turn of the century, the ruling political elements were able to develop the ideol-ogy of the *Volk* relatively continuously. In the propaganda of World War I, the conflict between a German culture with its own ideas and mores and an encroaching coalition of enlightenment values emphasizing egali-tarian individualism and natural rights emerged again (Dumont 1986, 134). The German national identity at this point, according to Ernst Troeltsch, took on a certain religious quality: "The 'mystique of the German state' is a secularization of the religious conception of the state, while the German idea of freedom is a secularization of the religious sense of duty" (1925, 96; my translation). The notion of a German national state hence took on more and more of the weight of sentiment originally assigned to the ethnic group and other memberships, and attempts to establish a uniform national-cultural membership continued following the failed experiment with democracy in Weimar Germany. In Nazi Germany these attempts took on an explicitly biological nature and culminated in efforts at racial purification through mass extermination and other means. Attempts in the course of the German reconstruction on the part of both the liberal-democratic and communist German states to distance themselves from the tradition of German particularism went only so far. The *Kulturnation* remains the basis of political organization, and reunification, with its slogan *Wir sind ein Volk* ("We are one peo-ple"), has led to an invigorated sense of national identity and pride that has defined itself further in opposition to the groups of foreign workers and refugees now present in Germany.

To summarize, the process of evolution from a decentralized group sharing certain common linguistic and cultural characteristics but without a common political or administrative base, into a relatively unified community claiming a common heritage, culture, and destiny — and even at times a collective *Volksgeist* — has occurred in a comparatively short time as a result of considerable effort on the part of elites and in a creative opposition to (and often at the expense of) other groups who have provided antitheses to certain values affirmed as "German." Military events have played a decisive role. The overtaking of an initial process of ethnic identification (nation-forming) by a concentrated period of linking cultural unity to national political aims (nation-building) has resulted in a consolidation of membership in a German nation based primarily on subjective characteristics. The composite member, the "German," speaks German and has, among other things, a "German" bloodline, an identification with "German" culture and history, a "German" pride and/or guilt, a "German" physical appearance, and a sense of belonging to the "German" community and polity.

State-Building

The development of the state society as an organ of German membership has occurred within a considerably shorter time frame than has that of the German national identity, although as with the German ethnocultural nation, the modern German state drew on traditions substantially predating its birth in 1871. Before thematizing this process, it is necessary to say something about what is meant by the state society as a membership group. As used here, the term refers to a group of governing and governed united by a set of differentiated institutions that order and control life within certain territorial boundaries. A significant aspect of this understanding is that membership in the state society is a *structural* matter as opposed to a question of identification or recognition. This is not to say that membership is wholly involuntary, nor, for that matter, that it is always possible to determine in an objective sense who is a member and who is not. Still, to a certain degree the extension of the modern mechanisms of state control has tended to render people its subjects willy-nilly, even as it has given them a say in its development through suffrage, interest groups, and the possibilities of mass politics.

In Germany, the development of a membership group defined by the state in this sense has naturally been intricately bound up with the process of building German national identity. The German case is distinctive in that these two processes have often worked apart from or against one another. The Prussian state was a subnational organization, and its expansion into a nation-state never truly attained the original supranational scope of the ethnocultural group; the post–World War II history, including the present German identity conflicts (for example, the "German Question" and the *Historikerstreit*), provides a good illustration of how state and nation have come in conflict. At the same time, of course, the two processes have greatly reinforced one another — nation-building in its function as a social cement necessary for loyalty to and effective administration by the state; and state-building as a concrete focus for the national pride of citizens and as a means for organizing the aspirations of ethnic Germans elsewhere.

At root, the processes of nation- and state-building have produced analytically separate collectivities that have evolved in comparable ways. As with nation-building, central themes for state-building have been the unification and homogenization of a German group on the one hand, and the exploitation of foreign groups on the other — both for purposes of differentiation and for satisfying the material requirements for building state control and a national economy. And as in the development of national consciousness, the creation of the state has relied heavily on the activities of elites and on military developments. A dynamic particular to the state-building process has revolved around the distribution of power. The German national state has long claimed a distinctive nature as a *Rechtsstaat*, a constitutional state. The building of this state has involved a dual process of *Verstaatlichung,* the increase of the degree and pervasiveness of centralized state power, and *Verrechtlichung,* the extension of rights and privileges of members of state society. This process is a common Western European development; in Germany, its specific course has resulted in a comparatively rule-oriented and authoritarian political culture.

In keeping with the federal nature of the German nation-state, statebuilding has occurred in two major steps in Germany. Like the process of building national identity, the construction of the German state after 1871 drew on a prior tradition of state formation. Of the various eighteenth-century states in German territories, Prussia was clearly the strongest. Yet before the Prussian state model took over a dominant role on German territory, a number of separate organizations with diverse state systems coexisted. The greatest contrast to the Prussian model was provided by Catholic states in the south with strong traditions of participatory democracy. The German states varied as well in their economic structures. But they had in common their successful restructuring of power from a purely local to a more centralized level. By comparison with other European states, local bodies of representative government were undermined by the German princes to an extreme degree (Tilly 1975a, 22). This was accomplished in part through the administrative establishment of memberships at a central level, coordinated by and among the states, eventually through a treaty system. The dividing up of the people was a function taken over from communities in order to carry out state policies regarding problems at a high structural level such as poverty. These memberships, and the services and obligations in terms of taxes they defined, remained primarily at the individual state level well into the history of the *Reich*.

In the *Kaiserreich*, this process was carried out on a broader scale and dominated by Prussia through a period of rapid industrialization and transformation of the economy. With the establishment of a set of consolidated boundaries, a new membership unit was created for the state in which a fixed, relatively liberal set of rights was established under Bismarck's constitution. However, this initial *Verrechtlichung* was accompanied by the establishment of a pervasive system of control and extraction formed by the alliance of Prussian military power-holders and the landholding Junker class in response to eastern Germany's need to compensate for its weak economic status (Rokkan 1975, 586). This alliance provided the political and military basis for advancing the central project of state-building, the bringing of territorial extremities under central control. Stein Rokkan has helpfully identified four tasks that were essential to the European state-building process: homogenization, penetration, participation, and redistribution (570–75). Whereas he sees these four processes as normally constituting consecutive phases, with the first two emanating from the geopolitical center and the second two from the periphery, in Germany's case these processes occurred to a significant degree contemporaneously, with the overall process dominated by the center.[14] *Homogenization* entailed nurturing a national culture that was bound to the political structure of the state through, among other things, the standardization of education, language, and culture, and the more or less forced assimilation of "non-German" social groups. *Penetration* consisted in the extension of state control into all levels of common life, but above all the economic realm, through the construction of unified legal and monetary systems and of a national market with fixed boundaries. *Participation* — the incorporation of the masses into the functioning of the overall state system — occurred through the expansion of suffrage and the acceptance, starting in the 1890s, of political parties, interest groups, a labor movement, and other instances of popular mobilization. *Redistribution* — the implementation of "safety net" measures and progressive taxation policies — was at first minimal but grew once the assembly of a modern welfare system began toward the end of World War I.

The construction of a unified state economy and the transition from an agricultural to an industrial base were crucial developments in the *Kaiserreich*. The establishment of boundaries defining a German market necessitated government control of labor admissions and the distinguishing of foreign workers from German workers; at the same time, foreign workers played a critical role in the success of industrialization, satisfying labor needs at a time marked by massive emigration to the United States. At first, state control in this area focused on admissions only, and the government was content to allow in a reserve population of foreigners who remained permanently on hand to meet the fluctuating demands for labor. Later, in the course of the transition from liberal to organized capitalism as capital became more concentrated, the state began to exert increasing control over the organization of the economy (Bade 1987, 60–66).

During World War I, the German government exerted complete control over the economy, establishing precedents that persisted afterward in a number of spheres. Administrative control of the labor market in particular led, in conjunction with the worker movement, to an organization of labor relations coupled with the provision of unemployment insurance (Bade 1984–85, 477–84). This step toward the formation of a welfare state was accompanied by limits on immigration and, in particular, strict regulation of foreign worker admissions.[15] As a result, a coherent strategy was developed for conditioning the flow of labor according to the needs of the economy through government intervention (Dohse 1985, 29–35). In effect, the reserve laborer population was placed outside the state with an accompanying externalization of costs. A growing set of administrative apparati marked the state expansion into new spheres of common life, a trend that continued under the National Socialist regime. The war economy under Hitler was also marked by extreme centralization and *Verstaatlichung*. In the Federal Republic, in contrast, the emphasis has been on *Verrechtlichung*. Considerable gains in the area of participation have been made on the strength of a constitution promoting basic human rights and a democratic political culture with a robust commitment to equality and redistributive values.

In the striking upswing of the postwar economy, labor demands resulted in a concerted effort to recruit foreign labor, the presence of which continues to be vital economically. The incorporation of the former German Democratic Republic (GDR) into the Federal Republic has placed a temporary strain on the economy; in the long run, however, it is clear that the economy will require a greater set of participants than can be accounted for by German nationals under present demographic trends (see, e.g., Geissler 1990; Cohn-Bendit 1993). This trend can only lead to further employment of non-Germans, a prospect that has alarmed many already worried about the present undermining of German cultural homogeneity. At this late date, of course, the cumulative effects of industrialization, urbanization, and developments in microcommunications have already exposed German society to much broader forces of assimilation. In fundamental ways, contemporary Germany has come to share with its North Atlantic neighbors all the characteristics of a classic welfare state, from the high centralization of power and the pervasive administrative presence of the government, to the compulsory education system and omnipresent mass media, to the great variety of protections, duties, and privileges assigned to individuals vis-à-vis the government.

To summarize, the process of German state-building has, as with other European states, been marked by the consolidation of an organized state society characterized by highly concentrated and centralized government power (*Verstaatlichung*) but also a considerable degree of representation and protection of members (*Verrechtlichung*). It has been distinctively "German" in its degree of centralization, in its military and geopolitical particulars, in its relationship to nationalism, and in its posture toward foreigners. Members of the German state society are those who, to apply Rokkan's model once more, (1) are objects of state penetration, that is, pay taxes, are held accountable to the law, and make the economy function; (2) are objects of homogenization, in that they undergo compulsory education and are exposed to the mass media; (3) are participants in the political life of the society, formally through their exercise of rights such as suffrage or less formally through interest group politics or mass mobilization; and (4) are included in the apparatus for redistribution, in that they are recognized as having equal claims of entitlement to collective resources in the form of welfare, unemployment, housing, and so on. These categories each admit of degrees, but in general they encompass those persons who live in and participate in German society. Thus, until reunification those German citizens who lived in the German Democratic Republic were excluded from the state society; while in the Federal Republic, permanent or long-term residents have enjoyed membership all along regardless of their citizenship.

Civitas-*Building*

The everyday reality of participation in and subjection to a concrete territorial society described by the notion of state membership stands in stark contrast to the dominant tradition in German citizenship policy, which juxtaposes to the state society a separate German membership determined partly through structural factors and partly through subjective identification. Where German national membership describes an ethnocultural group and state membership describes a class of persons fulfilling certain roles in society, citizenship, in theory at least, operates on the model of a *club*,[16] an organization predicated on common commitment to a purpose and on the principled exclusion of outsiders. The *purpose* of the German citizenry may be concisely identified as the self-determination of the German *Volk* or, formulated differently, the realization of a true German nation-state (cf. Fijalkowski 1991a, 2–3). In practice this realization has translated into a policy aimed at, crudely put, making all state members German and bringing all Germans into the state.[17] There are two ways of achieving such an end: making the state fit the Germans, or making the Germans fit the state. The first course has been attempted and, following a series of well-known imperialistic misadventures, failed; the second, pursued with more subtle means, remains the current strategy. The makers of citizenship policy have tried to attain their goal by, in effect, legislating it into existence. But because a state for and only for the historic German people has remained elusive for a number of geopolitical reasons, today's German citizenship laws remain attached to a "legal fiction" (Hailbronner 1989a) that collides with the reality of state membership and results in a politics of discrimination against non-Germans.

The laws that have given contour to German citizenship have aimed at the embodiment of a certain ideal citizen. This citizen is an active member of the state society, a bearer of German culture and language, and an engaged participant in the political life of a community viewed as worthy of his or her ultimate loyalty and sacrifice. Deliberately excluded from this category, as a rule, are ethnic Germans residing outside German territory and "non-German" members of the state society such as migrant workers; both groups possess other, competing citizenships.[18] As with other groups, the citizenry has developed through a process of identification and differentiation. Citizenship has been systematized in German lands over the last two hundred years through a largely problem-driven arc of development. In the course of this process, membership has come to be based principally on one's bloodline, although in exceptional cases other factors, such as assimilation to the national language and culture and commitment to the German *Rechtsstaat,* have also come to play a role. In Germany as in other countries, modern social movements have succeeded in securing the progressive extension of citizenship to various disadvantaged social groups: peasants, women, and children, for example. Of more especial significance to the German context, a crucial dynamic determining the boundary making of the citizenry has involved the ongoing development of formal distinctions between *Inländer* (native Germans) and *Ausländer* (aliens, resident foreigners). This distinction, which has important cultural and legal significance, has formed the heart of a distinctively German tradition of dealing with foreigners. The outcome of this tradition is the existence of two separate bodies of law dealing respectively with German citizens and with foreign citizens in Germany. The establishment of German citizenship has, through the *Inländer-Ausländer* distinction, severed a particular set of "civil rights" — including some fundamental political and civil rights[19] —

from the general set of human rights guaranteed to all in Germany. Moreover, one could argue, the fact that foreigners in principle possess no protection against deportation serves in practice to limit the extent to which they may safely exercise those rights assigned them.

In sketching the history of the institution of German citizenship, we may once again distinguish between a nascent period prior to the founding of the *Reich,* and a subsequent period of consolidation. Political memberships in German territories were for the most part informal and organized around cities, manors, or provinces until the seventeenth and eighteenth centuries. During this time, agreements among local communities were made with the goal of regulating treatment of beggars and the poor by assigning them home areas, determined by birth, from which they could not be expelled. As the growing mobility accompanying increased trade raised the number of foreigners present in German cities, a rudimentary system for licensing and regulating their movement arose (Dohse 1985, 12–14). Mass poverty and consequent internal migration led to state efforts to distribute the problem regionally. The initial attempt of the state to define "who its poor were" (Grawert 1973, 134) provided a criterion of belonging and marked the beginning of the practice of distinguishing legally between *Inländer* and *Ausländer.* At this point, the overarching legal status of citizen existed alongside the often more relevant categories of native, resident, burgher, and subject; yet, as intermediate political structures continued to be undermined in the state-building process, citizenship came to take on more and more significance.

In 1813 a passport system of sorts was introduced in Prussia along with a special police force (*Fremdenpolizei*) for dealing with foreigners. In the next decades citizenship remained assigned by and radically contingent upon the will of the representatives of the various state organizations. A certain guarantee for the passing on of membership through descent (jus sanguinis) was incorporated into law in Bavaria (1818) and Prussia (1842). Meanwhile, place of birth and mere residence ceased to suffice as criteria for membership, and mobility for foreigners became limited as a result. Following the revolution of 1848, a short-lived law temporarily established an imperial German citizenship based on reciprocity among states regarding their respective members. Around 1850, combined efforts at dealing with people who had become stateless in the period of unrest produced a further step: the explicit adoption in most German states of citizenship laws based primarily on the Prussian model (Grawert 1973, 199). On the eve of the creation of a German empire, however, citizenship remained at the level of these small states. At this point, German citizens were distinguished from *Ausländer* mainly in that they had a right to free movement within their particular state coupled with a right not to be expelled.

With the formation of the North German Federation in 1867 and the grounding of the *Kaiserreich* in 1871, this distinction was permanently raised to a federal level, with a corresponding transfer of the power to distribute membership from the state to the national level. Yet instead of creating a unified German citizenship, the federal model aimed at standardizing the individual membership practices across the German states. Under the new system, German *civitas* members — at this time, citizens and subjects (including women and children) — were technically no longer *Ausländer* everywhere outside their home state: they became entitled to treatment as *Inländer* throughout the *Reich.* The only ethnic German residents who could still to a limited extent be treated as *Ausländer* were those poor whom states were authorized to deport back to their home states (Dohse 1985, 18). As a result, the standardization of *Inländer* status linked the conception of *Ausländer* virtually exclusively with non-ethnic Germans.

The legislation accompanying the grounding of the *Reich* established a *Rechtsstaat* based on the Prussian model, which not only implemented a broad German citizenship but also provided for a set of individual rights and protections held for the most part equally by *Inländer* and *Ausländer.* Indeed, in the new state, both publicly and privately any disadvantaging of foreigners required a special legal ground as a general rule (Dohse 1985, 22). Finally, though, a bit of the police state remained in effect for foreigners who, in contrast to *Inländer,* remained ever vulnerable to expulsion at the discretion of the government — a situation that still exists today.[20] This vulnerability in turn placed the exercise of some rights within certain prudential limits. As the jurist Ernst Isay commented in 1923, "The sphere of freedom for *Ausländer* is reduced *in fact,* if not *under law* by the state right of deportation" (quoted in Dohse 1985, 24; emphasis in original).

For *Inländer,* the new state solidified not only the right to remain in the *Reich* but also rights to a place of residence, to practice a business, to serve in public office, to inherit land, and to enjoy those civil rights reserved for citizens in the various states. Since male suffrage had already been established in Prussia in 1849, citizens enjoyed some access to political participation, although the state formally remained under authoritarian rule and was on the whole immune to democratic influence.

During the period of intense state-building prior to World War I, the process of building distinctions between German members and others focused on foreign workers, whose admittance to and movement within Germany were increasingly controlled. At the same time, unambiguous efforts were made to accelerate the cultural assimilation of the German population. A militaristic attitude was an important component of the identity that developed at this time, and this attitude was reflected in the importance placed on the establishment of military service as a duty of citizenship. In addition, acceptance into the German civil service was effectively conditioned on subscription to official German values in a manner excluding not only Jews but also virtually anyone who was not a reserve military officer (Gilbert 1984, 86–87).

In 1913 a citizenship law (*Reichs- und Staatsangehörigkeitsgesetz*) was adopted which remains in effect today. The thrust of this law was to establish the principle of jus sanguinis as the basis for the attribution of German citizenship and to limit any further inclusion.[21] Any notion of a right to naturalization was dispensed with; naturalization was identified as an exception made contingent on full cultural assimilation, expressed commitment to German constitutional values, repudiation of previous citizenship, and the presence of a pressing state interest in accepting the applicant. Through this legislation, the political community was limited to a culture- and blood-related group for which considerations such as long-term residence or place of birth were irrelevant.

The strict limiting of citizenship to German ethnic members led to a deepening of the distinction between *Inländer* and *Ausländer*. As the bureaucratization of government progressed, separate administrations formed for each group. With the greatly increased mobility following World War I, immigration controls became widespread in Europe, and a complex system of residence permits with varying degrees of impermanence was devised for foreigners in Germany. In the Weimar Republic, labor policies restricted job prospects for foreigners by establishing a principle of priority for German workers. Even today, the system for policing foreigners still relies to a great extent on the structure developed under the National Socialists, although the special regulations for non-citizens[22] and revisions of laws for citizens enacted in the 1930s (such as the 1935 "Law to Protect German Blood and German Honor") are of course no longer valid, with the notable exception of a provision that transferred individual state memberships into a single national citizenship (Makarov 1971).

The turbulent postwar decades witnessed the creation and dissolution of a competing German citizenship in the German Democratic Republic. Yet citizenship in the Federal Republic has adapted to the new, postreunification scale of the state with a minimum of formal changes. In fact, no new citizenship law has been drafted. Policy has continued on the assumption that the *Reich,* for all intents and purposes, still exists, which means that the system for controlling foreigners without providing means for immigration or substantial naturalization has remained intact. Only two major revisions in citizenship policy have been made in response to changing conditions, both by way of the Basic Law.

The first of these revisions deals with the so-called *Aussiedler,* ethnic Germans from former German territories who elect to migrate to the Federal Republic. *Aussiedler* enjoy a constitutional right to take on German citizenship upon their arrival (German Basic Law, article 116). Since no separate citizenship for the Democratic Republic was ever acknowledged, refugees from East Germany were regarded as having always been German citizens. Ethnic Germans from elsewhere were guaranteed membership under the Federal Expellee Law of 1953. This policy was originally designed to accommodate the flood of over ten million German expellees and refugees from other countries that descended upon the Federal Republic in the years immediately after World War II. However, the policy has also been interpreted to apply to a continuous stream (for the most part, from Poland, Russia, and Rumania) of migrants with claims to ethnic German membership.[23] In many cases, these immigrants have little or no knowledge of German language and culture; nonetheless, by virtue of being related to a past member of the *Reich* they are entitled to receive citizenship status upon application.

The second revision has to do with the status of women. Under the law of 1913, German women automatically lost their citizenship when they married foreigners, while foreign women automatically became German citizens through marriage to a German man. In addition, a gender-based proviso of the German jus sanguinis principle held that children born to German women married to foreigners did not receive German citizenship. Following the founding of the Federal Republic, the loss-of-citizenship rule was rejected as incompatible with the ban on discrimination included in the Basic Law. Foreign spouses were required to apply for naturalization with no guarantee of success, although a general presumption was established in their favor. Only after a Federal Constitutional Court decision in 1974 was the provision for children born to German women in mixed national marriages declared unconstitutional and the policy revised (Huber 1987, 209–15).

The German Basic Law adopts as its main premise the idea that "the power of the state emanates from the people" (art. 20, sec. 2). The "people" (*Volk*), according to present legal standards, is the German people, understood as the collectivity of German citizens and German ethnic immigrants bearing a claim to citizenship. To summarize the process through which this group has been created, German citizenship has represented an attempt to transfer an emerging ethnonational identity to the concrete context of a developing state structure by limiting full membership in the state to a culturally homogeneous, consanguineous group and by creating differences of status between ethnic Germans and others present in the state. These others, deemed *"Ausländer,"* have been assigned a subordinate membership status. The distinction has been manifested legally in the creation of separate bodies of law for the two groups and the reservation of suffrage and other rights and duties for citizens, including the basic right not to be expelled. The citizenry that has emerged from this overall process views itself, in keeping with the ideology of the nation-state that its membership policy is designed to serve, as both the sole legitimate source of sovereignty in the Federal Republic and the designated bearer of German culture.

The three groups I have outlined might be said to constitute, in classic Hegelian fashion, a dialectic of German membership. The German *Kulturnation* in this formulation represents the original thesis that has been confronted historically by the antithesis of the emerging German *Rechtsstaat*. The synthesis that Germans have attempted to draw out of this conflict is the incarnation of the *Nationalstaat* in the form of citizenship. But like Hegel's "Absolute Idea," this synthesis seems an inexplicably static notion. More importantly, it has always been and is likely to remain in essence a *Sollen,* a telos, a utopia. As is the case in other ethnic nation-states, the institution of citizenship in Germany seeks to bind the responsibility for steering a concrete community into the future with an artificially constructed national past.

In the here and now, this synthesis is unstable in practice, challenged by evolving historical conditions. In the wake of reunification, German citizenship finds itself in an identity crisis exacerbated by economic inequalities and deep differences in social outlook among Germans. At the same time, the established presence of a disenfranchised foreign minority has increasingly highlighted the discriminatory character of prevailing citizenship practices and called into question the progress made toward democracy in postwar Germany. These changes in the structure of the nation, and especially of the state, have come to demand a more realistic synthesis for German membership, one that speaks to the present.

The Birth of the Migrant Worker Minority in Germany

In reunited Germany live over seven million foreign citizens (8.8 percent of the total population), roughly seven-tenths of whom are migrant workers or their family members.[24] The migrant worker population[25] has become, clearly and contrary to all intention, a fixed part of the German social landscape, and it is this development which is chiefly responsible for spawning the ongoing public discussion in Germany over citizenship, political representation, and the "multicultural society." An analysis of these membership debates must draw on an account of how this group became established in German society. The dynamic involved is the formation of a minority, a constant and distinct group marked off from the mainstream through a constellation of legal, political, ethnocultural, and socioeconomic differences.[26] German historians and social scientists have produced a wealth of detailed descriptions of the worker migration and its consequences.[27] Rather than portraying this history in all its complexity, my intent is to highlight those aspects of the process that have shaped judgments and positions regarding its aftermath. The following sketch of the birth of the migrant worker minority is, accordingly, a narrative that emphasizes morally relevant themes, such as responsibility for the migration or the basis of migrants' claims to stay, at the expense of other themes, such as the mechanics of recruitment or the international economic context.

Migration

The new minorities in Germany were formed through a policy of foreign worker recruitment that led gradually to an informal immigration process. This development had its roots in a sharply rising demand for labor that accompanied the rebuilding of the German economy following World War II. Traditionally, fluctuations in labor needs had been managed through the manipulation of foreign labor groups.[28] In the aftermath of the war, however, these labor needs were at first filled by a wave of *"Vertriebene"* — returning German refugees and expellees — and then by a wave of refugees from East Germany.[29] At the same time, the government and employers remained aware that a labor shortage loomed, and in 1955 a trial labor-recruitment agreement with Italy was initiated. With the building of the Berlin Wall in 1961, the attainment of full employment, and the coinciding rebuilding of the German armed forces, the shortage of workers became acute and policymakers turned in earnest to the recruitment of foreign workers. Throughout the sixties, Germany pursued and signed labor-recruitment agreements with Spain, Greece, Turkey, Morocco, Portugal, Tunisia, and Yugoslavia.

In keeping with the essentially economic character of the recruitment policy, each of the parties involved was concerned primarily with the pursuit of short-term interests, and the expectation on all sides was that the employment would be temporary. German recruiters saw the arrangement as an opportunity to build up the German economy through labor obtained with a minimum of financial investment and social costs. Policymakers in the countries providing the workers viewed recruitment as a chance to siphon off unemployed workers, bring in foreign currency, and gain trained workers who on their return would help develop their home country. And the workers themselves were confronted with the allure of good jobs that would allow them to provide for their families and improve their economic status following their return. Neither the Germans nor the other participants gave much thought to the somewhat foreseeable long-term social and economic ramifications of recruitment.

In the next years, millions of foreign workers — mostly men between the ages of twenty-five and forty — filled a variety of low-level jobs primarily in the industrial sector. Collectively, they played an essential role in the continued German ascent to prosperity and a high standard of living. Under the terms of their employment, they were officially granted the same status as German workers; however through a policy of "rotation" imposed through short-term contracts, they retained their role as a buffer in times of economic difficulty. During the recession of 1966–67 many were compelled to return to their home countries, and when unemployment threatened again following the oil crisis in 1973, the recruitment of foreigners was abruptly terminated.

Settlement

Following the ban on recruitment, many thought the foreign presence in Germany would eventually fade away, and after 1973 most national groups did see slight declines. Still, the majority of workers remained, and due to the activity primarily of one group, the Turks, in bringing family members to Germany, the overall number of foreigners continued to climb throughout the seventies. The migrants' continued presence was once more attributable to all of the parties of the original agreements. Before the recruitment ban, the German government's attempts to maintain a strict two-year rotation policy for workers had predictably met with resistance from employers, who protected their investments of capital and training by renewing the contracts of most workers regularly. At the same time, the governments of recruitment countries failed in most cases to provide adequate reintegration measures for returning workers, even as the amplified impact of downward economic trends after 1973 on developing countries greatly reduced the incentive of migrants to return. For their part, the migrants became accustomed to the consumer lifestyle and increased earning potential in Germany, and began gradually to raise families, to send their children to school, to invest in housing, to establish savings in Germany — in short, to put down roots. Over time, as ties to the new country began to solidify and those to the homeland to weaken, a phenomenological process of settlement took place. Communities of foreigners developed "hyphenated" identities (Rist 1978, 245), setting them apart from their conationals as well as the Germans.

Corresponding to this development, there evolved on the part of most

Germans a gradual recognition of the migrants' moral claim to a right to remain. That these workers had made their homes in Germany, raised families, invested labor and capital in the economy, and established entire communities, came to be understood as grounding a normative claim to membership, to belonging — to being able to stay if they desired, and to participate. This claim was reflected in the recognition of a constitutional right for foreigners to extend their residence and to bring their families, based on provisions guaranteeing the free development of the individual personality and the state's commitment to protecting marriage and family (German Basic Law, arts. 2 and 6). There grew as well a broad consciousness of the subordinate socioeconomic role played by foreigners and a sense of unfairness at the thought of forcibly expelling them once their usefulness was past. A mass expulsion consequently became both politically and legally impracticable, and by the end of the 1970s the governing social-liberal coalition officially recognized the necessity of a long-term integration of the increasingly settled foreign worker population.

Consolidation

In the early eighties, against the backdrop of a stagnating economy and growing sentiment against foreign workers, the newly elected conservative-liberal coalition government enacted a policy designed to encourage the return of the migrants to their countries of origin, partly through cash incentives. This program, however, was largely unsuccessful. It is true that to this day a majority of first- and second-generation migrants evince the intention, however vague, of at some point returning to their homeland for good (Friedrich-Ebert-Stiftung 1986). In practice, however, it has become clear that migrants generally remain permanently in Germany and, additionally, often retrieve family members who were left behind (Pöschl and Schmuck 1984). Further evidence that the Turkish community in particular has oriented itself to a long-term stay in Germany is provided by a shift in political focus away from issues in Turkey toward possibilities for collective action among Turkish migrants in the Federal Republic, as well as by increasing economic engagement in the new homeland (Özcan 1989; Hoch 1994).

The reunification of Germany complicated this picture by introducing a group of about 100,000 foreign workers from the former GDR. These workers, who had come to the GDR under agreements with Vietnam, Angola, Mozambique, Cuba, and Poland, served the purpose of meeting labor shortages in the East German economy. Ostensibly symbols of international socialist solidarity, in practice they were sequestered in isolated tenements, their stay made tenuous by a legal status purely contingent upon the interests of the state, under which, for example, pregnancy could constitute grounds for expulsion (Krüger-Potratz 1991; Cu 1992). With the collapse of the communist regime, many of these workers were quietly repatriated, while others sought political asylum in the Federal Republic. Following reunification, arrangements were made to secure the residence status of a portion of these workers, mainly Vietnamese, who now make up a distinct minority in Germany; many others, however, were marked for deportation.

Three decades of German experience with the guestworkers allow for a cautious assessment of the societal *consequences* of their presence. Critics have claimed that foreigners take away jobs from Germans, that they threaten the integrity of the German culture, that they are uninvited guests, that they sap the German social security system, that they encourage criminality and undermine order. The migrant workers and their allies meet these claims with various reminders: of the contributions made by the employment of foreigners to Germany's economic well-being, often at the expense of their countries of origin; of the need to respond to past injustices against foreign workers, most notably under National Socialism; of the fact that the presence of foreigners has actually created jobs for Germans and helped finance the German welfare system; of Germany's age-old status as a multicultural society; of the potential for mutual enrichment through cultural exchange; and — not least of all — of the long-term demographic prospects for a reunited Germany, which indicate a vital employment role for foreign worker families, the only growing sector of the German population. On balance, claims that the foreign presence until now has been harmful appear to be more emotionally than empirically based, while concerns about the difficulties of minority politics and the perils of pluralism tend to exhibit a firmer grounding in experience.

The Current Problem: Three Types of Subordination

The outcome of the recruitment and employment of foreigners in Germany—as in several other European countries—is a settled population of first-, second-, and third-generation migrants whose presence in the society is problematic in a variety of ways.[30] The troubled status of this group may be described with reference to the same broad categories used above in characterizing German membership. The central feature defining the *Ausländer* population is its subordination or exclusion, which arises in the intertwined processes of nation-building, state-building, and *civitas*-building, in the interrelated forms of discrimination, socioeconomic inequality, and legal disadvantage.[31] Characteristic problems falling under these three headings reflect the established status of the migrant worker population as a minority in the American sense, exhibiting all the social isolation and collective alienation that this term suggests.

Nation-Building and Ethnic Discrimination
As described above, the process of nation-building is one of marking off a distinct ethnocultural group from other comparable groups. The development of the German ethnonation has involved the valuing of certain central "German" characteristics and norms, and the heightening of differences between Germans and members of other national groups into oppositions and even into bases of enmity. It is difficult to identify precisely the sort of agency at work in this process, although as noted, intellectual and political elites play a disproportionate role. What is clear is that in the German case, as in others, nation-building has established boundaries for discrimination—for the preference of those sharing a common identity and for the exclusion or rejection of all others. The Holocaust saw the extreme side of this rejection, but the favoring of one's own group and the accompanying subordination of others takes place at the most mundane levels of human interaction.[32] In today's Germany, those members of society not sharing accepted "German" qualities experience considerable problems because of their otherness. Among the migrant worker groups, this applies especially to the Turks, who are perceived as a particular threat to Germans on account of both their numbers and the extent of their cultural distinctiveness.

Discrimination against foreigners in Germany takes place individually and collectively, in a variety of contexts, and with varying degrees of subtlety. Everyday instances of discrimination — isolation in a crowded subway or the refusal of admission to a disco — shade into more openly hostile forms of rejection. In the housing market, advertisements often specify that no foreigners need apply. In the workplace, foreigners are disproportionately assigned to poor working conditions and passed over for promotions (Schäfer 1985). Many foreigners complain about the harsh treatment they receive at the hands of the various administrators they are forced to deal with in the pursuit of work and residence permits, and statistics show that foreigners are more likely to be charged with crimes than Germans are (Pitsela 1986). A number of studies have focused on the images of foreigners presented in the German media, which, particularly in the case of Turks, tend to be mostly negative (Merten 1986; Galanis 1989).

The most striking aspect of discrimination against foreigners is the phenomenon commonly referred to as *Ausländerfeindlichkeit* — the wholesale rejection of non-Germans on ethnic or more often racist grounds (Struck 1982; Hellfeld 1986; Stöss 1989; Hoffmann and Even 1984). This sentiment, which tends to wax in times of economic downturn, manifests itself in a spectrum of actions ranging from antiforeigner graffiti to physical attacks on foreigners. An example of this trend is the manner in which the Turks have inherited that crude genre of jokes previously reserved for Poles and Jews. Scholarly analyses of the alleged threat posed by foreigners to the integrity of the German people (see, e.g., the Heidelberg Manifesto of June 17, 1981) were echoed in the late 1980s by a swell of political support for the Republikaner, a party advocating closed borders and the reduction of the foreign population. German reunification has revealed a particularly high level of hostility to foreigners among East Germans, an attitude not at all eased by the accompanying high rate of unemployment. But antipathy toward non-Germans is widely present in western Germany as well, and the sites of major outbursts of antiforeigner violence — Hoyerswerda, Rostock, Mölln, and Solingen — as well as the thousands of smaller incidents that take place yearly are distributed throughout the country. On the whole, discrimination is, due to its ethnic basis and face-to-face nature, a problem of particular moment for those mostly non-European foreigners bearing a conspicuously non-German appearance.

State-Building and Socioeconomic Inequality

A second type of subordination of foreigners corresponds to the structural realm described above as the state society and is characterized by the socioeconomic exploitation of foreigners. The inequality experienced by foreigners, while related to the active discrimination practiced against them, is essentially a systemic phenomenon, an outgrowth of the mechanisms of the state-building process. In this process, foreign labor has provided a class that is not excluded from the German state, but rather subordinated within it. With reference to the categories of state-building used above, foreign residents as a group are (1) more subject to centralized state power than other members of German society, (2) less integrated in terms of language, education, and public life, (3) less involved politically, and (4) less likely to benefit from economic redistribution. The migrants' occupation of the lowest rung in the German socioeconomic hierarchy has not been the least of their contributions to the postwar stability and prosperity of the Federal Republic.

Of course, to a certain extent the worker communities in Germany have benefited from the general push for social equality in welfare states. Even so, the forms of structural inequality with which foreigners must contend remain manifold. In the area of employment, the situation of foreign workers is characterized by disproportionately hazardous conditions coupled with low wages. Foreigners, the traditional "industrial reserve army" (Fijalkowski 1984) for the German labor market, also experience unemployment rates that are more than double the national average, and in the past many have found their only prospects for work in illegal employment under particularly bad conditions. Although the gap is gradually closing, those with jobs have considerably lower chances of advancement than their German coworkers (Friedrich-Ebert-Stiftung 1986). In general, the average income of a migrant family falls notably below that of a native German family.

These trends in employment have a great deal to do with inequality in the school system, and both are aggravated by language deficits on the part of the migrants. The number of foreigners who enter the German schools at a late age skew the statistics to a certain extent; nonetheless, it is clear that foreigners are considerably behind other Germans in terms of high school graduation rates. Moreover, they are greatly underrepresented in higher education as well as in vocational training programs, where their entrance rates are a third those of Germans (Berlin Commissioner for Foreigners' Affairs 1989; *Die Zeit,* June 11, 1993, 12).

Housing is another realm in which foreigners fare considerably worse than the German population at large. The dwellings occupied by migrant worker families tend to be inexpensive and poorly maintained, and often occupy areas that are practically devoid of ethnic Germans. It is important to note that the "ghettoization" of the migrants is partly a matter of choice reflecting the desire both to save money and to live in a particular cultural subcommunity. At the same time, few opportunities exist for a standard of housing equal to that of most Germans. Indeed, it seems clear that in the area of basic social and economic living conditions, foreigners have taken on the role of an underprivileged class.

Civitas-*Building and Legal Disadvantage*

The differentiation process associated with the institution of citizenship has produced a third fundamental type of subordination for the migrant worker minority, namely the systematic disadvantaging of its members through laws and regulations. The historic collective political-legal attempt to make full membership in the German political community contingent on the possession of German ethnic characteristics has resulted in a denial of many of the commodities of membership for the non-German portion of the society. In the course of *civitas*-building, the status of "foreign national" has established itself as the basis for the institutionalization of subordinate rights and separate treatment. Just as the category of citizenship mediates between efforts to define ethnonation and state society, the legal disadvantaging of long-term foreign residents provides an arena for translating active ethnic attitudes into the basis for systemic inequality.

This process is reflected above all in the general legal strictures that apply to foreigners, including many second- and third-generation migrants born and raised in Germany. In many areas of life, foreigners with legal residence in Germany possess, it is important to note, the same rights as Germans. In their legal personae as workers, for example, they enjoy virtual equality with German citizens. Nonetheless, as foreign citizens the overwhelming majority of migrant workers and their families find many of their horizons shaped by the restrictions applying to them under the German Aliens Act (1991). This means above all that they do not have a legal right to stay in Germany, but rather require a residence permit, and that they may be expelled for a number of reasons including criminal activity, drug addiction, and endangering the interests of "state security."[33] It also means that they require work permits in order to hold jobs, and that they are ineligible for many careers — as civil servants, for example, or as chimney sweeps. Certain legal limits apply to the political activity of foreigners (see Hailbronner 1989a, 183–203; de Groot 1989): they are not allowed to vote, run for office, or form political parties, and additional restrictions apply to their rights of speech, association, and assembly (Berlin Institute 1987). The lack of venues for political expression is not total for this minority — they have advisory bodies in some local governments and also exert indirect influence on political parties — but it is sufficient to ensure that they can do little to prosecute their own interests.

Foreigners face additional legal disadvantages in the job market (where Germans have priority for open positions), in the commercial spheres, and with regard to privacy regarding personal data (Berlin Commissioner for Foreigners' Affairs 1994, 24). Communities with a certain percentage of foreign residents can legally ban additional foreigners from moving into them. In the sphere of religion, the overwhelming majority of Turks find their faith denied the legal status and privileges accorded the two major Christian churches (Berlin Institute 1989). In these ways, having the status of foreigner conditions the entire sphere of possibilities for shaping one's life. This disadvantage is partly ameliorated for those foreigners who benefit from membership in the European Union. For others, apart from emigration, the only way to transcend this pervasive handicap is through acceptance into German citizenship. Yet, although most foreign workers are now eligible for naturalization, the costs and requirements involved — especially the disavowal of all previous citizenships — discourage the overwhelming majority of migrants and their families from taking this step.[34]

Although the relationship among them is complex, in general the various sorts of subordination of migrants tend to reinforce one another. This interdependence is illustrated in the case of housing, where discriminatory letting practices, structural inequality in the form of "ghettoization," and legal bans on moving to some areas combine to limit seriously the living conditions of foreigners. A fundamental change in the subordination of the foreign minority would ultimately require changes in all three areas. Altering patterns of ethnic discrimination and socioeconomic inequalities is inherently difficult, however, because of the complex and indirect forms of collective agency they involve. Consequently, the area of legal disadvantage and *civitas*-building — that is, the sphere of the international political structuring of societal membership — suggests itself as the area where change might most fruitfully be sought.

In any case, it remains difficult to avoid the recognition that foreign workers and their families have become de facto immigrants and must be dealt with as such. Since the early 1980s, efforts to integrate these minorities into the German mainstream have been increased. These efforts have been marked by virulent discussions regarding various facets of the question of membership for this group. Should integration or assimilation be the goal for incorporating them? What sort of society should be aimed at — a homogeneous one or one respecting and perhaps even encouraging cultural diversity? Should political inclusion be conditioned on citizenship and if so, under what terms should naturalization be available? Should a single status of full membership in German society be pursued, or should a hierarchy of variegated categories be imposed in recognition of the desire for and attainment of partial membership?

H ow is membership in a given political entity determined? Who does the including and excluding? A basic ethical question regarding membership status is the question of agency. In the case of the migrant worker families in German society, this question becomes, Who is responsible for the ethnic isolation, for the economic inequality, for the political and legal disadvantage experienced by this group?

As we have seen, the boundary-making processes that shape the relations between the foreign worker population and their German "hosts" combine different forms of activity focused on, among other means, political rules, economic structures, and ethnic identification. Since these forms are so intimately bound up with one another, it is difficult in most cases to specify the role played by each. Take, for example, the question of how to account for the low number of naturalizations among eligible Turkish workers. Some claim that the individual workers themselves are solely responsible for this result, that each simply chooses freely not to take on German citizenship. Others claim that the low rate of applications for citizenship is attributable to the manner in which German officials (legislators, the government, civil servants, the courts) have shaped this choice — for example, in making naturalization contingent on the renunciation of all other citizenships. Still others may find decisive deterrents to efforts at attaining full German membership in the collective phenomenon of active discrimination against non-Germans, or in the "illusion of return" actively nurtured by representatives of both the Turkish and German governments. These explanations are by no means mutually exclusive; indeed they tend to reinforce one another and are further buttressed by the structures of the German economy and the relations between industrial and developing nations.[1] We might say generally that in questions such as that of naturalization, a complex dialectic of agency is at work involving individuals, collectivities, and the structures they create. But this is not a very satisfying response, nor does it provide us with a promising starting point for probing and criticizing the exclusion of foreign residents in Germany.

In order to make the problem more manageable it is necessary to set some limits to our considerations. This can be done, first, by focusing our examination of membership processes on the realm of political debate and lawmaking — that is, on *civitas*-building. This strategy allows us to narrow our field of inquiry to that sphere of membership definition in which developments are most susceptible both to analysis and to concerted change. Although the socioeconomic and cultural activities that produce inequality and sharpen prejudice are not simply detached objective processes — they are undeniably perpetrated by people — the precise way in which this occurs, and consequently ways in which these processes could be altered, remain opaque to us.[2] That which distinguishes the activity of politics,[3] in contrast, is its explicit apprehension of the possibilities of social agency — in its characteristic focus on the problems of shaping human interactions, and in the chance it presents of effecting changes in the structures conditioning them. Politics in this sense is an ethical practice par excellence, and its inherent activism endows it with a unique, controlling status in questions of membership. It is through this sphere that we find the best chance of attending not only to formal disadvantage but also, if less directly, to the other aspects of subordination. Political discourse and action alone cannot solve the problems of discrimination and inequality, but they may represent the key to an overall solution.

A second way of narrowing our exploration is to concern ourselves specifically with the normative concepts employed in the process of *civitas*-building. The taking of a position on questions of political inclusion and exclusion is an action guided by norms about membership. These norms may be more or less explicit, but we must recognize that they are always there, unless we wish to assume that at least some attitudes toward membership literally do not make sense.[4] Even when we deem a given perspective to be incoherent, this judgment itself takes place with reference to the norms we understand to be invoked by the perspective we criticize. In political discussions about membership, competing norms find expression in the presentation of the disparate views of participants. An individual view is always at once an interpretation and an application to specific circumstances of the norm or norms that inform it, and for this reason a few basic norms can support a great variety of different positions. My proposal here is to examine various debates about membership in Germany in an effort to delineate the basic normative schemes at work in them and to explore their conflicts. By identifying the central normative points of difference regarding German membership in the political sphere, we can establish the basis for a nuanced evaluation of the overall grounds for the subordination of the foreign worker population.

This approach is empirical in the sense that my characterization of normative views of political membership is based on an account of current debates instead of the other way around. Yet, as with any such investigation, the way in which the phenomena are described and classified is unavoidably conditioned by the terms in which the project is cast. This process ought always to be made explicit. Consequently, it is necessary to note that normative perspectives on political membership in the modern West are all deeply influenced by the idea of citizenship first developed in the Greek city-states. The core of this notion lies in the idea of a "bounded equality" preserved within the context of a political community.[5] Modern notions of political membership characteristically involve both a certain definition of equality (for example, of specific rights and duties) and a set of criteria according to which eligibility for this equality is limited (for instance, membership in an ethnocultural group, or residence in a specific territory). From this observation it follows that the norms underlying various positions on membership may fruitfully be distinguished with respect to both their *form* and their *basis*. These in turn will always be shaped by beliefs about the *purpose* of the political community in question, as well as the *character* this community should have in terms of, for example, ethnic, religious, or linguistic diversity.[6]

What follows is a brief description of the participants in the political and legal processes surrounding the treatment of migrant workers and their families in Germany, and an account of two sets of debates, one set centered primarily on the concepts involved in questions of inclusion and citizenship for the migrants and another concerning basic political alternatives for dealing with the problems of membership raised by this minority. Based on this treatment, a number of fundamentally different understandings of political membership that have decisively shaped policy discussions are identifiable, setting the stage for a more extensive consideration of conflicting normative perspectives on citizenship.

The Players

The political and legal structuring of the status of the migrant minority is the product of a collective process involving a variety of actors. The sketch given here of the different roles in the boundary-making process for German citizenship aims at providing a basis for assessing the political cal weight of different arguments bearing on the inclusion or exclusion of Germany's permanent foreign residents (cf. Bade 1990, 35–86; Sieveking et al. 1989).

The dominant role in determining national policies toward foreign worker families has been played by the German government, since long before a policy of recruitment was enacted. In keeping with the exclusively economic focus of the original "guestworker" policy, the Minister of Labor has always been a central actor; in recent years, the Minister of the Interior has also taken on large responsibilities toward the new minority. Since the late 1970s, Germany's official strategy for dealing with this group has aimed at (1) preventing its growth by limiting further migration wherever politically and legally possible, (2) reducing it by encouraging the return of foreign nationals to their countries of origin, and (3) absorbing it through various measures aimed at integration. Although the liberal-socialist (1979–82) and liberal-conservative (1982–97) coalitions gave different weight to its individual components, on the whole there has been a great degree of continuity in this policy. However, the basis of parliamentary approval for this policy has steadily eroded over the last decade.

Germany's federal system grants each individual state a large say in setting and implementing its own policy toward aliens. This has produced a great diversity of measures and made a unified policy impossible. In general, states governed by the social democrats have adopted more liberal, integrationist policies, while states governed by the Christian Union parties have preferred to emphasize limiting new migration and encouraging remigration. At the federal level, these respective orientations clash in the Bundesrat, the parliamentary body constituted by the heads of the state governments.

The particular legal basis for the foreign presence has led the government to create a large and complicated system of controls regarding residence and work permits, accompanied by a highly developed bureaucracy that possesses a considerable amount of discretion in decision making that affects the membership status of foreigners. In addition, the German administrative courts have greatly influenced how officials who deal with foreigners practice, although in which direction is not clear. Some (e.g., Quaritsch 1981, 35–45) claim that the courts are largely responsible for the unintended consolidation of the foreigners' stay in Germany, while others (e.g., Franz 1990a) accuse the courts of establishing exclusionary precedents concerning the migrants.

Not surprisingly, political parties in Germany have been leading participants in discussions concerning policy toward the foreign minority. Their differences have contributed to the creation of a variety of policies, particularly at the regional level. At the same time, the foreigner issue itself has played a major role in shaping the party-political landscape in Germany since the early 1970s. Thus 1988 saw the rise to political viability of the far-right Republikaner party on the basis of their opposition to the foreign presence and commitment to reducing it. At the other end of the political spectrum, the Greens have likewise made the equal treatment of foreigners a cornerstone of their platform, which calls for the recognition of a "settler" status for long-term foreign residents that would include full political rights and dispense with residence and work permits. The allied parties of the right, Kohl's Christian Democratic Union (CDU) and the Bavarian Christian Social Union (CSU), have—with notable individual exceptions—backed the government in maintaining a restrictive policy aimed at preserving German national identity. In their view, this means limiting the size of the foreign population wherever possible and conditioning full membership rights for foreigners on a completed process of integration. Their primary opponents, the Social Democrats (SPD), have pushed for limited political rights for foreigners as well as for greater efforts at integration. The Free Democratic Party (FDP), in keeping with its liberal centrist orientation, has resisted efforts to limit the number of foreigners through restrictions on family reunification and has strongly supported political rights for resident foreigners, particularly in the context of a unified Europe. The political newcomers on the left, the Democratic Socialists (PDS), formed following German reunification, lack experience in foreigner policy but have tended in most questions to side with the Greens (see party literatures; cf. Bukow and Llaryora 1989, 35–93; Bade 1990, 35–67).

The original nature of the admission of foreign workers as a national economic strategy ensured that both the German Federation of Trade and Labor Unions (DGB) and the Federation of Employers (BDA) have since had much to do with shaping the conditions under which migrants live. At first these organizations worked together fairly closely in securing foreigners a status in labor issues equal to that of German workers. Since the mid-1980s, however, while employers have remained close to the government line on migrant worker issues, the DGB has taken an increasingly inclusive position that has propelled it toward an alliance with churches and welfare organizations (Dohse 1982; Bade 1984–85; Schäfer 1985; Esser et al. 1983).

Since the early 1970s, these groups, including Catholic- and Protestant-based charities as well as voluntary associations such as the Red Cross, have fulfilled a lobbying function on behalf of foreign workers and their families, taking the form of both political and scholarly efforts at securing recognition of the migrant population's claim to broad social equality as well as to specific rights such as family reunification (Esser 1983; Barwig and Mieth 1987).

On the whole, the foreigners themselves have been unable to exert much influence on the decisions that structure their existence in Germany. While a very few naturalized foreigners have begun to establish a presence in the party system, the disenfranchisement of the overwhelming majority has combined with competing national identities within the group to make concerted action difficult. It is important to note that resident noncitizens are able, in an advisory capacity, to participate politically in a variety of "foreigner councils" that provide input in local government (Puskeppeleit and Thränhardt 1990; Wichmann 1989; Federal Commissioner 1988). Yet, since these councils lack any decision-making powers, this form of participation is highly limited in its effectiveness. Other foreigners' organizations such as the Council of Turkish Citizens in Germany, an umbrella group founded in 1993, must rely primarily on their freedoms of expression and assembly in pursuing their political aims. In general, these aims include a more secure legal status regarding work and residence, equality of opportunity with Germans, political rights, and minority protections such as classes in the native language for children of foreigners (see Sen and Jahn 1985; Berlin Commissioner for Foreigners' Affairs 1989; Özcan 1989; Bischoff and Teubner 1990; Hoch 1994).

Foreigners have found valuable advocates at various levels of government in certain official agencies entrusted with coordinating the integration of the migrant worker minority. The Federal Commissioner for the Integration of Foreign Workers and Their Family Members has actively pressed for more liberal policies toward the migrants, with occasional success. At the regional level, the influential Berlin Commissioner for Foreigners' Affairs and the Office of Multicultural Affairs in Frankfurt provide examples of effective activism in the interests both of specific minority concerns and of mutual tolerance among German citizens and foreign residents.

It would be remiss not to mention the ever-increasing influence of external actors on the legal and political membership processes affecting the migrant minority in Germany. Governments of sending countries, for example, are able to influence the treatment of their citizens through treaties with Germany. They also play a role in the organization of community life for the migrants, for example through the provision of resources and funding for religious instruction (Thränhardt 1986; Bade 1990). A number of the social and economic rights enjoyed by migrant workers — including the right to family reunification — are guaranteed by international treaties and customary law. Furthermore, policies developed by the European Union (EU) and supported by decisions from the European Court have created a special status for workers from other European countries in Germany. These workers enjoy freedom of movement in Europe and are thus entitled to residence and work permits in the Federal Republic. In addition they may vote for the European Parliament, and EU policymakers foresee in the future the standardization of local voting rights for all Europeans who have established residence in another European country. To a certain extent EU policies dealing with migrant workers have been broadened to apply to non-EU workers (Turpin 1987, 93–94; Kühne 1995). Nonetheless, the general effect of the European unification process has been to strengthen distinctions between worker families from other EU member-states and those from non-EU countries such as Turkey and the former Yugoslavia.

Of this great variety of actors, the most influential has been the CDU-dominated government, which, supported by other like-minded groups, has succeeded in maintaining a policy of exclusive political membership modeled on the nation-state principle — on, that is, the ideal of a state of and for Germans and only Germans. At the same time, this policy has been tempered through the efforts of supporters of a more inclusive stance. This dynamic process has been reflected in a range of public debates over questions of German membership.

Three Conceptual Debates

In the early years of the foreign worker migration, their role in German society was a topic of political discussion only during economic hard times. Yet, with the undermining of assumptions about the temporariness of the "guests'" stay, and the increasing visibility of a second generation of foreigners, especially in the schools, the "foreigner issue" became politically unavoidable. As questions of policy toward the new minority became the subject of parliamentary debates and electoral campaigns, legal scholars, social scientists, and theologians joined politicians in an effort to define the basic issues at stake. In the last decade or so, three conceptual debates have been particularly influential in fixing the terms of the political discussion over foreign residents.

Germany: A Country of Immigration?
Since the mid-1970s, a common assertion in official statements of foreigner policy has been that Germany is not (and cannot be) a country of immigration. This claim has been amply echoed throughout those parts of the political spectrum opposed to the incorporation of a foreign minority in Germany. The rebuttal that Germany is (and always has been) a country of immigration has likewise become a byword for advocates of inclusive policies toward the migrant worker population. The heated

exchanges over this theme have, on the whole, been characterized on both sides by dogmatism combined with a failure to specify the actual point of contention. In actuality, the two sides have tended to address fundamentally different aspects of the question regarding Germany's relation to immigration. On the one hand, disagreement has concerned the permanence of the foreign worker population; on the other, disagreement centers on the issue of the formal induction of new members into the German polity. When both of these points of difference are laid bare, it becomes clear that both sides are right — and both sides are wrong.

At first, one major objective of those who denied Germany's nature as a country of immigration was to prevent the recognition of an established "guestworker" minority. In this regard, the question was primarily a social-scientific one: Have those workers who originally came as guests become, in effect, *immigrants* who have turned the Federal Republic into a plural society? The answer in the negative asserted that most of the workers intended to return to their home countries and that their presence was in fact temporary. The goal of this claim was to underscore a particular conception of membership in German society, namely that of belonging to a continuous, enclosed and homogeneous national culture. The opponents of this view drew on a wealth of social scientific data to show that the foreign worker population showed every sign of permanence and indeed exhibited all the classical characteristics of an immigrant minority. That the migrants had become de facto immigrants was undeniable by 1984, when the failure of the government's policy of re-migration incentives became clear. Indeed, the extent to which the modern West German state was constituted by immigration is revealed when one considers that including German expellees and repatriates, roughly one-third of the population before reunification consisted of immigrants (Bade 1994, 89). And it is hardly unrealistic to portray the East Germans as another set of immigrants who migrated into the political system and society of the Federal Republic.

From the question of the *process* of immigration we may distinguish the question of the *acceptance* of immigration, and it is here that the conservative position has its most force. In an important sense, whether or not Germany is a country of immigration is a matter of political self-understanding incorporated in legal policy toward admissions and naturalization. The government has traditionally defined Germany as a country of emigration in contrast to classic North and South American countries of immigration, states that historically have geared their membership policies toward the acquisition and legal integration of new citizens.[7] As a result, German naturalization has been legally defined as an exceptional case and administered accordingly. Consequently it is undeniable that Germany is *not* a country of immigration, if this is understood to mean having a political orientation toward the taking on of new citizens. Moreover, the resulting fact that a negligible number of migrants have become naturalized supports the assertion that in a formal sense Germany has not experienced appreciable immigration in the last decades.

A relativization of this position, however, is called for by the wide extent to which the migrants have found a legal basis for their presence in the Federal Republic. It can thus be argued that, insofar as foreign workers and their families enjoy a secure social and economic citizenship, Germany has become — in spite of political intentions to the contrary — a formal as well as de facto country of immigration. Lobbyists for the foreigners argue that the government should recognize this situation and complete the legal integration of de facto immigrants by naturalizing them. Even if this were to happen, however, in the absence of the establishment of any mechanisms for accepting new immigration, it would remain the case that as a matter of political will and official self-definition, Germany cannot accurately be labeled a country of immigration.[8]

Integration and Assimilation
As the established nature of the guestworker minority became clear, "integration" became the keyword of policy debates over the foreign presence in Germany. It was agreed that some measures must be taken to "integrate" the new minority, yet what this means has been a topic of disagreement ever since. In a general sense, integration has been understood to involve the reduction of tensions and the encouragement of equality between native Germans and the foreign residents. As a result, it has not been difficult to identify specific measures in the areas of German language instruction, education, job training, or housing as encouraging

integration. Beyond this, however, what the broader goals of integration are, how they are to be attained, and who is to secure them are issues that have proved fertile ground for the cultivation of ideological differences.

A central concern of this discussion, the relation between integration and assimilation, has provided the focus for a number of conflicting positions on policy toward the migrants. Although some have posited these two processes as identical and others as opposites, for the most part integration has been seen broadly as the *binding together* of discrete social groups in a manner aimed at removing conflicts and inequalities between them, while assimilation has been understood as the *removal of differences* acting as barriers to cultural homogeneity.[9] A consequence of this usage is that integration falls more readily into the realm of government action, whereas assimilation emphasizes the adaptive act of the migrants in relinquishing an old identity for a new one.

As objectives in themselves, assimilation and a pluralist model of integration do not necessarily favor any particular ideological orientation toward foreigners.[10] Integration strategies emphasizing the nurture of distinctive cultural traditions in ethnically segregated classrooms, an approach employed for instance in Bavaria, may be supported by foreign groups committed to preserving their culture in the German diaspora as well as by those wishing to improve the chances that foreigners will return to their homelands. By the same token, assimilation may be seen as a desirable goal both by nationalist defenders of the German culture and by proponents of social harmony and full equal rights for the migrants. What distinguishes conflicting ideological approaches is the way in which they conceive the relation between assimilation and integration, that is, whether both are to be pursued and if so, in which order or with which priority.

One might distinguish (Esser 1983) among models of societies that are integrated but not assimilated (cultural pluralist), assimilated but not integrated (marked, for example, by class conflict), assimilated and integrated (culturally homogeneous), or neither assimilated nor integrated (marked, for example, by ethnic strife). Integration will be viewed by most as desirable, but whether it should be coupled with assimilation depends on a normative stance regarding the relative value of homogeneity and ethnic or cultural diversity. Many participants in the German discussion understand assimilation as forced Germanization and reject it as tantamount to an assault on the ethnic identity of foreign residents.

For the many advocates of both integration and assimilation, the question arises as to which is to take precedence. Many conservatives assert that integration in the form of a fully equal position in society can only follow a completed process of assimilation (Hailbronner 1989a, 79; Quaritsch 1981, 53–65). Some of their opponents argue the opposite: that integration, possibly even including the nurture of separate ethnic identities, is an essential precondition for successful assimilation in the long run (Esser 1983, 32–34; Francis 1983; John 1987). The most crucial point of difference between these views concerns who is to assume primary responsibility for the overall process. Where assimilation plays the central role, the burden is placed on the migrants to conform to German culture, with equality held out as a reward for the arduous transferal of identity. In the opposing view, establishing the necessary legal and political equality and promoting tolerance are tasks that fall on the indigenous population and its government. Assimilation is then expected to take place as the natural result of living together peaceably and in equality.

The discussion of integration since the early 1980s has kept pace with political developments affecting the foreign workers. Thus the trend toward recognizing the legitimacy of the migrants' continued presence has been reflected in the increasing currency of a notion of integration emphasizing social and economic equality as well as the preservation of separate cultural identities — or, alternatively, the development of a new (that is, not simply German) common identity. Politicians of all stripes are quick to distance themselves from understandings of integration that equate it with Germanization. Slowly participants in the debate over integration are recognizing that the full incorporation of permanent residents into German life cannot be a one-sided process carried out through the adaptive efforts of the migrants or by legislative decree. Mutual tolerance and concessions are required. At the same time, most involved parties have come to appreciate that assimilation is something that occurs whether one likes it or not, not so much along ethnic lines as through the impersonal technological forces of modernization, in a manner impinging on German and foreign lifestyles alike. If the general outlines of what integration means have become less controversial, however, debate has become all the more heated concerning the sort of society an integration policy should attempt to create.

The Multicultural Society

In the last decade, the notion of the multicultural society has provided a vital conceptual conduit for the discussion over how to cope with the ethnic stratification and increased social tensions in Germany. The term itself was appropriated from Australian debates over minority policy and introduced into German academic circles by Protestant scholars in 1980; it was then injected into policy debates by the General Secretary of the CDU, Heiner Geissler. The theme has since been invoked in contexts ranging from immigration policy to educational curricula, from social services to ecumenical debate. Moreover, it has found proponents, often for different reasons, in the progressive wing of the CDU as well as the SPD, the FDP, the churches, and the parties of the left. It is, accordingly, difficult to identify multiculturalism as a single position (Fijalkowski 1991b); it is perhaps best understood as an ongoing theoretical project fostered through continuous debate.[11]

There are two basic aspects of this project, a descriptive one and a normative one. First, "multicultural society" is used to describe the reality of cultural diversity in German society. At a minimum, it is a factual claim about the cultural heterogeneity that has come to characterize Germany in the wake of the post-war labor migration. Taken further, it asserts that Germany and indeed all societies have always encompassed a variety of cultural strands, even if some have been systematically subordinated and successfully repressed. In this view, the denial of diversity in nationalist ideologies is a harmful distortion of reality that may be corrected only through the recognition of the multicultural nature of modern societies.

A normative component enters the multiculturalist project with the claim that cultural diversity should be not only recognized but *affirmed*. Both the historical legacy of German nationalism and the prospect of a unified European political entity add to the force of this imperative. This claim establishes a particular context for considerations of how the multicultural society should be ordered so as to enable a peaceful and just coexistence. The central question of multiculturalism in this sense is, as Axel Schulte formulates it, "According to which point of view is common life between the native population and migrant minorities to be shaped, and what role are 'structural' dimensions (economy, politics, laws, etc.) on the one hand and cultural dimensions on the other to play?" (1990, 3). There is of course no consensus regarding an answer. One can, however, identify a number of issue areas that together constitute a multiculturalist agenda.

First, multiculturalism defines cultural diversity as a positive value. This dictates that integration policies should aim not at assimilation but rather at preserving difference. The question that follows is, to what extent and for which groups? Are, for example, all migrant workers to be taken as a group with a distinctive minority culture,[12] or is each nationality or ethnic group to be treated separately? Are German refugees from, say, Rumania to be encouraged to cultivate their otherness?

A second issue for multiculturalists is structural equality for non-German groups. This point is a response to the problem of ethnic stratification, the systematic disadvantaging of the non-German minorities. It is an article of faith for proponents of the multicultural society that the subordinate *Ausländer* status of the migrants should be replaced by measures guaranteeing them equality of opportunity in German society. Without such a structural reorientation, cultural diversity is doomed to lapse into ethnic strife. Considerable disagreement, however, surrounds the question of how this reorientation is to be attained — whether, for example, affirmative action or even some form of positive discrimination should be introduced.

Third, cultural minorities should enjoy certain group rights, that is, some measure of structural autonomy — from other groups, and above all from the state. The obvious point of dispute concerns how much. Some contend that self-sufficient ethnic communities play a positive role in providing a sense of place for members and in easing the integration of new arrivals into the society at large. Yet too much autonomy and isolation, others fear, may result in ethnic segmentation and overall societal disintegration (Esser 1983). Another point of disagreement is the extent to which cultural autonomy should be politically institutionalized, for example in the form of group rights.

A further programmatic feature of a viable multicultural society is intercultural dialogue. The isolation and separation of cultures does not bode well for long-term social harmony; according to a catchphrase of multiculturalists, instead of an existence "next to one another" (*Nebeneinander*), living "with one another" (*Miteinander*) should be encouraged. Beyond this sphere of agreement, some emphasize the aspect of mutual tolerance in contacts among cultural perspectives, while others underline the importance of engaging in argument and not shying away from conflict within certain boundaries.

What these boundaries are raises a final multiculturalist topic, namely, the minimum shared conditions necessary for multicultural coexistence. Here, two types of conditions are usually debated. One is the overarching *cultural* baseline required for a functional society, which most would argue includes acceptance of the German language and respect for human rights, in particular gender equality. Equally necessary is a basic *institutional* consensus over the authority of the constitution and the role of the state in adjudicating conflicts.

Due to its broadness and flexibility the multiculturalist agenda has found support in a number of quarters, often for quite different reasons. The more progressive advocates of the multicultural society see it as a *chance* (Miksch 1983) to secure societal stability and to pave the way toward a new European and — eventually — world order. Multiculturalism is also championed by those who see the pursuit of social equality, the protection of minority cultures, and the promotion of intercultural conversation as a moral or religious *duty*. Still others see in this project the *enrichment* of German society, be it superficially in the form of a greater variety of ethnic food and folklore, or more profoundly in the fostering of a more tolerant, cosmopolitan ethos. From a more pragmatic perspective, a departure from a monolithic German national culture is seen as a dictate of *prudence,* since demographically the German population alone is aging rapidly and failing to reproduce itself (Geissler 1990). Finally, from the point of view of some migrants, the acceptance and affirmation of their cultural otherness is seen as their (long overdue) *due.*

Among those who do not subscribe to the multicultural discourse there are two camps. Multiculturalism finds opponents on the right of the political spectrum and critics on the left; together these two groups sharpen the question of the depth and significance of cultural differences in German society.

The opponents of the multicultural society emphasize the unity of national cultures and especially of the German national culture. They object to the program of multiculturalism on two main grounds. Pragmatically, they see the promotion of minority cultures as a suicidal course that can lead only to ethnic strife, societal discord, and the destruction of German national unity.[13] Foreign residents who wish to stay should be assimilated; those not capable of being integrated in this manner should be encouraged to leave. At a different, ontological level, the acceptance of alien ways of life is seen by some opponents of multiculturalism as imperiling the very essence of the German people. To expose the German people, understood as a living organism, to the alienating influence of a multicultural society would be tantamount to genocide (Heidelberg Manifesto of 1981, 1986).

Critics of multiculturalism attack it not for underestimating but for overestimating the unity and significance of culture. They tend to sympathize with the broad objectives of pluralist integration, but view the idea of multiculturalism as overly ideological in character (e.g., Hoffmann 1990; Schmid 1990; Radtke 1993). Its ideological nature is manifested mainly in its hypostatization of societal diversity into a network of coherent cultures. Because these cultures tend to be identified in national terms (the Turks, including Kurds; the Vietnamese), critics further accuse multiculturalists of supporting the perspective of their nationalist-conservative opponents. And echoing the American debate over affirmative action, they express concern that support for cultural diversity can tend artificially — or at least unnecessarily — to strengthen ethnic identification and increase the potential for social conflict. This criticism implies a hope for the long-term development of a society of individuals whose ethnic identities have withered away.

The discussion over the multicultural society is a membership debate about the place of foreign members in German society and the shape their relations to the dominant German culture ought to take. At the heart of this debate is the issue of the separation of societal spheres, of whether the cultural realm may be treated as separate from the realm of politics. Proponents of multiculturalism seek to wed political unity with cultural diversity on the assumption that the world in which religions, languages, and ethnic traditions confront one another may successfully be severed from the world of political, economic, and social organization. Some critics also subscribe to this project. Lutz Hoffmann (1990), for example, advocates a "multiethnic" (as opposed to multicultural) society in the context of an overarching "republican" political order. Opponents, however, uphold instead the nation-state principle: the intrinsic claim of a sacred and monolithic national culture to political authority in a culturally homogeneous state. As we will see, these different prescriptions for how to link political structures and cultural identity constitute a crucial determinant of conflicting normative positions on membership.

Three Policy Debates

The various disputes over concepts dealing with the foreign presence in Germany have been paralleled by debates over membership policy regarding the migrant workers and their families. Three interrelated topics touching on different aspects of membership will be examined here: the government's basic policy orientation toward foreign residents, the propriety of extending voting rights to these residents, and the advisability of allowing multiple citizenships.

Priorities in Foreigner Policy: Integration or Reduction?

With the consolidation of the foreign worker population in the Federal Republic, the question of state policy toward this group took a permanent place on the political agenda. As in other European countries with guestworker histories, a broad consensus has arisen around two general goals for foreigner policy: limiting the growth of the foreign population and incorporating it into the overall society. Within this strategic framework, however, wide differences of opinion concerning priorities and specific strategies have emerged. The trend in Germany since the early 1980s has been toward ever greater disagreement over the priorities for policy toward the non-German population.

In the late 1970s, as it first became apparent that the guestworker population had come to stay, the SPD / FDP coalition government established a set of basic policy guidelines intended to buttress Germany's claim to not being a country of immigration. The policy consisted in a tripartite strategy of immigration restriction, repatriation assistance, and integration. The objective of restricting the numbers of the migrants was pursued primarily through the maintenance of the ban on recruitment set in 1973. Repatriation assistance combined financial aid for workers who wished to return to their homelands with reintegration programs in the sending countries. Integration, finally, was promoted in two ways: through attempts to stabilize the residence and work status of migrants wishing to stay, and through increased access to naturalization. The overall emphasis of this policy on integration was reflected in the government's sponsorship of a broad competition for ideas on integration programs during 1979–80 (Meier-Braun and Pazarkaya 1983, 52–53).

A major shift in this orientation followed the economic downturn at the beginning of the 1980s, as unemployment rose sharply and popular sentiment against foreigners grew. The opposition CDU made foreigner policy a cornerstone of its campaign and began to exert pressure on the government to increase state control over the migrant population. The coalition responded by enacting a set of stricter measures emphasizing the reduction of the foreign population; these were not, however, enough to prevent their loss at the polls. In 1982, a new coalition with the CDU, CSU, and FDP took office and announced its intention of cutting Germany's foreign population by half. The change of orientation in foreigner policy was quickly sealed with the adoption of measures that in effect presented foreigners with the choice of assimilating or leaving.

Superficially the new policy retained the former emphasis on restriction, repatriation, and integration. These objectives were, however, rearranged in terms of priority, and the first two were pursued with increased vigor. The policy's new focus, restriction, was extended to apply to family reunification, and in the following years the permissible age for retrieving children was lowered, waiting periods were introduced for bringing spouses from the homeland, and a number of other restrictions, including visa requirements, were enforced. Repatriation efforts intensified under a 1983 law designed to promote actively the readiness to return. Most significantly, integration was reconceived as a process leading solely along the path to naturalization. The fundamental distinction between the rights and privileges of citizenship and the human rights enjoyed by aliens was reaffirmed, and the body of law applying to foreigners was shaped in a manner emphasizing the subordinate nature of their status. The aim of this policy was clear: the development of a permanent minority in Germany was to be prevented at all costs. The strategy for achieving this goal involved limiting the growth of the non-citizen population as much as possible, reducing its numbers by encouraging repatriation, and then absorbing the remainder into German society through assimilation and naturalization.

The initiation of this policy unleashed a public discussion over the foreigner question. The government justified its actions on a variety of grounds. One argument, which found general agreement, was that restrictions on migration were needed in order to ease tensions that could jeopardize the integration of the present migrants. More controversial were assertions that the maximum level of acceptance of foreigners had been reached and that the foreign population must be reduced to free more jobs for German citizens and to preserve social stability. The claim that the new policy pursued the interests of foreigners, both by strengthening the expressed will of many to go home and by supporting their "right to a homeland," met with considerable skepticism.

The most effective rationale for the coalition's efforts referred to a particular vision of how German society should be structured. A restrictive foreigner policy was defended as necessary to protect a homogeneous German national culture from an impending collapse into a multicultural society with minority problems comparable to those in the United States. The existence of minorities, it was alleged, would gravely endanger the chances for German reunification. Proponents of the "assimilate or leave" approach raised the specter of a future in which a radicalized Turkish minority bloodily carried out Turkish political conflicts on German streets, sought to establish the cultural and legal hegemony of Islam, and through its high birth rates eventually turned ethnic Germans into a minority. Such exaggerated images found a receptive public. At the same time they generated considerable protest from opposition parties, the churches, the labor unions, and many other political actors.

The aspect of the new policy which drew the most fire from critics was its fundamentally contradictory nature. For many, the notion of increasing efforts at integration while simultaneously creating incentives to leave made little sense, even after the government suggested that the former strategy applied specifically to the second and third generation aliens while the latter was aimed more at the original migrants. This contradiction, it was suggested, only made more difficult an unwanted choice forced on workers in many cases unprepared to make such a consequential decision. Opponents of the policy drew attention to statistics demonstrating the unreliability of the intention to return, and predicted — correctly — that incentives to return would have little success. Additional doubt was cast on the decidedly unscientific claims that the tolerance level of German society for foreigners had been surpassed, and that foreigners were taking away jobs from Germans. Some emphasized that the foreign workers had earned their place in the Federal Republic, and that it was unjust to prevent them from bringing their families together or to push them into the extremely insecure process of remigration. Integration, critics finally underscored, cannot simply be equated with assimilation; rather, it must be sought through active strategies adapted to the needs and desires of the migrants themselves.

Despite its announced intention of setting its policy into a new, reformed Aliens Act, the government delayed such a step for most of the 1980s. In 1988 a proposal finally appeared, couched in language championing the homogeneity of the German national society (Heldmann 1989, 215–19). Its terms were so strict that a unified opposition was able to force its withdrawal. Soon after, a somewhat milder draft was introduced and enacted with a haste spurred as much by the need to undermine support for the extreme right[14] as by the expectation of an impending SPD majority in the Bundesrat. The new law, which went into effect on January 1, 1991, for the most part simply codified the administrative practices that had evolved according to the government's guidelines. It did include some necessary reforms, such as reduced naturalization requirements. Yet at the same time it furthered the goals of restriction and repatriation by instituting strict living space requirements for family reunification and by considerably expanding the legal grounds for the expulsion of noncitizens. In addition, it established the duty of social workers to report data on aliens and opened the possibility of future foreign labor recruitment under full government control. As a result, this law may be seen as essentially a continuation of the government's efforts at preventing the long-term presence of minorities.

For this reason, the passage of the Aliens Act sparked a new round of criticism. The new law has been characterized as aimed more at repelling than at incorporating foreign residents and criticized for sending a message of distrust to those who had hoped for acceptance. Opponents of the law claim that the membership status of migrants has been made less secure in many respects, a development bound to complicate rather than aid integration. Particularly strong disapprobation all across the political spectrum has been expressed in response to the overall conception of membership inherent in the new legislation. Given that migrant worker families have clearly established themselves in Germany, is it appropriate to continue to disadvantage them as "foreigners," particularly when members of other, in many ways comparable, minorities such as East Germans and other ethnic German refugees are treated as equals? The permanent residents, many feel, should have equal rights and should no longer remain without fundamental protections against the will of the state. The human rights of these "Germans without passports" should be given priority over the ideology of German national unity. Government policy that continues to suppress the multicultural character of Germany society can only cause harm in the long run.

These criticisms bring into focus the primary disagreements at the core of deliberations over policy toward the migrants. The central question is whether the permanent existence of distinct ethnic groups within German society is to be affirmed or prevented. An important secondary question is whether the migrants should be able to choose how they shape their lives in Germany, or whether they should be forced either to adapt fully to German standards or to leave. These questions will likely continue to animate the debate over the fundaments of policy toward the migrants for some time to come.

Voting Rights for Foreigners

According to one estimate, roughly ten million European residents are ineligible to vote because they maintain no domicile in their home country and have not taken on the citizenship of their country of residence (Turpin 1987, 71). Hence it is not surprising that in most European countries some form of political rights for this group has been discussed.[15] In the Federal Republic, local voting rights for foreign residents were first proposed in 1971 by the churches. A lively debate ensued over the next two decades. In the course of this discussion, foreign-voting-rights advocates in the churches, welfare associations, foreigner organizations, and the Greens were gradually joined by the labor unions, the SPD, the FDP, and isolated members of the CDU. The federal government, the Employers' Federation, the CDU, the CSU, and parties of the far right have remained staunch opponents of any such measure.

The debate over political representation for foreigners has focused primarily on local elections, for two reasons: first, this focus has been the only politically feasible one, and second, the constitutional situation of local bodies is, arguably, unique. As a consequence, two types of considerations—political and legal—have shaped the discussion. For proponents of voting rights for foreign residents, moral and political arguments and the constructive possibilities of legislation have been the means of choice (Zuleeg 1987; Hoffmann 1990; Sieveking et al. 1989; Franz 1991; Rittstieg 1981 and 1988; Sievering 1981; Bukow and Llaryora 1989). Opponents have organized their arguments mainly around constitutional constraints on extending the vote (Doehring and Isensee 1974; Quaritsch 1981; Hailbronner 1989a, 1989b; Stöcker 1989).

The political arguments have revolved around three topics. The first and most important is the understanding of democracy to be embodied in policies defining political membership. Here, where foreigner advocates assert the central significance of *subjection* to democratic authority (*Betroffenheit*) in determining the right to political participation, their opponents see democratic rights as grounded in a sort of national *club membership*. The argument of those who favor allowing long-term residents to vote runs as follows: Foreign residents are not in principle distinguishable from German citizens in the extent to which they are affected by political decisions; indeed, if anything they are more subject to state power than their coresidents. At the same time, they contribute as much as citizens do to the life of the society: they pay taxes and fulfill all the same obligations as citizens apart from jury duty and military service, a duty applicable only to men and for which foreigners are at least theoretically eligible.[16] Together with citizens they are part of a "community of life and destiny" (*Lebens- und Schicksalsgemeinschaft;* Zuleeg 1987, 157). This involvement entitles all long-term residents to democratic expression—to the right to help shape decisions affecting this community. For democracy is grounded in the human right of individuals to self-determination, and only this right forms the basis of the state's claim to sovereignty. In this context the purpose of the vote as a democratic process is to mediate among the conflicting interests of autonomous individuals.

Opponents of the vote for foreign residents counter this view with a nationalist conception of democracy. For them, democracy is likewise grounded in self-determination — but in that of a fixed group, namely, the nation defined in ethnic terms. The task of democratic participation is not conflict resolution but the building of a unified national will, and this requires a high degree of homogeneity — of cultural similarity and common interests (Schmitt 1970, 223–39). The fact of subjection is no more an argument for inclusion in decision making for residents than it is for prisoners facing capital punishment. The category of residence fluctuates constantly and is no substitute for the permanent commitment to the state demanded by citizenship. For this reason, citizenship — full and official membership in the body of the German nation-state — is the only permissible foundation for political participation. Voting rights are exclusively citizens' rights. Foreigners may freely choose to take on full political rights by naturalizing. Yet to extend the vote unilaterally to noncitizens would compromise Germany's democratic order and undermine the value of citizenship since foreigners (1) have no obligation of loyalty to the state and indeed as a rule hold competing loyalties, (2) would not be bound by their decisions since they can return to their home country at any time, and (3) do not share the full range of duties incumbent upon German citizens.[17]

A second area of difference concerns the significance of voting rights for the integration of foreigners. The argument of those in favor is that increased political rights would constitute a step toward the structural and social integration of Germany's long-term foreign residents. Having a political voice, at least in local decision making, would increase the sense of belonging, of being at home in Germany, of having a stake in community affairs.[18] This sense of inclusion would in turn encourage further integration, including naturalization (here the experience of other countries is often cited as evidence). Moreover, establishing the vote for foreigners would bring Germany into line with EU policy and thus aid her external integration into a unified Europe.

The counterarguments to this position portray even limited participation for foreigners as an obstacle to integration. Foreigners, it is claimed, are uninterested in voting in the first place — or in existentially belonging at all — since otherwise they would long ago have taken advantage of the opportunity to naturalize. To give them the vote would not solve their problems, rather, it would increase them by removing a major incentive for them to adapt and to pursue citizenship. As it is, this view holds, the number of privileges aliens already enjoy has the consequence of undermining their resolve to return to their countries of origin. Moreover, regarding the question of European integration, there is simply no need to prefigure future decisions regarding political rights for foreign residents.

Additional disagreement, finally, concerns the effects that including foreigners would have on the political landscape of Germany. Opponents assert the effects would be overwhelmingly negative. The vote for foreigners would lead to a fracturing of political life and a radicalization of the populace. It would introduce the danger of the formation of foreign political parties that might import their own national conflicts and, for example, attempt to replace the Basic Law with the Koran. At the same time, foreigners — overwhelmingly workers — would imbalance the German political spectrum by throwing their weight behind communist parties (Quaritsch 1981, 52). The effect would be a strengthening of social tensions in general and especially of hostility toward foreigners. Reserving the right to vote for citizens, on the other hand, would uphold a source of identity, namely that of the nation, of especial importance to young Germans.

Advocates of the foreign vote provide a different assessment. They cite studies showing that foreigners would not significantly depart from German voting patterns (see Koch-Arzberger 1985).[19] Entitling foreigners to vote would benefit them not only by giving them a voice but also, just as importantly, by forcing parties to pay more attention to their needs. At the same time, it would serve the interests of some German voters by forcing fairer gerrymandering practices, since at present, districts with high foreign populations are correspondingly underrepresented. Finally, the political integration of foreigners would work against a political radicalization stemming from the isolation of the foreign population. The message sent by taking such a step — the departure from a narrowly nationalistic conception of politics — would moreover help Germany's credibility as a liberal democracy.

The differences in the political debate are reflected in the discussion over the constitutional implications of voting privileges for foreign residents. The basic position of those opposed to extending the vote is that such a step is unequivocally ruled out by the German Basic Law. Those on the other side contend that the Basic Law not only leaves considerable leeway for interpretation[20] but moreover contains warrants for a more inclusive voting policy that would take account of the fundamental changes in German society following the worker migration. The constitutional issues revolve around five points: the constitutional definition of democracy, the concept of the "people" or *Volk,* the status of local assemblies, the guarantee of equality, and the procedure for constitutional changes.

The competing views of democracy in the political discussion find separate loci in the German Basic Law. The "subjection" notion of democracy held by supporters of a broadened electorate finds its ground in article 1: "The dignity of the human being is inviolable. To respect it and protect it is the duty of all state power." This "anthropological premise" (Hoffmann 1990, 133) is held to establish the human rights of individuals as the basis of the democratic state and to justify the political inclusion of all those individuals whose dignity is fundamentally contingent upon the actions of the state. The prevailing nation-statist conception of democracy, on the other hand, is based on article 20, paragraph 2: "All state power emanates from the people." According to this view, not the individual, but the "people" (that is, the collectivity of national members) is the basis of democratic sovereignty.

This definition of the "people" forms a second point of controversy. The conventional, restrictive position is that with the term "people" nothing other than the totality of German citizens can be meant. The modifier "German," it is conceded, is not applied in this connection as it is in specifying other rights.[21] However, it is argued, the "German people" is mentioned in comparable contexts in the (nonbinding) preamble and in the last article regulating the replacement of the constitution (art. 146); and this notion, in turn, is defined with reference to article 116 as the union of German citizens and those ethnic German repatriates who enjoy constitutional equality with them ("status Germans"). This understanding of *"Volk"* as the German nation is backed by a long tradition of state theory and legal precedents (see Grawert 1984). Proponents of voting rights for foreign residents argue for a considerably different understanding of *"Volk."* They see the wording of article 20 as deliberately agnostic about the ethnic or national character of "the people." In principle, they argue, there is no reason why "the people" should not be understood to comprise the entire long-term resident population; indeed, only such an understanding would comply with the commitment to human rights in article 1. In addition, they point out that even in the conception of their opponents, citizenship is neither a necessary nor a sufficient condition for being eligible to vote, since nonnaturalized repatriates have the right to vote, while certain citizens — those below a certain age or without the required duration of residence — do not. A reasonable understanding of *"Volk,"* they conclude, is one in which German citizens make up the core, but in which there is room for other members of German society.

The third point of debate concerns the legal admissibility of extending voting rights at the communal level. At issue is the interpretation of the "homogeneity clause" of article 28, which specifies that "in the states, counties and municipalities, the people must have a representation determined through a general, direct, free, equal and secret vote." This clause is interpreted restrictively to mean that both the group of eligible voters and the form of democratic process must be the same at all levels of German government. It follows, according to opponents of the foreign vote, that no separate provisions at the local level are permissible. The counterargument denies that this interpretation is compelling and contends further that significant structural differences, for example the lack of territorial sovereignty, separate the local level of government from the state and federal levels. Indeed, this argument runs, communal political associations are in their nature much closer to other sorts of organizations, such as unions or universities, in which foreigners already enjoy full membership rights. Representatives of this view attempt to anchor their claim with reference to the constitutional concept of "local community" (art. 28, par. 2), which they claim is to be distinguished from that of the national electorate (*Staatsvolk*).

A fourth area of difference regards the question of equality and discrimination. Article 3, paragraph 3 states, "No one may be disadvantaged or privileged on account of his sex, his descent, his race, his language, his homeland or place of origin, his faith or his religious or political views." Local voting rights for foreigners, their opponents insist, would violate this provision by creating two unequal electorates. By the same token, advocates argue that denying political rights for permanent residents on account of their nationality is a direct violation of their right to equality.

Finally, the two sides disagree over the possibility of clarifying the constitutional situation through a revision. Citing article 79, paragraph 3, which prohibits changes affecting either the federal order or the principles advanced in articles 1 and 20, opponents deny that any such change is possible. In their view, this prohibition, together with the univocal nature of the constitutional definition of the electorate at all levels, effectively renders voting rights for foreigners impossible. Proponents of these rights, for their part, assert that the room for interpretation of the Basic Law makes official changes unnecessary; nonetheless, revisions that would anchor their understanding more clearly are not only possible but also desirable insofar as they would provide an opportunity for public debate of the basic issues. The passage of legislation specifying the right of all long-term residents to vote would be a vindication of both the human rights foundation of German democracy and the democratic will of the people.

In 1989 SPD-Green coalitions in the states of Hamburg and Schleswig-Holstein passed resolutions extending voter eligibility in local elections to certain classes of foreigners. Parliamentary members from the CDU and CSU brought suit against this step, and on October 31, 1990, the Federal Constitutional Court nullified the laws on the constitutional grounds discussed above. In spite of this development and given the precedence of European law over the constitutions of member states, in the context of European integration the German *Länder* were obliged to extend political rights at least to resident citizens of other European countries by the beginning of 1996. European policymakers recognized the unacceptability of introducing freedom of mobility in a manner that would compromise equality of political representation (Sieveking et al. 1989, 72). As the European Union continues to develop its own form of political membership, it will become increasingly difficult to maintain a link between political rights and assimilation to a specific national identity (Meehan 1993). In this context, the most pressing issue for electoral policy is likely to become the extent to which non-Europeans should be given a political voice.

Viewed in terms of membership norms, the debate over voting rights for foreign residents reveals a clash over two fundamental determinants of political inclusion. The first is the *ground* for inclusion. At issue is whether the reason for being politically represented is located in an identity, in actions, or in a context. The arguments for excluding foreigners invoke the first two reasons, that a person is entitled to vote either in virtue of being a German (an attribute conveyed through birth) or in virtue of having committed oneself to the German state (for example through naturalization).[22] The third reason, advanced in arguments in favor of a more inclusive membership policy, seeks to tie the right to political participation to one's context of subjection to both state authority and the consequences of the state's acts.

The second determinant is the *unit* of inclusion. Here the question is whether political membership is to be attributed on an individual or on a group basis. The restrictive position advances the view that political self-determination is an action engaged in by groups with internal decision-making structures. Persons are entitled to political participation only in a derivative sense defined wholly through their membership in such a group. The opposing view focuses on individuals as the primary ontological possessors of political rights. In this view, it is the authority of states that is derivative.

From these beliefs regarding the appropriate ground and unit of political inclusion emerge two competing images of political membership. One image is that of the political community as an exclusive club in which membership is passed on from one generation to the next and in rare cases extended to new members under conditions set forth by the club. Guests are allowed in but rarely initiated. The other image is of a more open community defined by common circumstances and interests. Membership is not handed out as an act of benevolence, it is rather open to all those who are involved to a certain extent in the society and who wish to belong.

Naturalization and Dual Citizenship

Encouraging naturalization—the induction of new members into the full rights and duties of citizenship—has been recognized by almost all participants in the foreigner debate as a desirable policy toward Germany's new minority. Some see naturalization as a means for absorbing the newcomers and preserving the homogeneity of German society; others emphasize the role of citizenship rights in dismantling the subordinate status of the migrants and in aiding in their integration. Naturally, foreigners also stand to gain a number of material benefits through naturalization. The question that has dominated debate in this area since the late 1970s is, On what terms should citizenship be granted?

Naturalization has traditionally been conceived of in Germany as an exceptional act presupposing full assimilation and a clear state interest. Legally, naturalization has been governed by the German Citizenship Law of 1913, paragraphs 8 and 9, and a set of internal guidelines regulating the decisions of naturalization officials. The law of 1913 sets forth a few minimal requirements: a permanent place of residence, a good reputation, the capacity to support oneself. The administrative guidelines have established a number of further criteria, including ten years of lawful residence in Germany, a commitment to the democratic order of the Federal Republic, a basic knowledge of its political and social structures, a certain degree of cultural integration and mastery of the German language, and a "voluntary and permanent attachment to Germany." This attachment is understood to rule out the cultivation of another national identity and culture, for example through activity in foreign political organizations. Finally, candidates for naturalization are required to pay an application fee and to relinquish all other citizenships.[23] When all these conditions are satisfied, a large area of discretion remains for naturalization officials. Naturalization is to be granted only when it lies in the interest of the state, that is, when the applicant is seen as a "worthy addition" to society whose acceptance is politically, culturally, and economically desirable (cf. Berlin Commissioner 1990).

This policy is among the strictest in Europe, and Germany, despite the fact that roughly two-thirds of its migrant population fulfill the basic criteria, has had far and away the lowest rate of naturalization among European countries with guestworker populations.[24] Several factors contribute to this. Until a recent reform, the fee represented a considerable barrier to many. Beyond the financial aspects, in the view of most foreign residents the overall cost of naturalization has been too high, or the benefits too low. Many feel unwanted by German society and recognize that citizenship in itself cannot solve problems of inequality and discrimination. More important, nearly all are unwilling to sever their ties to their homeland. Doubtless there is some truth in the claim of some politicians that, in light of the status they already enjoy, many migrants simply do not aspire to more.

In the conviction that a permanent, disenfranchised minority is, in the long run, insupportable, policymakers of all persuasions have produced proposals for easing naturalization requirements and thereby lowering the cost of citizenship.[25] One oft-repeated suggestion — establishing a claim to naturalization for first- and second-generation migrants fulfilling basic requirements of long-term lawful residence and self-sufficiency — was incorporated in a limited form in the recent Aliens Act (arts. 85 and 86). Another proposal involves a one-time decree extending an offer of German citizenship to guestworkers along with an option to refuse it (see Hoffmann 1990, 168). In recent years the parties of the left have argued for introducing a right to naturalization with birth in the Federal Republic (jus soli) to all with at least one parent born in Germany. An alternative strategy would legally declare the migrant worker families "status Germans" in the same sense as German repatriates, thus qualifying them for all the constitutional rights due to "Germans" — including the claim to be naturalized upon application. With the exception of this last, hardly feasible proposal, however, none of these strategies comes to terms with the problem at the heart of naturalization policy regarding the migrants: the demand that one give up one's former citizenship in order to take on full German membership.

There is no doubt that the official refusal to accept dual citizenship is the main determinant of the reluctance of migrants — especially the Turks — to naturalize. For members of this population, giving up one's citizenship is attached to great costs, both symbolic and material. For one thing, it is perceived as a betrayal of one's country, people, and relatives. First-generation migrants in particular are defeated by the prospect of breaking their ties to family in the homeland and giving up their hope of eventually returning. Even for younger members of this community, important ties to the homeland exist that often do not stand to be replaced through the German society. At the same time, the loss of citizenship has weighty legal and financial consequences in the homeland. Thus, former citizens require visas to return to their country of origin and — in the Turkish example — lose the rights to operate businesses, to own land, and to inherit. The deterrent effect of these factors is reflected in a poll in Berlin in which 61 percent Turkish and 72 percent Yugoslavian respondents said they would apply for German citizenship if they were not required to give up their old one (Bischoff and Teubner 1991, 173).

For these reasons, considerable debate has arisen over the policy of not allowing dual citizenship. The various proposals for easing naturalization have each appeared in two versions allowing or prohibiting the maintenance of other citizenships. Some support has been garnered by the Federal Commissioner for Foreigner Affairs for instituting a type of dual citizenship already employed by Spain together with certain Latin American countries. According to this model, citizenship in the country of residence is understood as "active," meaning all duties and rights are in force, while other citizenships are seen as "dormant" and only to be activated through the transferral of residence. Such an arrangement requires a complex set of treaties, however, and for this reason many instead advocate simply allowing dual citizenship as it arises.[26] In general, the discussion of dual citizenship has encompassed five main topics: the legality of allowing double citizenship, its desirability, the problem of loyalty, the question of inequality, and the likely effects of such a policy.

Strictly speaking, naturalization officials are bound by neither international nor national law to refuse citizenship to those unprepared to give up other national attachments. However, as opponents of dual citizenship are quick to note, under customary international law, states are in no way hindered from including such limitations in their own citizenship policies. Moreover, a positive legal basis for the prevailing policy exists in a treaty from 1963 aimed at reducing instances of multiple citizenship and preventing conflicts over mandatory military service among Council of Europe countries. This treaty has been accepted in court cases as the basis for the administrative ban on dual citizenship worked out by the Minister of the Interior and individual states. Dual citizenship supporters point out, however, that the treaty itself does not license denying naturalization to potential dual citizens; rather, its letter obligates states to denaturalize those of their citizens who have taken on another citizenship (Zuleeg 1987, 255–62). In addition, they challenge the legitimacy of the central role in naturalization policy that the Ministry of the Interior, on the basis of a law dating from the Nazi period, enjoys while at the same time they deploy constitutional arguments in favor of the position that naturalization policy is a matter for individual states rather than the central German government (Rittstieg 1990, 131–40).

The doctrine at the heart of the 1963 treaty — that multiple citizenship is a general evil to be avoided whenever possible — is also controversial. The argument against dual citizenship is that for the persons and states involved, it results in disadvantages that considerably outweigh any advantages it may bring (Kammann 1984). Dual citizens must contend with an unclear legal status, above all, in matters of international private law; their countries are unable to extend them diplomatic or consular protection in their other country of citizenship; in addition they may face doubled tax or military obligations. Opponents of this view argue, first, that multiple citizenship is unavoidable. The establishment of gender equality in many jus sanguinis policies has alone meant a massive increase in the number of children of binational marriages who now receive both citizenships. In Germany, many additional dual citizens are accounted for by German repatriates (who are not forced to give up their other citizenship) and by foreign citizens granted German status in order to participate in professional sports.[27] Second, the argument runs, the scope of dual citizenship has meant that conflicts and other disadvantages must be dealt with in any case — indeed, many have already been satisfactorily regulated. Thus, techniques such as the principle of "effective citizenship" (membership in the country to which one is most strongly bound) have been developed to resolve legal unclarities. The above-mentioned treaty has contributed greatly to resolving the (almost exclusively male) problem of multiple military obligations. In general, this view holds, what few problems remain either may be resolved without much trouble or will fall away through international processes such as European integration.

Perhaps the main objection to double citizenship is often expressed in the catchphrase, "One cannot serve two masters." Double citizenship is seen as leading to inevitable conflicts of loyalty, which in situations of crisis such as war produce dangers for the citizen as well as the countries involved. According to this view, the total and undivided loyalty of citizens is a fundamental requirement for the democratic order of the nation-state (Hailbronner 1989a). Citizenship is seen as an ultimate bond of commitment, a manifestation of a unique, indivisible, sacred loyalty to one's nation (Brubaker 1989b). Correspondingly, naturalization is conceived of as a rare and solemn transfer of the profound dedication presupposed by the fundamental privileges and duties of membership — above all, military obligation and political rights. The tendency of this position is to view the interests of the state in matters of membership as supreme.

The opposing view challenges this assumption and asserts the primacy of citizens over the state. Here the most important criterion for citizenship is not the dictates of state policy but rather the free consent of the individual. It is incumbent on the state to merit the loyalty of its members, and one way it may do this is by guaranteeing their full rights and equality. This position further attacks the idea that loyalty is indivisible by posing the question, In a society that tolerates cultural difference, why can one not remain loyal both to this order and to his or her nation of origin? The answer that proponents of dual citizenship supply is that there is no reason why support for the democratic system of the Federal Republic should require giving up non-German national identities. Admission to citizenship may rightfully require loyalty to the German political order, but not to the German ethnic nation. What is needed is a "de-ethnicisation of demands for assimilation" (Fijalkowski 1991b).

An additional claim of defenders of current German policy is that allowing dual citizenship would establish unfair advantages for certain groups, resulting in an unjustifiable inequality of membership statuses. Two classes would emerge, one with the normal rights of citizenship and one with voting privileges in two states, as well as the additional right to withdraw to another country when wished. Opponents meet this argument with the reminder that the sizable population of ethnic German repatriates already has a practical right to dual citizenship. In addition, they point out that since voting rights in general presuppose fixed residence, in practice double voting rights do not exist as a rule (Kaskin 1990, 43–44). For cases in which they do, for example in the European Parliament, two views prevail. One is that double voting rights should be ruled out; the other is that a double vote where two memberships are legitimately held is unobjectionable (Bade 1990).

A last area of disagreement concerns the effects a policy allowing double citizenship would bring. As in other areas of debate over foreigner policy, radically different assessments exist of the impact more inclusive policies would have on integration. The conservative position continues to hold that only naturalization at the end of a long process of assimilation will ease the societal tensions surrounding the migrants, and that only strictly regulated citizenship attribution will contribute to better relations among states. The opposing line is that successful large-scale integration requires full legal equality as a precondition, and that to allow multiple citizenships is to move in the direction of cooperation and closer ties among nations.

Defenders of the German nation-state fear that allowing jus soli and dual citizenship would compromise German traditions and devalue citizenship. They also fear that a population of dual citizens would give other countries an unwarranted influence on German politics. Both these worries are viewed by their more internationally oriented opponents with equanimity. Advocates see the acceptance of dual citizenship as a positive step away from a nation-state ideology shaped by the legacy of National Socialism, the doctrine of German blood, and the myth of an organic *Volkskörper* (Decision of the Bundesverwaltungsgericht E 8, 340, cited in Franz 1990b, 195). Finally, however, it is not clear how they would cope with a last concern of their opponents, namely the long-term legacy of double citizenship. For many, the prospect of a thoroughly assimilated population in the Federal Republic still holding foreign citizenships, or worse, an emigrant population in, say, Turkey, with no more ties to Germany other than German citizenship, remains unsettling.

An overview of the discussion of naturalization and dual citizenship reveals differences on several basic aspects of membership. One question is whether the extension of citizenship is to be seen primarily as a right of the applicant or as an act of generosity carried out by the state on behalf of its full members. A related question is whether in its essence citizenship as an institution should be shaped by state interests and requirements, in which case citizens are largely reduced to subjects, or whether it should conform to the real ties and conditions experienced by the individual. A third issue is whether the decision to leave or assimilate may rightfully be demanded by the host state, or whether an obligation exists to reduce as much as possible coercive influences on the decision to apply for citizenship. Bound up with this issue is the question of the extent to which citizenship may be conceived of as a willed attachment, and the extent to which it is an involuntary category. A final issue high-lighted in this debate concerns the type of assimilation required for acceptance into citizenship. The question here is whether or not assimilation into the structures and commitments of the state should suffice, or whether a cultural assimilation may legitimately be demanded as well.

Five Conceptions of Political Membership

How might we best characterize the basic positions at odds in the making of German membership policy? A common interpretation of this process understands it as, at root, a contest between nationalism and republicanism.[28] On this view, two constitutionally anchored political ideals are locked in a struggle for dominance: the traditional German nation-state versus a democratic order grounded in human rights. This conflict inevitably surfaces in discussions over political rights or naturalization for foreigners, pitting defenders of the integrity of the German national culture against supporters of a more diverse, inclusive, egalitarian society. If the Federal Republic is to succeed in establishing itself as a credible democratic state, holders of this interpretation argue, it must place the universal values of the liberal republic above the nation-state principle and establish a basic equality of rights for all residents independent of nationality. "Constitutional patriotism,"[29] as Jürgen Habermas (1987) argues, must trump national patriotism.

There is much to recommend this analysis. Nonetheless, the dichotomy it assumes fails to do justice to the complexity of the conceptions of membership that clash with one another in debates over Germany's foreign residents. One reason for this is that the distinction between republicanism and nationalism is drawn too sharply. Many supporters of a German national state have incorporated core republican ideas into their position and are thus willing, for example, to concede most basic rights to non-Germans. At the same time, alongside its cosmopolitan tendencies the republican view also echoes the nationalist position by upholding the notion of the state as a fixed territory set off from others and integrated under a particular constitution.[30] A second shortcoming of this classification is that it fails to take account of trends that have undermined citizenship as the foundation of state membership. Its assumption that an equal citizenship status for all should be the goal of membership policy is not shared by all parties in the debates.

The preceding discussion of membership debates has shown that a complex set of normative questions serves to distinguish the various views on how foreigners should be treated in Germany. What is the relationship between cultural identity and political membership? Does democracy require cultural homogeneity? Is political membership best assigned on grounds of individual commitment, subjection to the state, or membership in an ethnic community? Is it a right? A privilege? May it be earned? Answers to these questions necessarily invoke interrelated beliefs about the purpose of political membership, the basis on which it should be distributed, and the form it should take. These beliefs may be explicit or implied; taken together they constitute more or less coherent orientations toward political membership. Reflected in German membership debates are at least five fundamental normative orientations toward membership, which I call the closure, culture, choice, coexistence, and cosmopolitan positions.[31] These positions, it should be emphasized, are something like ideal types that as a group represent the spectrum of responses to the complex of normative issues regarding German political membership. As it happens, they correspond—very roughly—to the stances of, respectively, the far right, Christian, liberal, social democratic, and far left parties in Germany.[32] The following sketches characterize each position with reference to its attitudes toward equality, diversity, and the meaning of political community. In addition, I suggest how these attitudes lead to different membership strategies and incorporate differing assessments of the nation-state system.

The *closure* position assesses membership on the basis of belonging to a racial or ethnic entity. Represented by the slogans "Germany for the Germans" and "Out with Foreigners," this view posits political participation as the exclusive domain of a closed community defined through heredity. The purpose of political organization is the preservation of the group conceived as an ontological entity. "Peoples," according to this view "are (biologically and cybernetically) living systems of a higher order with distinctive systematic characteristics which are passed on genetically and through tradition" (Heidelberg Manifesto of 1981, 1986). Attempts to integrate foreigners would lead to the destruction of this entity. For this reason, the presence of members of other peoples is not to be tolerated in the long term. When necessary, foreigners may be allowed into such a society, but only for limited purposes and under a fundamental denial of membership rights. In this view, the bounded equality of full membership is reserved for the ethnic group, and diversity is perceived as a fundamental threat to be avoided at all costs.

The *culture* position differs from this view in two important respects. The basis of belonging is defined in terms of culture and commitment to the nation instead of in purely ethnic terms. And the society is not wholly closed but rather open to new members willing to transfer their national loyalty and to take on a German cultural identity. This view, which has marked the approach of the German government since the early 1980s,[33] presents foreigners with the choice of assimilating or being excluded. The premise is that the democratic order of the state (as opposed to the hypostatized nation) depends on the basic cultural homogeneity and indivisible loyalty of its members. Democracy may function fully only in a society limited to like-minded political actors; to tolerate the growth of cultural minorities is a recipe for chaos. Membership policy should therefore aim at preserving a homogeneous culture. Thus the basis of inclusion becomes the possession of certain central characteristics of the national culture, including the language and an identification with the German community. Membership is to be extended only to the extent that it accords to the interests and will of the group itself (Hailbronner 1989a). A foreigner may be granted the rights and responsibilities of full membership if it is recognized that he or she (1) has assimilated to the degree demanded by the state, and (2) is prepared to pledge exclusive fidelity to it. If these conditions are not met, then certain basic rights may legitimately be denied and his or her departure may be actively encouraged. Here, equality of status is bounded by participation in the national culture. Diversity is to be discouraged.

The central value in the *choice* approach is the freedom of the individual. In order to maximize the sphere of choice, the option of fully belonging or leaving is replaced by acceptance of a wide range of degrees of membership. Here, the guiding principle is that no coercive pressure should be applied to the prospective member. There should be neither a demand to assimilate nor pressure to leave: whether a foreign resident pursues citizenship or settles for living with a more uncertain and limited resident status should be that person's free and independent decision.

The contours of membership arrangements should be tailored to the needs of the various sorts of members, with an eye to maximizing their ability to shape their life plans. It may well be the case that many migrants in Germany are happy to remain politically and socially marginalized foreign citizens. For this reason, a category of "denizens" with secure residence status and limited political rights should be tolerated. At the same time, in order not to discourage naturalization, the option of accepting the risks and benefits of dual citizenship should remain for individuals. In accepting a plurality of unequal statuses matched to the level of commitment of members, this model encourages institutional as well as cultural diversity and moves beyond traditional notions of citizenship.

The *coexistence* orientation toward membership envisions cultural diversity under the aegis of political and social equality. The basis for inclusion is membership in the state society (that is, involvement and participation in the economic and social structure of the community). The main measure of this sort of membership is the duration of residence, the assumption being that after a certain amount of time — say, five to ten years — one becomes integrated *nolens volens* in the society. This integration, combined with the fact of subjection to state power, is held to provide the normative basis for political inclusion. All members in this sense are entitled to full political membership, contingent upon their commitment to observing the order ensconced in the constitution. For this orientation, citizenship is not contingent on assimilation; it is rather established by the fact of structural integration into the society. Cultural minorities are not to be suppressed. Indeed, cultural identity is seen as a right of members that is to be ensured or even protected through political measures. Other citizenships do not compromise the basis for political rights, although there is no reason to encourage them. In sum, citizenship based on coexistence implies full equality of rights among members of the fixed resident population of a given territorial organization, as well as a positive assessment of cultural difference.

A *cosmopolitan* stance, finally, grounds claims to political membership in the worth and dignity of the individual. On this view no admissible justification exists for confining basic rights to a certain hereditary group or political club. Political representation is a human right due all persons — or at least all adults — in a given territory, irrespective of their national or state affiliation. Other rights as well are viewed as linked primarily with where one lives. The purpose of any government is to serve the human rights of its resident population. On the whole, this view tends toward the separation of political rights and traditional citizenship. Proposals for full voting rights for foreigners, or for a "settlers law" that would establish the full equality of long-term residents and citizens thus fall within this rubric. Cosmopolitans argue for open borders and global politics, and their position is fundamentally opposed to the nation-state system and the institution of state citizenship. Membership is conceived in the Enlightenment terms of cosmopolitan solidarity. The more utopian strains of this orientation aim at a society in which national associations have been transcended. The equality sought by cosmopolitans is unbounded, and while diversity is tolerated, it is hoped that a harmonious world culture may be developed in the long run.

In these perspectives the task of democracy is conceived of respectively as the exclusive preservation of the ethnic group, the maintenance of a society of cultural and political equals, the libertarian maximization of individual free choice, the regulation of order among diverse constitutive groups, and the fulfillment of inherent human dignity. These orientations are in essence normative logics of membership that serve to justify the specific arguments made in debates over foreigner policy. They stand in varying relation to the current structures of societal membership in Germany, which waver between national and postnational forms (see Soysal 1994; Bauböck 1994). In these positions, the possibilities for different conceptions of membership are by no means exhausted. At the same time, these constellations of beliefs are not arbitrary. They inform policy debates over citizenship and political rights in Germany because they draw on and embody entrenched traditions of Western thought on political membership. In order to engage in a critical assessment of these positions it is necessary to say more about their historical provenance and broader philosophical context.

Chapter Three

Political Anthropologies

I n the arena of contemporary German membership debates five basic conceptions of citizenship contend against one another. The task of this chapter is to assess their strengths and weaknesses. But before embarking on such a task, something must be said about both the nature of the views involved and the criteria for judging their respective merits.

What separates these conceptions of citizenship? What is the nature of their disagreement? As competing *normative* conceptions of political membership their differences are not simply attributable to failures of reasoning; it is not the case that a single ethically correct method of defining political membership might be determined if only the proper conclusions were obtained, in a rational and consistent fashion, from objective premises about political order. Nor is their disagreement purely of an empirical nature, although some of their differences revolve around their divergent interpretations of social scientific data. At issue, rather, are conflicting accounts of the nature of human agents, the purpose of their communities, and the form their political organizations should take. These orientations embody, in short, what I will call conflicting political anthropologies.

A Methodological Excursus

"Since there are many forms of government there must be varieties of citizens," declared an influential political thinker long ago. In his *Politics,* Aristotle develops a typology of governments based on their divergent conceptions of the citizen and then goes on to describe monarchy as the "first and most divine" form of government (1941, bk. 3, especially chap. 5, 1278a 15–18; bk. 4, chap. 2, 1289a 40). Aristotle's method, if not his conclusion, lies at the root of the approach I take to assess the various positions on membership reflected in the German debate. Arguments about who should or should not be accepted as citizens necessarily contain premises about the political nature of people — about how they act, the extent to which they may be conceived of abstractly as individuals or as groups, their capacities for knowledge, their relation to the world in which they live, and the source of moral constraints on them. For instance, as we have seen, arguments that would ground citizenship in ethnonational membership involve a quite different view of human actors and the purposes of political community than, say, arguments that invoke an individual human right to democratic representation. But how are such differences to be resolved? Some may claim, as Alasdair MacIntyre (1984) does, that they represent the clashing of incommensurable traditions of thought on morality and politics. In actuality, however, the picture is somewhat more complicated.

The concepts deployed in contemporary debates on citizenship in Germany and in other Western countries do not spring full-grown from the furrowed brows of politicians.[1] They are, rather, part of a rich legacy of thought on politics and human nature. Western ideas about democracy and the citizen have emerged and been refined in the course of ongoing debates about questions such as the form of the perfect state, the source of sovereignty, the nature of democracy, and the basis of political obligation and the right to revolt. Political anthropologies reflect the presuppositions of seminal thinkers as well as those of later theorists who have reinterpreted them and applied them in new surroundings. The changing religious context of discussion has also deeply informed conceptions of the human subject of politics in Western cultures. These understandings have been stamped by the Hellenistic, Judaic, and Christian traditions, shaken and broken in the cosmological and epistemological shift to modernity, and reforged and reinvented in the battle between the secularized humanism of the Enlightenment and the sacralized nationalism of the Romantic Era.

Political ideas develop in a dialectic not only with other ideas but also with their environment. Thus political anthropologies have been formed in, and have come to reflect, concrete historical communities, even as they have conditioned the evolution and occasional restructuring of these settings. Our inherited ideas about democratic membership are indelibly marked by their origins in those societies and periods in which the institution of citizenship has played a prominent role — most notably, in the Greek city-states of Athens and Sparta, in republican and imperial Rome, in medieval and Renaissance cities such as Geneva and Venice, in the fledgling United States and revolutionary France, and in modern nationalist and welfare societies. Arguments about the proper nature and scope of citizenship are to a large extent culture-bound, in that they most often take the form of either apologia for or criticisms of policies reflecting the political status quo in a given society. For this reason, we are as unlikely to accept Aristotle's criticism of democracy as we are to think that his idealized conception of the polis is a viable political alternative for our day and age.

Yet bereft though it may be of its context, Aristotle's theory retains a certain relevance today through its embodiment of a fundamental attitude toward politics, a particular view of the human *as a political animal* — a being that attains fulfillment only in a cohesive and well-governed community. And other conceptions from other eras and societies likewise continue to exert an influence on contemporary imaginations. For our critical assessment of contemporary accounts of membership in the demos, it is necessary to gain an understanding of how these historical views of the citizen continue to play a role in political discussions of the enduring question, Who belongs and on what terms?

One way to do this would be to examine "traditions" of thought on citizenship. There is, of course, no dearth of continuities among theories of political membership from different eras; indeed, identifying traditions has become an industry of its own in recent years. Consequently, it is possible to portray the contending positions in contemporary debates as representative of the "republican" or "virtue" tradition (Pocock 1975; Oldfield 1990), the "common-law" tradition (Whelan 1981), the "cosmopolitan" tradition (Heater 1990), and the "consent" tradition (Schuck and Smith 1985) of citizenship. As tools of analysis, these constructions represent valuable devices for characterizing common lines of thought in different thinkers; they also help in understanding the history of central terms and institutions. However, at the same time they often suggest the discreteness — perhaps even the incommensurability — of different lines of thought that in fact may have much in common.[2] Moreover, a focus on traditions is susceptible to the danger of emphasizing continuity at the expense of attending to the ways in which socioeconomic conditions and power relations shape particular theories.[3] Most decisively for my purposes, employing the idea of traditions suggests that political theories may be compartmentalized and categorized as self-contained wholes. My interest, however, is in conceptual elements often shared by rather different thinkers — in the building blocks, as it were, of a variety of more developed systems of political thought.

In my analysis, instead of speaking of traditions, I make reference, in a style similar to that of Hannah Arendt (1958), to some common anthropological images of the citizen that have, in various shapes and forms, emerged repeatedly in normative theories of political membership. While the citizen has been imagined in many ways by many different theorists, I consider three basic anthropological images that have been particularly influential in the development of membership practices in the Western world. These images, I propose, may play a heuristic role in assessing the contrasting positions in the German debates.

Who is a citizen? A citizen, according to one view, is a person who is a native member of a particular group or communal entity with a historic claim to self-determination — for example, a born and bred Swede, or Inuit, or Jew, or Tibetan. A citizen, from a different perspective, is someone who actively commits himself or herself to being a participant in the political community — say, an emigrant come to join and participate in Plymouth Colony. Or a citizen, according to a third account, is anyone who fulfills certain objective, universal criteria dealing with membership in a given territory — for instance, a free inhabitant falling under the jurisdiction of Imperial Roman Law. These three images of political personhood — the communal self, the voluntary self, and the universal self — do not, it must immediately be noted, necessarily exclude one another.[4] Rather, each captures a powerful and arguably essential aspect of what it means to be a member of a political community. The compelling question, indeed, is not which one of these images is objectively the best portrait of the ideal citizen, but how all three are to be balanced with one another and whether they may be fashioned into an overall account of citizenship that is both coherent and appropriate to its social and political content.[5]

One problem in balancing these images comes from a tension among their respective ontological commitments, for each assigns a primary value to a different anthropological unit. To emphasize the communal self is to establish the ontological priority of the group: Each person's status becomes defined through his or her acceptance in the group and through decisions made by the group or its leaders. By way of contrast, the universal self takes as its frame of reference all of humanity, so that one's particular political membership is lexically subordinated to one's membership in the human race. Meanwhile, theories premised on the notion of the voluntary, self-constituting subject privilege the individual, exploring membership as a status one determines or accepts for oneself.

These respective foci give rise in turn to competing normative contexts for resolving questions of membership. With regard to the communal self, the relevant criteria of justice are seen as group-specific, determined with reference to the values of the community in question. In ethical conflicts over who belongs to the group, *Sittlichkeit* possesses the highest authority, and the stranger, excluded, has no court of appeals. Insofar as the citizen is conceived of as a universal self, however, more objective rules are held to apply. Impartial considerations regarding a person's relation to the society in question (whether or not he or she is protected by it, is subject to its laws, or contributes to its well-being) — judged without reference to that person's particular characteristics — will be taken as the basis for membership decisions, not that person's heritage. The rationale behind these decisions is grounded in convictions about human beings generally, and in notions of justice on a universal scale. Finally, in settings where the voluntary self holds the stage, the self-constituting individual is understood to be the arbiter of meaning and value, the only actor qualified to assess his or her ends and to determine his or her political allegiances. In this rather existentialist framework, the willing political subject becomes the sole creator of political obligations; criteria regarding membership receive their validity as posits of the individuals constituting society.

Variations on these images have been employed by thinkers throughout the Western political tradition, and over time they have become associated with important themes or motifs in the discourse on member-ship. Three of these motifs help to illustrate the manner in which these images are often applied. The concept of *sovereignty* — the incorporation in a single governing entity of legitimate authority over an entire com-munity and territory — has often been enlisted in the service of claims for the hegemony of the communal entity in determining membership (see Hinsley 1986). Theories in which the self-constituting or voluntary self has played a central role have tended to make use of the metaphor of covenant or, more prosaically, *contract* in their descriptions of the basis of societal organization (see Gough 1978). And arguments about the uni-versal self as the basis of citizenship have often invoked some form of the idea of *natural law,* including natural rights and human rights (see Pas-serin d'Entreves 1970; but also Gierke 1957).

The political-anthropological images of the communal self, the volun-tary self, and the universal self and their accompanying motifs help de-scribe and differentiate the normative structures embedded in the com-peting conceptions of membership with which we have to deal in the German case. There remains the matter of how we might then evaluate these positions. Given the historicity of political arrangements, we can-not simply ask what the best means for defining political membership generally is. We must ask what means of determining political member-ship is best suited to a situation such as that which currently prevails in Germany and other like states.

In the view I propose, membership positions may be judged accord-ing to the extent in which they (1) exhibit a balanced concern with the primary values of citizenship (namely community, agency, and rights; see below), and (2) do so in a way adapted to the characteristic needs and capacities of humans in their current social environment. In short, we should favor those conceptions of political membership that contain the most insightful understandings of human nature. This type of eval-uation might be called a modest naturalist approach, for while I want to say that the best policies are those that best assess the good for people as they really are, I do not wish to claim that the human good is a static or objectively ascertainable value. Rather, I hold that we can argue about human nature and human goods only in a relative and contextual way, by trying to show, for example, that some positions construe people in a manner so individualistic as to be irreconcilable with our experiences of commonality; or that some theories do not credit persons with the sense of moral agency presupposed even by the very act of theorizing; or that some accounts provide a more plausible view than others of the moral significance of economic and cultural coexistence. The more a theory of politics succeeds in matching its conception of human goods to existing moral conditions, the greater normative force it will have.

A corollary of this approach is that while certain sorts of views may simply be universally unacceptable, within a certain range societies may vary in what constitutes a suitable membership policy for them. Thus, one might argue that a political community with a long tradition of institutionalized individualism such as the United States is more justified in pursuing membership policies that emphasize individual consent than is a society with a historically communal structure such as China. And for communities with a self-understanding as a democracy — that is, with an entrenched collective commitment to equality of political status — universal and voluntaristic criteria of citizenship will bear more normative weight, relatively speaking, than in other communities. They will be weightier because they will construe political membership and, more basically, human potentialities in a way that is more consistent with a view of fundamental human equality, agency, and dignity than are other, competing views. It must be noted, however, that such generalizations hold only so long as societies remain more or less physically, economically, and administratively distinct from one another. The characters of political communities are not static. As economic and governmental institutions evolve and political barriers change, so too do the moral considerations that a membership policy must take into account.[6]

Five Political Anthropologies

What follows is an explication and critique of the political anthropologies embodied in the competing German conceptions of membership, carried out with reference to what I have called the communal, universal, and voluntary selves. In criticizing these views, I attempt to point out some of their empirical shortcomings and logical flaws. My main concern, however, is with their plausibility as accounts of the structure of political membership understood as a human good.

The Closure Position

When politicians claim that the German people is an organic entity whose survival depends on its purity, that Germany is for Germans only, or that persons of foreign origin should be expelled or denied rights, they are expressing what we have called the closure position. This position has had a striking resurgence in Germany and elsewhere in recent years. The core of this view, which defines membership in ethnic, tribal, or racial terms, is based on an extreme version of the communal self. The form of political organization it recommends may be called the *organic polity,* a body defined by the nation-state principle — the rule that political boundaries should correspond to divisions among discrete and cohesive "peoples" or "nations" that are held to have corporate rights to the territory they occupy. Political membership is determined by birth, while changing polities is ruled out in principle.

The closure position is a reflection of hereditary membership practices that have prevailed throughout much of human history. Accordingly, it has been expounded by a variety of influential thinkers: In the West, Richard Hooker, Edward Coke, and Robert Filmer in the British common law tradition; Jean Bodin and later Jacques Bossuet in France; and Johann Herder and a whole succession of theorists of the nation in Germany provided influential formulations of the essential link between birth into a historical community and political membership. Accompanying the modern move from monarchy, there has been some evolution in this basic perspective. The idea that states are hierarchical corporate entities under divinely ordained sovereigns has given way to a view emphasizing self-determination for and greater egalitarianism within ethnic groups. Although its theoretical exponents have over the years become fewer and farther between, the position — primarily embodied in jus sanguinis citizenship policies — remains entrenched in the practice of most states.

The prevalence of policies reflecting the principle of closure by no means establishes the ethical force of this position. Exploration of this issue begins with the basic normative question for polities: What is the appropriate unit of self-determination?[7] The answer of closure advocates is that the relevant unit is the ethnic community. Political control should be exercised by the members of and on the territory occupied by a group defined by blood ties, a collective history, a common language, mutual loyalty, and the other shared characteristics of communal life: culture, economic activities, religion. The structuring activity of politics is best engaged in within a naturally emergent group of persons not only committed to one another but also *related* to one another in a profound manner wholly beyond their individual control. The primary requirement for admission to political membership becomes existence as part of a preexisting ontological nexus, the *people*.

This strategy has the pragmatic virtue of rooting political obligation in the fertile soil of consanguinity. It responds directly to what Roger Scruton has called "the indispensable need for membership" in the "we" of the nation (1992, 94). Perhaps the greatest merit of this position, however, lies in its acknowledgment of the importance of the communal aspects of human life. Those collective goods that arise only through life in community, it holds, are of paramount importance and hence should not be subject to external political forces. Self-determination of the ethnic group means valuing traditional structures that provide persons with a context for social activity, ethical judgments, self-understanding, and agency in general.

That this is an important goal is demonstrated to some extent by the historical success of the nation-state principle. With time, however, the shortcomings of the closure position's anthropology of community have become increasingly evident. Problems with this view begin with its empirical assumption of the cohesiveness and homogeneity of national groups and are compounded by modern demographic and political realities. The closure stance does not account for crucial ways in which, as Michael Ignatieff writes, "modern life has changed the possibilities of civic solidarity" (1984, 138). In addition, as we will see, in its focus on communality, this view ignores other important moral dimensions of politics.

The notion of the organic nation or "people"[8] is problematic in both its historical and ontological dimensions. Nations, it is often assumed in political discussions, are enduring natural communities united by a common language, lifestyle, and set of commitments. Yet as a wealth of recent scholarship by historians such as Benedict Anderson (1983), Ernest Gellner (1983), and Eric Hobsbawm (1990) has shown, these communities have to a large degree been created quite recently, for political purposes, through the standardization of language and education, the consolidation of centralized state power and borders, and the rewriting of history. Often, coercive means have been employed to erase regional variations and produce cultural homogeneity within broad political boundaries. Such research has called into question the extent to which there existed at all "nations before nationalism," as John Armstrong (1982) puts it. It seems, indeed, that in many areas of the world, cultural groupings exhibited much greater diversity and existed on a much smaller scale than the model of nation-states implies.

The knowledge that nations bear little resemblance to historical reality challenges in turn the plausibility of the ontological notion of the organic nation. It becomes difficult to imagine the nation as the sort of group-person assumed, for instance, in the Heidelberg Manifesto, when it is revealed to be not a timeless and cohesive entity but an "imagined community" (Anderson 1983) wrested from a background of local diversity. It is true that the concept of group personality given its classic exposition by Otto Gierke (1957) is independent from the mental states of individual members. Even so, the image of the German people as a cohesive historical person entitled to self-determination through the legal trappings of an ethnically exclusive state makes little sense in light of the record of migrations, regional variations, and cultural cross-fertilizations that long kept the population of central Europe in a state of ethnic flux. The imposed myth of Aryan supremacy provides sobering testimony that the illusion of the pure ethnonation may in the end be sustained only through the exercise of raw coercive power.

Doubts about the idea of the nation undermine in turn the force of the nation-state principle. If the nation is in fact neither a single coherent cultural entity nor simply the naturally preeminent level at which persons form and maintain communal ties, then the claim of nations to an exclusive right of political sovereignty is correspondingly weakened. Yet one need not deny the historical reality of nations in order to question whether nationhood gives rise to a right to self-determination. If one concedes that nations are constructed largely through coercive means, one may well reach the conclusion that as a matter of justice, the harm done particular subcommunities in the process of incorporation may nullify the claim that they belong to a given nation.[9]

The notion of independent national cultures defined by blood, tenuous to begin with, has been dealt a decisive blow by modern historical developments. The twentieth century has been an era of migration on a grand scale, of global integration through economic exchange and communications, of massive shifts in borders and spheres of political influence. Historically separate communities have grouped together, interpenetrated one another, and together experienced the homogenizing effects of intermarriage, technology, and trade. Notions of distinct national characteristics remain as stubborn remnants of times past, but their empirical basis can only shrink as the populations of states become at once increasingly multiethnic and increasingly stamped by the character of postindustrial society. In this composition there remains little place for the closure advocate's image of unique, separate, and pure nations based on birth.

The closure view of the nation is further confounded by territorial realities. To begin with, very few borders in the contemporary world coincide with traditional definitions among ethnic groups. Most reflect instead the political expedients of colonists or conquerors, and as a result many divide and group ethnic populations indiscriminately. Very few states in today's world might be called ethnically homogeneous in any strict sense.[10] In addition, territorial sovereignty has in recent years been impinged upon by international political organizations as well as by transnational integration. As a result, a world neatly divided up according to the nation-state principle has become, quite simply, impossible.

Germans are no exception to this state of affairs. In a country with a noncitizen population of seven million, a significant proportion of permanent residents are of non-German ethnic origins. Yet as we have seen, many of these residents, born and bred in Germany, are much better integrated into German society, linguistically as well as socially, than many ethnic Germans who immigrate from other countries—or who hail from the former German Democratic Republic. Indeed, the same might be said for some other Europeans not of German descent. At the same time, entire populations of ethnic Germans living in other countries such as Switzerland or, most obviously, Austria challenge the notion of the German state as the legitimate political expression of the German nation. Given these conditions, the view that Germany is for all ethnic Germans, and only for ethnic Germans, appears at best a chimera and at worst a harmful and potentially dangerous delusion.

A third set of problems for the closure ideal of political membership stems from its focus on one normative conception of citizenship at the expense of all others. Its exclusive reliance on the communal self as the guiding image for political organization opens this perspective to the critiques of the voluntary and universal models. These critiques gain in force when one considers the implications a closure-based policy could have.

The closure view implies a total absence of individual choice or voluntarism in the ascription of membership. One's political identity is determined wholly by the allegedly objective criteria of ethnic or national membership, through birth. For those outside the group, there is in principle no way to gain entrance. Even more poignant, for those born into the group, there is no way out. In Germany, this view has the consequence that native Germans necessarily remain citizens regardless of their commitment to or rejection of the aims of the German state.

At the same time, establishing the ethnonational community as the source of absolute political authority carries with it the rejection of any universal norms dealing specifically with political membership. The nation as such is viewed as comprising a natural and self-contained moral unit. The sovereign judgments of the state as to who belongs to it and to what degree are not answerable to any external standards of justice; at the international level, a Hobbesian state of nature prevails. The consequences of this parochialism are twofold. For citizens, the state's rejection of any legitimate supranational ethical controls results in the likelihood of nondemocratic forms of government and the absence of human rights protections for citizens. Citizens of foreign countries, meanwhile, find themselves with no independent rights and, indeed, no intrinsic moral status in relation to the state. Such a status may be awarded by the state, but standards protecting foreigners must be voluntarily entered into by representatives of the closed state—and are unenforceable in principle. And for a state that would remain ethnically pure, there is little incentive to enter into such agreements. In Germany, according to this view, if the sovereign state were forcibly to expel all non-Germans, even those born and raised there, it would be within its rights unless it had explicitly committed itself not to do so.

These two implications of the closure position—the denial of any role for human volition in determining political status, and the absence of independently binding extranational considerations of law or justice—

demonstrate how the closure position rests on moral grounds that are at odds with important, widely held values. The picture of the political nature of persons on which it bases its norms for attributing membership hence appears skewed; that human beings are, at root, mere components of morally self-sufficient and organic national entities is an implausible claim in our modern clime. As a simple theory of group rights writ large, the ideal of closure ignores the interdependence of group rights and the rights of willing, acting persons. A more nuanced version of the communal self model, which integrates aspects of the voluntary self, is incorporated into what we have described as the culture position. This view draws significantly on the classical model of the polis and, on the whole, provides a more powerful normative account of political membership than does the closure position.

The Culture Position

The culture position distinguishes itself from the closure position by emphasizing cultural rather than racial community and by including a role for individual choice and commitment. In doing so it seeks to combine the basic anthropological insights of the communal and voluntary selves. From this perspective, the legitimate unit for political self-determination is a collectivity of persons united by a common culture and sense of mutual commitment. The case for self-determination is thus grounded in both a claim for the integrity of a given cultural group and a claim for freedom of association among its members.[11] The right to self-preservation of the group, coupled with the belief that cultural homogeneity is a precondition for a viable democracy, gives rise to the claim that the community has the exclusive right to limit membership to those it deems culturally assimilated and suitably committed to it. This means that although political membership is not closed, to gain admission requires considerable effort and remains contingent on the approval of the community.[12]

In its linking of community and self-determination, this view evokes the normative contours of Aristotle's political account of the communal self. It is hence not without reason that the comparison with the classical Athenian polis is often drawn in German debates. The culture position endorses Aristotle's central claim that the human is a *zoon politikon* that truly flourishes only in a well-ordered political community exhibiting a basic consensus about the good. A flourishing community requires the participation of equals in making decisions and in the administration of government (1941, 1221). Citizenship is a highly valued privilege deserved only by those who belong to the community, nurture its values, and are prepared to devote themselves to its maintenance. This notion of the political importance of culture, often associated with Edmund Burke (1987), has been expounded at various times and in varying degrees by a line of republican thinkers stretching from Cicero to John Adams to Hannah Arendt.

That current German membership policies have largely been shaped by the culture perspective is illustrated by how much they have in common with citizenship practices in ancient Athens. In the most democratic of Greek city-states, citizen status could be claimed only by native males who could prove that they were at least eighteen years of age and had been freely born to two lawfully married Athenian parents; native women and children possessed quasi-citizen status.[13] Only in exceptional cases was citizenship extended to foreigners. The status of citizen brought with it a number of privileges and duties, including participation in religious ceremonies, voting and serving in office, obedience to the laws of the polis, the provision of military service, and the payment of taxes. Citizens were sharply distinguished from slaves, foreigners, and *metics* — resident aliens who shared the duties of military service, taxes, and participation in public liturgies yet were denied a political role and other important rights.

Guestworkers in European countries have often been compared to metics, yet on this point German policy departs somewhat from the Athenian model. Metics, unlike citizens, could lawfully be tortured, which illustrates that they were viewed as fundamentally less valuable than native Athenians.[14] In postwar Germany, however, such a far-reaching double standard is hardly sustainable, for obvious reasons. The idea of a permanent subordinate status for foreign residents has come to be viewed as incompatible with the Federal Republic's commitment to democratic self-determination. Resident aliens are consequently to be given a choice: they may either depart or assimilate themselves with the goal of naturalization. A corollary of this stance, nonetheless, is that as long as they refuse the choice offered them, their civil rights and privileges may justifiably be limited by the community whose guests they are.

There are several clear merits to the culture position. Central among these is its acknowledgment of the moral importance of the communal nature of humans. Human beings are after all, as the liberal theorist Joel Feinberg allows, products of the social, political, and linguistic communities in which they are raised:

> As soon as they think of themselves at all, they think of their identity as determined by their membership and group-assigned roles. They may form purposes of their own, but even when these are nonconformist or rebellious, they can be understood only against a background of community practice and tradition. Their original purposes, values, and conceptions, all socially assigned, play a decisive role even when, as budding adults, they choose to alter or transform them. A complex modern community will even provide them with antitraditionalist traditions to identify with and be comforted by. (1988, 39)

As the culture position recognizes, cultural membership is of extraordinary importance for human identity, and indeed, human agency. This observation provides the basis for the claim that cultural groups deserve the right to be politically self-regulating. By framing their argument in terms of the right that members of a common culture have to shape their political life, culture theorists avoid many of the difficulties that the hereditarily defined, organic conception of the nation advanced by closure proponents demonstrates.

Another strength of the culturalist argument is that it supports a high level of political commitment by focusing cultural attachments on the political sphere. Even such a champion of universal rights as Rousseau was forced to acknowledge the psychological importance of communal solidarity in the business of running a state; for this reason, his conception of *humanité* remained bounded, for political purposes, by the borders of the republic (Vernon 1986, 39–40). Identifying the political community with a particular cultural group improves the chances of generating a strong sense of cohesion and loyalty to the state. It makes possible the cultivation of what Alasdair MacIntyre calls the virtue of patriotism (1984, 254).

At the same time, this membership orientation adopts a broader normative base than does the closure approach by including a measure of openness to outsiders. It is possible for persons demonstrating sufficient dedication and cultural assimilation to become new members, which represents a nod to the importance of the voluntary self in defining political communities. The notion that consent and contract are important components in political organization thus receives some accommodation. The difficulty of becoming a member, moreover, serves to affirm the *value* of political participation and citizenship in general. When citizenship is simply ascribed, by birth or by right, it may well be taken for granted. When, on the other hand, citizenship is seen as an identity earned through commitment and effort, it may be expected that its responsibilities and duties will be highly prized and discharged accordingly.

Although it escapes some of the difficulties to which the closure view succumbs, the culture argument is hardly immune to criticism. To begin with, some of its empirical suppositions are open to question. For example, one of its crucial assumptions — that cultural homogeneity is required for the success of democratic government — has been hotly debated for centuries and is by no means resolved.[15] Even if evidence could be found to vindicate this premise, the tangled question of what constitutes a sufficient degree of assimilation would remain open.

This problem suggests another in turn: Do cultures actually exist in the cohesive way posited by this view? In many respects this question does not differ from the problem of nationhood discussed in connection with the closure position; thus the notion of a discrete culture must cope with the attendant problems of local diversity, migration, and suppression of diversity. Assuming for the sake of argument that one can speak intelligibly of a unified German culture, the question remains as to whether this is an appropriate unit for political self-determination on the logic of the culture position, or whether it is simply too large and unwieldy.

This complication is perhaps best illustrated with reference to the form of organization on which the culture position is based: the polis. As Robert Dahl remarks, Greek democracies were not Greek, but rather Athenian, Spartan, Corinthian, and so forth: Although ancient Greeks saw themselves as members of the Hellenic culture, their political institutions required an intimacy and proximity naturally available only at the level of the city (1989, 3). Such theorists as Plato and Aristotle perceived that an active democratic culture relied on a concrete sense of participation in shaping a shared life—a sense that was diluted, the more political boundaries were extended and populations increased (see Wolin 1961, 69–71). With the rise of the Macedonian empire, as with the imperial expansion of the Roman republic, the question arose, At what point does the communal form of democracy lose its character and, with it, its normative cogency? Conversely, at what point of growth does the state lose its significance for the moral life of the citizen? It seems, finally, that the sort of democratic citizenship found in the polis and in classical republics depended on a sort of community characterized, if not by face-to-face interaction, at least by a sense of immediate involvement with one's fellow citizens. And this is a context that no amount of economic integration, common education, and telecommunications is likely to reproduce in today's large and complex nation-states. The modern German social setting, it seems, simply cannot sustain the sort of citizenship envisioned in the culture model.

Apart from these empirical drawbacks, the culture position also exhibits shortcomings of a more normative nature. One has to do with the territorial aspect of political organization. Where a single coherent culture exclusively occupies a clearly defined region, the principle of control of membership by the group according to cultural criteria might well carry decisive weight regarding admissions of new residents. It is a different matter, however, when a sizable number of nonmembers already reside in the territory.[16] The situation might then arise—and there is no reason to think it would not—in which people not belonging to a dominant culture are faced with the choice of leaving or changing their cultural identity in order to gain political rights. This, it can be argued, would place an undue burden on them tantamount to a form of harm. Yet in such a case, these residents would have no basis for demonstrating that they were being wronged. For the logic of the communal self embedded in the culture perspective recognizes no moral authority outside the community, and the logic of the voluntary self could be seen as satisfied by the choice offered the residents.

This possibility points to a second shortcoming this view shares with the closure position—namely, the failure to accommodate considerations of justice or human rights bearing on membership. For German representatives of the culture position, the shape of the German polity is a matter that arises prior to any considerations of justice or entitlement; as a result, the idea that a non-German resident might have a universally grounded human right to political membership simply does not make sense to them.[17] Their view does not recognize the political relevance of what we have called the universal self, the self possessed of intrinsic political rights grounded not in particular communities but in membership in the generic community of humankind.[18] As in the closed society, foreigners have an inferior moral status in principle. Whether or not they might be eligible for membership and if so under what conditions is determined wholly by the political community. The noncitizen's fundamental lack of standing in regard to the distribution of membership under the culture position is a shortcoming that is to an extent remedied in the choice position.

The Choice Position

The choice position takes as its highest value the autonomy of the individual political actor. It holds that each person should be able to choose not only the political organization in which he or she is a member but also the extent of membership and participation. The resident alien, therefore, should have a full range of options, including remaining a political outsider, becoming a naturalized citizen, or adopting some intermediate status including, perhaps, limited voting rights. In this strategy a positive value is placed on citizenship, in that successive levels of political inclusion are accompanied by increasing costs — in terms, for example, of length of residence or military service — and full inclusion requires maximal involvement on the part of the prospective member. Uniformity of political status within the state, on the other hand, is neither required nor especially valued. Instead, a layered polity is accepted, and the lack of political representation for some is justified on the grounds of their personal decision not to "purchase" a fuller form of membership.

This position is perhaps as thoroughgoing an embodiment of the anthropological image of the voluntary self as current political structures permit. It conceives of government as subordinate to, and firmly grounded in, the interests of the individual. It is, in short, a liberal individualist strategy, and although it draws on a tradition of consent reaching back to the Sophists, it is essentially a modern outlook expressed initially and in varying degrees in contractarian thinkers such as Locke (1967), Rousseau (1947), and Jefferson (see Whelan 1981, 649–50). According to this view, within the constraints of social utility the unit of self-determination ought to be defined in terms of individual choice and commitment on the principle of freedom of association. Thus the political community should coincide with that group of persons that elects to administer its affairs collectively within a given social sphere. This group may vary according to the scope of the issues concerned, and a local polity might therefore include persons who are not members of the national polity, or vice versa. The key claim is that political membership should conform to rather than determine the conjunctions of individual interests that occur at different levels of social organization.

This tolerance of organizational diversity is a major strength of the choice stance, for in much of the world, and especially in Western Europe, migration and international integration have produced a situation conducive to partial and multiple memberships. An ethnic Algerian residing in France may well have a significant stake in the governance of several communities to which he or she has ties, including Algeria, his or her town, France, and Europe. The choice perspective offers the possibility of giving each of these attachments some political substance in complementary fashion: some political rights may be ensured by the country of residence, others by the country of origin, still others by international organizations.[19] In fact, current practices regarding citizenship and permanent residence in Europe and North America reflect the choice perspective to a great extent. The guiding principle of this position — a respect for individual autonomy — has been manifested most notably in the general reluctance of governments to impose uniformity of citizenship on settled foreign residents who do not pursue naturalization.

Respect for autonomy is the principle that produces most of the normative force of the choice stance. At its core this position conjoins the fundamental conviction that human beings deserve control over their individual lives and projects, with the recognition that one's political membership represents a crucial aspect of this control. From the point of view of isolated and mobile individuals — or of individuals within a constantly fluctuating world polity — the value of this position is clear.

The choice position enjoys moral plausibility not only from the perspective of the atomistic individual but also from its reliance on the

principle of freedom of association that lies at the core of modern-
day democratic politics. The idea that political communities should be
grounded in the consent of the individuals they comprise is as old and
distinguished as the contractarian tradition. So long as a set of individuals clearly wishes to establish and maintain a political organization,
there seems to be no prima facie reason to deny them. Consent, as many
have argued, provides a strong ground for political obligation. As far as
membership policy goes, there is clearly something to be said for allowing the desires of the collectivity of members pride of place, as Michael
Walzer emphasizes in his analogy between countries and clubs.[20]

The choice system, finally, also incorporates an important element of
fairness. The voluntary model on which it is based is committed to
defining eligibility for political membership primarily in performative
terms, that is, in terms of what someone — anyone — might *do* in order to
qualify for membership. Political membership is open to one's efforts to
change it, and generally one is free to earn political status by fulfilling
requirements established by the community in question. In contrast, the
communal and universal models make one's eligibility dependent upon
involuntary criteria: respectively, *who one is* by birth and *in what situation
one finds oneself* as a human being.

Along with these merits, there are some serious disadvantages to the
view that political identity should be established wholly on the basis of
individual choice. We may begin once more with some relatively empirical considerations. First, there is no reason to assume that a choice principle of political membership is ethically appropriate simply because it
reflects many current membership practices. One must further inquire,
for example, whether stable political structures and effective governance
are possible on the terms of the choice principle. As migration increases,
the tendency of choice-based political membership moves away from the
rigid structure of the nation-state toward more complex and interwoven
political forms. One worry is that this movement may lead to a radical
undermining of political cohesion and stability. If all within a territory
are free to reassign their loyalties and commitments as and when they see
fit, those institutions of the state that rely on patriotic feeling and civic
commitment can only be undermined. In the longer term, modeling
political membership according to individual preferences will seem dangerous to anyone who holds, in the tradition of Plato, Aristotle, Saint-

Simon, and Hegel, that human well-being depends on the maintenance of concrete political structures.

These pragmatic issues quickly give way to difficulties of a more normative nature. For example, the notions of choice and the will on which this view depends become problematic once subjected to close examination. For a start, choice does not occur within a vacuum. Although the choice position seems to assume that individuals exist in some way prior to the political organizations they form, in fact the opposite is true. Until they reach maturity, people are hardly capable of determining their political membership; they simply belong willy-nilly to the community in which they are raised. At what age and on what basis may persons be expected to make decisions about their political membership? The problem is partly definitional in nature. Should choice of membership take the form of an active selection among possible communities or that of a response to an offer of membership? Or might it be inferred, in Lockean fashion, from one's tacit consent? Beyond this question, there are deeper problems with the way in which the will and choice are assumed to generate moral legitimacy for modern-day political systems. These problems arise from the tension between the will understood as a psychological function—a broad notion that encompasses even such simple physical motions as breathing—and the will understood to be an active, focused moral faculty capable of producing obligations (see Riley 1982, especially chap. 7).[21]

The problem with the idea of a choice of membership becomes clearer when we consider the case of the many migrant workers in Germany who, laboring under the "illusion of return" nurtured by host and sending governments alike, remain political outsiders all their lives because they feel they will wish to return one day to their country of origin. Should it be assumed by default that such workers do not choose membership because they do not demand it? On the evidence, it is highly probable that such workers would choose German membership if their choice were structured differently, for example as an option to turn down citizenship granted by statute. In any event, decisions regarding membership are in practice always severely constrained by social ties and obligations experienced as prior to choice. In phenomenological terms, choosing one's political membership is somewhat akin to selecting one's ethnic identity or religion. It is far from clear that such a choice is willed in a manner strong enough to ground either political obligations or their lack, hence the difficulty in accepting the proposition that the continued existence of foreign residents in a disenfranchised status may be taken as evidence that they choose it. Socrates, a "guestworker" of sorts himself, may have grounded his political obligations in his submission to the laws of the polis, but in our modern times this justification no longer seems compelling.

The premium placed by the choice position on maximizing personal autonomy may also be expected to have some undesirable moral effects. The choice orientation emphasizes autonomy at the expense of political obligation. Citizenship comes to be experienced less as a set of objective duties and privileges than as a range of insurance policies that may be mixed and matched as seen fit. As a result, the option of being apolitical gains in acceptability, even in respectability. The choice to exempt one-self from some of the basic duties and privileges of the society becomes a viable possibility. The effect is a depreciation not just of citizenship but of politics in general, as many have warned (see, e.g., Heater 1990; Oldfield 1990). And there is a further implication. When isolated residents freely choose not to belong to the polity that shapes the life of their community, this choice might at first be defended on an individual basis as an expression of personal autonomy. On a larger scale, however, when a system of subordinate political membership becomes entrenched, those in the polity are placed in the situation of ruling over nonmembers who remain subject to the laws the polity makes, and the policies it chooses. The society as a whole becomes implicated as a state ruled by, in Walzer's words, a "band of citizen-tyrants" (1983, 58), whose claim to govern legitimately and democratically is no better founded than the claim that the acquiescence of slaves justifies slavery.

This difficulty is generated in part by the territorial dimension of political organization. Like the culture position, the choice position must cope with the overwhelming probability that those willing to form an exclusive political association will not occupy a territory devoid of other persons. But the difficulty also has to do with a problem inherent in the principle of freedom of association undergirding the choice per-spective. The essence of this notion is that political groups should be self-defining: only collections of like-minded individuals have the authority to constitute groups bearing a right to self-determination (see Beitz

1979; Philpott 1995). But what happens when there is disagreement on the shape of the relevant groups? It may be true, as Charles Beitz argues, that an encompassing group does not have the right to restrain a separatist subgroup that seeks autonomy; but this does not resolve the conflict that arises when a large group seeks to exclude a smaller group that wishes to belong to it. There is no reason to think that agreement could be obtained among all political actors about their respective memberships without some such problems of exclusion arising. Yet when the operative principle of organization is free association, that is, when no appeals can be made to either community standards or standards of justice transcending individual choice, then there are no resources for resolving such an issue other than force.[22]

This problem points to a final pair of limitations exhibited by the choice perspective, which have to do with its narrow emphasis on the political anthropology of the autonomous self. On the one hand, this focus exempts membership policy from important considerations of community. The values sought in the culture and closure positions of ethnic and cultural solidarity, loyalty and obligation to country, and maintenance of a coherent moral community are all subordinated or dropped in favor of individual autonomy. The result is an impoverished and perhaps dangerously fractured political culture. On the other hand, the emphasis on choice also comes at the expense of broader considerations of justice. A rough structural fairness is indeed evidenced in the linking of different political statuses with different levels of personal commitment, but there remains no authoritative standard to appeal to when specific membership criteria set by a political group are seen as unreasonable, unfair, or inegalitarian. It becomes impossible to argue from human rights premises except in the sphere dealing directly with individual autonomy. It is this last problem—the problem of how to admit concerns of justice and egalitarianism in membership policy—that the coexistence position addresses.

The Coexistence Position

The coexistence position, like the culture position, is a political-anthropological hybrid. Both value the political commitment of the voluntary self, but where the theorist of culture additionally extols the particularistic identity of the communal self, the theorist of coexistence emphasizes the significance of the universal self's integration and participation in society. Eligibility for full political membership is determined not by one's membership in a particular cultural or ethnic group, but by the role one occupies in a given territorial society: All those living, working, and participating over time in the life of a community are held to have a warrant to being included, subject to consent. From this perspective, full citizenship rights should accompany birth into the society — birth, that is, to resident parents. In addition, these rights should be offered to all those with origins elsewhere who have resided in the society long enough to become integrated into its social structure and patterns of daily life, contingent only upon acceptance of the constitutional order of the society. The universalist aspect of this orientation is reflected in its subscription to the idea that, since all persons are in essence equal, all those subject to the power of a government possess the same right to representation. Its voluntaristic aspect is captured in the notion that one's existential contribution to the overall project of life in society morally grounds a say in collective decision making.

The appropriate unit for self-determination, according to the co-existence position, a territorial community exhibiting a structurally cohesive character. Political membership, in short, should be congruent with economic and social membership — memberships determined primarily through long-term residence. The reasoning behind this view is grounded in that aspect of states which sets them apart from other sorts of groups and associations, namely, the claim to exclusive dominion over a given territory. The central idea is, simply, that territorial sovereignty should be exercised not by an ethnic nation or cultural group, but by the collectivity of those living under the laws of a spatially defined society. Of course, territorial "societies" are shaped through a complex dialectic including political, economic, and social factors, and it is dangerous to view them as "natural" groupings. Consequently, the coexistence view sees territorial societies as providing a legitimate basis for political organization only within certain constraints of justice regarding the circumstances in which borders are established in the first place.[23] This position, it is worth pointing out, does not rule out the existence of nation-states, but in cases of ethnically or culturally diverse regions, it establishes a principle of the priority of residence over nationality in determining citizenship.

In holding that citizenship rights remain subject to the assent of long-term residents, the coexistence position draws in part on the legacy of theorists of consent. However, its core claim — that one's place and role in society ground an entitlement to the status of citizen — is founded on the universalist notion of justice embodied in the tradition of natural law, natural rights, and what are now known as human rights. This line of thought, the logic of the universal self, has its roots in the cosmopolitanism of the Stoics and ancient Roman law; it was also deeply influenced by the spiritual egalitarianism of the nascent Christian church. In the early modern period it was pursued most notably in the work of the natural law jurists. At the heart of this school was the attempt to establish the notion of jus gentium, a system of law and morality binding for all states.[24] The notion of natural law played a large if ambiguous role in Rousseau's thought (see Shklar 1969), and in the French and American Revolutions the notion of natural rights helped shaped the new states and their jus soli citizenship practices.[25] Eventually, traditional notions of natural law were largely superseded by the Kantian project of grounding rules for the state in a rationally ascertainable universal law.[26] With or without a theoretical grounding, the notion of the fundamental equality of humans — or, more often, of the fundamental injustice of certain inequalities among humans — has continued to play a major role in the evolution of citizenship. The constant thread uniting these developments has been the conviction that the definition of citizenship should be subject to standards that reach beyond simple consent or communal membership — standards that have to do with membership in the community of all humans.

The coexistence position combines the anthropological images of the universal and autonomous selves by defining *eligibility* for citizenship in terms of impartial criteria while leaving the *assumption* of citizenship status subject to a right of refusal for those already holding other citizenships. There are three important normative implications that flow from this stance. The first is the recognition of socioeconomic participation as a primary political value. It is the performance of "socially necessary work" (Walzer 1983, 60), more than one's personal characteristics, that grounds one's claim fully to belong. The second is the lack of a requirement for an exclusive citizenship. Where integration, and not first and foremost national identity, provides the basis for political membership, there is no reason to make inclusion contingent upon the relinquishment of attachments to national groups abroad, even if these links include a foreign citizenship.[27] The third is the need for a viable constitutional system to support the tolerance of ethnic diversity. The cement of the coexistence polity must be a common commitment to the rule of impartial law — a "constitutional patriotism" — rather than ethnic solidarity (Habermas 1994, 134).

A great merit of the coexistence approach is that it provides a model with a strong potential for implementing the equality of citizenship in a world of large-scale industrial societies and ethnic diversity. Where the sort of inclusion envisioned by the culture and closure models would require substantial, perhaps even impossible, changes in the ethnic or cultural composition of present states in order to achieve equality of political membership, the coexistence model is constructed to apply to more or less current conditions. In addition, where these competing models ideally require a relatively small scale of political organization in order to buttress the thick political attachments of traditional citizenship, the coexistence model, with its emphasis on individual protections and impartial criteria, is designed to cope with the size and impersonality of modern states.

A territorial basis for defining political membership recommends itself on two additional counts. First, in practical terms, a territorial community is considerably easier to demarcate than a racial, ethnic, or national community.[28] Second, the coexistence model avoids the problem the territorial aspect of states presents other models since it leaves no basis for fears that large populations within the state will fail to qualify for political membership and remain permanently disenfranchised. We live in political communities, this view recognizes, that are closer in scope and structure to the Roman Empire than to the Greek polis; accordingly, we require something more akin to the universal Roman citizenship that so impressed Augustine than to Aristotle's ideal of Athenian citizenship.

The central virtue of Roman citizenship after the *Constitutio Antoniniana* was its guarantee of equality for all within a given territory under a strong system of law (see Sherwin-White 1973, especially 287, 461–68; cf. Balsdon 1979). This feature is shared by citizenship on the coexistence model. Where citizenship is based on integration understood in terms of residence and socioeconomic participation, no separate set of laws can exist for long-term residents who are citizens and long-term residents who are not. Subordinate political membership is not allowed as a matter of structure, even though individuals possessing political membership elsewhere may choose not to accept the formal status of citizenship or not to exercise their political rights. In today's world many find normatively appealing a system in which membership is based not simply on the vagaries of one's heredity but also on one's situation within and contributions to the political community. There is a similar appeal in protections that are founded not in the will of a particular group but in laws thought to embody norms applying to all humans regardless of particular attachments.

For many communitarian thinkers, however, the coexistence model represents a fatal corruption of the very notion of citizenship. There are two points to this objection. First, defining citizenship in exclusively political and socioeconomic terms means detaching it from those ethnic and national ties that have historically given it its affective power. This split, some predict, is likely to lead to a decline in loyalty and commitment to one's country of citizenship, a trend that cannot bode well for questions of, for example, national defense. In addition, where citizenship can be obtained simply as a matter of impersonal right, as opposed to communal identity or individual election, it may be expected that a climate of civic-spiritedness is not as likely to prevail. A state whose citizens lack a basic cultural homogeneity, this criticism adds, will be wracked by ethnic antagonisms that will exert a constant strain on common political institutions.[29]

The second communitarian objection to the argument for coexistence is that it disregards the moral significance of community. By adopting purely socioeconomic criteria as the basis of political membership, it ignores the fact that human flourishing requires a culturally and linguistically coherent environment as its context. Instead, the coexistence position contributes to the breakdown of moral community by denying it the political incorporation it requires to survive. In short, it denies the moral claim of the communal self.

Even if one accepts the basic logic of the coexistence approach, there remain some potentially large problems concerning its applicability. One such problem is how universal requirements regarding citizenship might be agreed upon, a quandary, of course, faced by human rights generally.

Various arguments have been advanced as to why political representation is a fundamental human right (e.g., Shue 1980; Finnis 1980; Gewirth 1982). But agreement has proved elusive as to which argument is best or most true, a state of affairs that could have important implications for the criteria for citizenship recognized in actual policies. This issue is likely to be particularly important in connection with restrictions on political rights. Is it unjust to deprive persons of citizenship if they are acknowledged to represent a threat to collective security? If they are convicted felons? If they refuse to provide military service? How long must one live in a country before he or she becomes "integrated"? The basis for deciding such questions will always remain open to debate and disagreement. Yet a primary tenet of the coexistence position is that it is unjust for membership criteria to be subject simply to the preferences of a majority of those who are already members. Some overarching standard is necessary to which those who are excluded may appeal; but at present international norms that might fulfill this role in regard to political membership have not yet emerged with any definition.

A second problem of application involves the nature of "societies" in general and of contemporary societies in particular. The question of what defines a society has long been a central concern of sociology, and stipulating a territorial component by no means resolves this problem. Do actual territorial entities truly exhibit the moral characteristics required by the coexistence model — relative self-sufficiency, self-containedness, sovereignty over their own affairs? It is, in fact, the divisions among societies — or the lack thereof — that present the greatest difficulties for the normative logic of coexistence. Why should political membership not be drawn on the scale of "industrial society" as a whole, or on the scale of the global economy? It is difficult to see how the coexistence position can maintain a basis for separate citizenships. In a world in which political divisions have to do less and less with economic or social divisions, the adequacy of this view is increasingly challenged. The final position, that of cosmopolitanism, gains its focus in response to this problem.

The Cosmopolitan Position
The cosmopolitan position is in important respects the antithesis of the closure position; together, the two represent the extremes in modern

debates on political membership. The fundamental cosmopolitan claim is that political participation is a human right of the first order.[30] Simply by virtue of being human, and irrespective of their contribution to society, all persons have a right to an effective voice in any decisions that significantly concern them. For this reason, questions of political membership should be determined according to the scope of the effects of political decisions. It is immediately apparent that in its disregard for ethnicity, affective ties, and long-term individual involvement or commitment, this logic leads away from traditional conceptions of citizenship and political closure. This tendency is borne out in the sorts of policy suggestions that arise out of the cosmopolitan stance. In Germany, human rights advocates have argued for full political rights not only for long-term residents such as guestworkers but also for migrants with as little as six months of residence. A further extension of this argument would, in response to increasing global interdependence, necessarily make the right to political participation transnational.[31] Ultimately, its logic leads to the establishment of a system of world citizenship (see especially Heater 1990). Cosmopolitanism represents, in short, the eclipse of national citizenship.

The cosmopolitan view that political inclusion is a human right has been developed in a tradition dating from the Stoic philosophers. In the modern era, the idea played an important, if not finally decisive, role in Rousseau's thought; for Kant, it was an even more central notion. And although Marx saw citizenship itself as a corrupt bourgeois institution, his alternative vision of the communist society was similarly an expression of the cosmopolitan ideal. An innate universal right to political representation was furthermore assumed by many important republican thinkers and early theorists of representative government. Yet it was only in response to the vast sociopolitical changes of the twentieth century that much attention came to be focused on the inherent conflict between this right and the existence of separate sovereign states. The progressive extensions of suffrage in many countries over the last century and more recent steps toward international organization have arguably made cosmopolitanism a more viable idea than ever before, even though it remains unlikely that a right to political membership will gain international support so long as human rights mechanisms depend in practice on individual state interests.

Several points are worth making about the normative character of the cosmopolitan position. The claim grounding political participation in a human right to self-determination is, first of all, essentially an individualistic, as opposed to a social, conception. At the same time, it is essentially contextual, in the sense that it depends on a structure of actions that affects the liberty or well-being of the person concerned. The duty correlative to the right to participate is — in addition to the duty to participate — the duty of the individual to abide by political decisions. Since the arena in which this right is to be exercised is a function of the *position* of the individual in various different contexts, its social or political referent need not remain constant. This means, however, that in principle, the concept of a system of fixed and mutually exclusive political communities is undermined; indeed, the notion of having a determinate *particular* political membership is challenged (see Bader 1995). Indeed, cosmopolitanism militates against the intrinsically territorial concept of sovereignty. It challenges not only the right of any particular political group to exclusive control over a given territory but also the very legitimacy of political borders (see Bauer 1975; Carens 1987). Consequently, cosmopolitan theorists are highly skeptical of the claim that one has special moral obligations toward one's compatriots that do not exist toward noncitizens (see Shue 1980, 134–49; Goodin 1988). A consistent prosecution of this logic of individual human rights leads finally to a denial of the moral force of any distinction between citizens and (noncitizen) human beings — and consequently, of the validity of any constitution that sets up special political privileges for its citizens while denying them to others.

The normative strength of this approach lies in its principled pursuit of a radically democratic view of politics. Through its rigorous upholding of a human rights standard it challenges the monopoly of power assumed by states and strongly asserts the inherent moral value of each individual. At the same time, it seeks a thoroughgoing observance of the principle of the fundamental equality of all human beings. In doing so it seeks to fix a ground for political and other rights that is arguably stronger and more concrete than a notion of citizenship founded on community or contract. As Alexander Bickel writes, "Emphasis on *citizenship* as the tie that binds the individual to government and as the source of his rights . . . bodes ill for the endurance of free, flexible, responsive, and stable institutions and of a balance between order and liberty" (1975, 53; emphasis added). The objective of a world polity embraced by the cosmopolitan position represents, finally, a far-sighted goal that is perhaps uniquely appropriate to an increasingly integrated world in which common concerns — nuclear arms control, overpopulation, the environment — are likely only to grow in scope.

But there are also drawbacks to this position. The most obvious problem with a cosmopolitan approach to political membership is the question of its practicability. Certainly a long-term trend is observable in many countries toward less exclusive membership policies. Yet this development has for the most part been within individual sovereign states; only in the European Union has even slight progress been made toward supranational membership, and this may indeed prove to be simply a new level of national membership. A global political entity that would standardize the individual right to political representation continues to seem unattainable, and there are many who doubt that an organization possessing such massive centralized power would be desirable even in principle.

But this matter aside, let us consider the most immediate and realizable prescriptions of the cosmopolitan position. It supports a political inclusiveness at the national level that would embrace anyone likely to be subject to state policies for any substantial length of time — a category excluding tourists but including recent migrants and all official residents. In practical terms, it may well be asked whether such a policy might have unacceptable effects for the state. The political inclusion of new and socially unintegrated immigrants might easily lead to social and political instability. New immigrants might also be expected not to exhibit the loyalty to the political community and the attachment to its laws that are bred by socialization in a society and are necessary to its security.

At a more theoretical level, a difficulty arises with the conception of individual rights that the cosmopolitan position seems to presuppose. The moral right to political inclusion in the state is often invoked as if it were an innate, natural quality of individuals possessed independent of their social setting. This abstract view is, however, incoherent; for a right is, analytically speaking, a relational concept that makes sense only given the existence of some moral-political context in which rights may be held.[32] If we cannot speak of rights as simply innate, then we must inquire, In which context might a human right to political membership obtain? In practice, many human rights, such as the right to welfare or to personal security, find their expression within the setting of individual states and political cultures. But the same cannot be said of a right to state membership. In large part this is because by its very nature this right challenges the notion of state sovereignty. At the same time, the particularist framework of nation-states simply does not provide an adequate arena for evaluating rights-claims regarding political inclusion. The putative member — as a rule, a citizen of another state — is not yet a part of the community to whose norms such an evaluation would have to refer. As a consequence, we must recognize that if it is to be a viable concept, the right to political membership must assume a transnational, if not global, context marked by shared moral understandings and political institutions. The extent to which such a context already exists is, of course, debatable.[33]

This criticism leads to another of a more explicitly anthropological nature. Somehow it seems unfair to include someone in political decisions who has not contributed to the life of the community, who has not been attached to it and experienced its ups and downs, who has not demonstrated a commitment to the society's well-being. I suggest this appearance of unfairness derives from the value we place on the notion of the voluntary self and lies in the belief that political membership should at least be *chosen,* and in certain senses even *earned.* From this perspective, the political community rests on a metaphorical contract, a moral understanding developed over time and honed through the practice of self-determination. Newcomers must become parties to this contract in order to take up political rights; yet this would seem to involve not only an act of commitment on the part of prospective members but also some sort of acceptance on the part of the community. *Political* membership, according to this common intuition, cannot be established simply through objective criteria such as a conception of human rights. More is needed to establish a sense of shared obligations among the members of the political unit.

This objection is related to another anthropological criticism leveled from the perspective of the communal self. Where the constitution of political communities is determined through strictly universal and impartial criteria, the thick basis of politics in historical communities is seriously undermined, with the consequences not only that social solidarity is eroded but also that community values are harmed and individuals morally impoverished. Michael Walzer puts the case in these terms:

> Politics (as distinct from mere coercion and bureaucratic manipulation) depends upon shared history, communal sentiment, accepted conventions—upon some extended version of Aristotle's "friendship." . . . Communal life and liberty requires the existence of "relatively self-enclosed arenas of political development." Break into the enclosures and you destroy the communities. And that destruction is a loss to the individual members, a loss of something valuable, which they clearly value, and to which they have a right, namely their participation in the "development" that goes on and can only go on within the enclosure. (1979, 236)

This argument points out in turn a further danger of cosmopolitanism. It is true that in its immediate practice a cosmopolitan ethic works against the internal homogeneity of ethnic or national communities and thus encourages diversity. But its individualist logic leads ultimately to the reduction of national differences, to a sort of overall human homogeneity—and conceivably, to the destruction of the cultural diversity that many take to be an essential human good.

Toward a Balance

In this chapter, five basic normative positions on membership have been considered, primarily in light of the assumptions they embody about the political nature and requirements of persons. In terms of the three basic symbols of the communal self, the voluntary self, and the universal self, three of the positions—the closure, choice, and cosmopolitan models, respectively—focus on a single image. The other two, the strongest of the five, are hybrids: the culture position develops a logic that is at once communal and voluntaristic, and the coexistence position a logic that is both voluntaristic and universal. Although each of these views has distant historical roots, there is a sense in which, taken together, they represent a historical evolution, in the order in which I have treated them: As human societies have become ever more complex, centralized, and interwoven, the anthropological focus of political theory has shifted from the primacy of the community toward the will of the individual and, increasingly, toward universal aspirations to democratic ideals. This evolution has been a function of complex developments in technology, social organization, and cultural interaction, matched by shifts in epistemological conceptions, religious consciousness, and historical awareness; the only point I wish to make here is one that did not escape Aristotle, namely, that political norms are in part historically contingent.

But at the same time, the shift in political norms has been just that and only that — a shift in emphasis among fundamental concerns that have in themselves remained more or less constant. What our survey of normative orientations to membership has illustrated is this: The images of the communal, voluntarist, and universal selves each represent important moral aspects of political life as we know it, aspects that continue to exert forceful claims, in different measures depending on the national context perhaps, but generally across the entire human range of political communities. Not incidentally, each image further provides some basis for criticizing its counterparts, which explains why the attempt to balance some or all of these anthropological facets is an unvarying, if often implicit, component in those political theorists whose work continues to influence and provoke us most today — in Aristotle, in John Stuart Mill, in Locke, in Hegel and Marx, perhaps preeminently in Rousseau. And as the shortcomings of the positions I have examined indicate, the most compelling argument for appropriate norms of political membership is likely to be one that gives earnest attention to all three.

Such an argument will place considerable value on, first of all and commensurate with its importance in the present age, individual choice and commitment as an element of political morality. At the same time, it will acknowledge that choice alone cannot be absolutized at the expense of the values of political structure and communal cohesion. Second, in keeping with the emergent international morality of human rights and democracy, this argument will assign an important role to justice concerns and other universal criteria bearing on the question of political inclusion. Finally, it will devote attention to an area of concern that has suffered somewhat under the tenure of liberal ideologies in the modern West, namely, the question of the moral and political significance of cultural identity and communal ties. A theory that succeeds in forming a synthesis of these three elements will not of itself solve specific problems of political membership, for these are always concrete and vary from setting to setting. Developing adequate normative responses to membership issues will always involve empirical arguments about the scope and nature of the political entity in question, as well as judgments about its values and normative structure. What a theory of the ethics of political membership may aspire to is a defense of parameters within which specific solutions should be considered.

Chapter Four

Inequality, Nondomination,

and Human Rights

S ome of the crucial points of disagreement in modern membership debates are of an empirical nature. To what extent does
the acceptance of immigrants harm or benefit the national
economy? How much cultural homogeneity is required for
the smooth and effective functioning of a democratic system of
politics? How much and what sort of civic loyalty is necessary to preserve
the character of a political community against its enemies? Such questions immensely complicate discussions concerning the extension of political membership, yet are, at least in principle, amenable in some degree
to solution through social scientific techniques of investigation. This
does not hold, however, for the ethical questions that circumscribe these
issues and lend them their significance with respect to the distribution of
membership. In the formulation of empirical questions, the weight assigned to a certain level of well-being among citizens, or to the maintenance of explicitly democratic institutions, or to the survival of a certain
type of political community depends on broader commitments regarding the moral significance of autonomy, human rights, individual welfare, special relations, and equality. In this chapter, I examine these moral
factors in the course of developing an argument for a set of basic normative guidelines for membership policy.

Naturalism and Political Membership

As we have seen, within political communities citizenship policy is a
means for fixing the bounds of "in-equality" — the exclusive equality of

an in-group, and the inequality of excluded groups. Thus, in the German case we have been examining, despite a broad consensus that long-term political inequality for established minorities is an unacceptable prospect, disagreement continues to reign over how the sphere of equality should be defined — and over who should be left out of this sphere and excluded from what we might call political personhood. This central issue has two sides, one concerning the appropriate sphere of equality within modern states and the other, the basis for exclusions. Should the sphere of equal citizenship be delineated according to lines of ethnocultural division (the culture position), or expressions of individual preference (the choice position), or integration under a territorial authority (the coexistence position)? Might candidates for political membership be excluded on the basis of the lack of a certain cultural identity, or a failure to pledge exclusive loyalty to the state, or the absence of qualities viewed as essential for political participation? In addressing these sorts of questions, I attempt to set out a theory of membership that retains the deepest insights of the various positions we have examined without incorporating their shortcomings.

My main premise, introduced in the preceding chapter, is that human beings are in morally important ways at once communal entities, individual agents, and universal beings. These human characteristics, I argue, have important political implications. They determine that vital human goods depend upon the maintenance of some forms of community, upon the free and protected exercise of individual volition, and upon the secure enjoyment of certain generic requirements of human being. The goal of an ethical membership policy should be to balance these concerns in the structuring of political membership. The balance need not be identical for every political community; indeed, we may expect just policies to vary in accordance with local calibrations of the relations among communality, individuality, and universality.[1] Yet where these three concerns are not all adequately attended to, it should be recognized, human goods are denied and human beings are, in more or less obvious ways, harmed.[2]

The argument is a naturalist argument, in the sense that its warrants derive explicitly from what I take to be defining moral aspects of human beings. It is, however, a naturalist argument of a deliberately modest sort. In making my case I admittedly rely on a teleological conception of overall human well-being; yet my suppositions about human nature and the human good are intended to remain few and limited. I do not wish to invoke a timeless theological or philosophical conception of ideal human nature. Rather, as I will treat it, human nature is neither uniform nor static. Its contours evolve over time, in response both to changed material circumstances and to changes wrought by humans themselves. The argument I make about political membership depends on cautious judgments — plausible ones, I think — about what humans are under present conditions, about what contributes to their good, and about how they may be harmed.[3] It is thus an argument about the direction, not the goal, of a just politics, about immediate political ends, not ultimate ones.

This theory is developed in two stages, a critical one and a constructive one. I first trace the broad outlines of my position through a critical assessment of a powerful contemporary treatment of political membership. In *Spheres of Justice* (1983), a work that has in great part defined the terms of current ethical discussions of citizenship, Michael Walzer presents a normative account of democratic membership as part of a broader theory of distributive justice. Overall, this "defense of pluralism and equality" represents an extension of Walzer's work on individual consent and contract,[4] but in his treatment of membership he seeks precisely the sort of anthropological balance I have suggested an adequate theory demands. He combines a sensitivity to problems of individual consent with a strong defense of the right of communities to protect their own character, and at the same time a recognition of requirements of transnational standards of justice. Although his argument focuses on shared understandings of social goods, he also acknowledges the constraints of broader moral principles. Moreover, in many respects he is sensitive to the ways in which modern conditions shape and alter the demands of justice.

I endorse several basic elements of Walzer's theory, including in particular his evaluation of relations of domination and subordination as the moral basis of claims about equality, including equality of membership. However, there are several points at which it is necessary to supplement or move beyond his analysis. Walzer leaves much to be said on a number of topics: the role of universal moral factors, the self-containedness of states, the problem of conflicting equalities, the distinctiveness of the political sphere, and the legitimacy of willed political subordination. In treating these themes, I set about developing a modified theory more appropriate to the realities of an increasingly post-national world.

The constructive theory of membership I develop is grounded, in a manner Walzer is loath to follow, in an account of human rights. Such an account provides a useful framework for articulating the moral force of Walzer's central categories of subordination and self-determination. It also has the virtue of placing claims about the rights of states, groups, and individuals within a common setting. As I demonstrate, the view that political membership is a matter first and foremost of human right has implications both for general criteria of political inclusion and for the political structuring of democratic states.

My argument proceeds through four steps, addressing in turn the basis of norms bearing on political membership, the content of these (human rights) norms, their general implications for the structuring of political communities, and their specific dictates in regard to the distribution of citizenship. First, I show that the very nature of modern political membership determines that its distribution should be subject to, or at least constrained by, norms that transcend both the decisions of the polity as a whole and the desires of individuals — norms that are today best understood as the requirements of global justice, or human rights.

Second, I argue that human rights are best understood as rights grounded in the requirements of human being as revealed through the experience of domination. In political terms, this requirement translates, first, into an injunction against specific forms of domination, and second, into a generic right to self-determination. Nondomination and self-determination are rights that apply not only to individuals but also to certain morally significant human collectivities, collectivities that crucially determine the possibilities for human dignity and agency.

Third, I make the case that in modern states, the human right to nondomination supports a provisional right of the political community to exclusion, and a categorical right of all settled residents to political membership. At the same time, the imperative of nondomination supports the claims of some collectivities, such as religious and ethnic minorities, to institutionalized group rights. The rights of groups need not include a positive right to political autonomy; usually, they will take a negative form, such as protections against domination within an overall context of common political membership.

Finally, I address the role of consent in political membership, arguing that the appropriate structure for citizenship policies is one in which residents are at a certain point presumed to be citizens unless they explicitly demand not to be included.

Walzer on Membership

In *Spheres of Justice* (1983), Walzer innovatively examines political membership as a *social good* that, because it is in some sense *distributed* to persons, is properly considered in the context of an inquiry into distributive justice. For this reason it is helpful to begin our examination of his view with a few words about his theory of justice.

Distributive Justice

Walzer's core idea is that criteria of justice are determined by social understandings about the nature of specific goods and are hence both historically particular and pluralistic in nature. Philosophers who seek a timeless single principle of distributive justice are misguided: "Justice," Walzer states, "is a human construction" (1983, 5; unless otherwise specified, all references to Walzer are from this book). Developing a theory of justice, it follows, is a matter of identifying the normative logics that inhere not in actual distributions — which may be unjust — but in the "roughly knowable" (16) meanings people within a society hold about how specific goods should be distributed.[5]

The account of distributive justice that Walzer sketches is, from the start, limited by three important assumptions he makes regarding social goods. First, while acknowledging that they are not self-contained distributive worlds, Walzer explicitly identifies national political communities (that is, states) as the appropriate setting for an investigation into criteria of justice (28). Second, his entire discussion relies implicitly on a belief that meanings about social goods will be more or less coherent and shared within such societies. Third, he similarly assumes that while social goods are perhaps not entirely separable from one another, they are as a rule distinct, so that there exists, in any society, a "separation of spheres" within which different distributive principles should apply. He thus posits a world divided into distinct societies, each with its own coherent geography of distributive spheres. In this landscape, the task of the ethicist becomes a sort of moral cartography.

Having set out this basic picture, Walzer goes on to introduce two basic normative maxims that presumably hold for all human societies. These maxims are framed in terms of a distinction he draws between "dominance" and "monopoly." Dominance involves the abuse of goods in one sphere to gain advantages in other spheres, while monopoly refers to the control of a given social good by a single person or minority group. The first maxim asserts that distributive spheres ought to remain autonomous from one another[6] — that advantages in one sphere should not enable the establishment of advantages within another sphere. Money, for example, occupies a sphere of its own, and its possession should not bring power within a different sphere involving, say, the distribution of political office. In support of this "non-convertibility" principle, Walzer adduces a number of historical examples illustrating the injustice of the dominance of a single sphere within society. Ultimately, however, his stance appears to be grounded in his initial account of social goods and the structure of justice. Built into his picture of plural spheres is the presumption that they ought to be kept apart. It is because Walzer sees distributive spheres and their accompanying criteria of justice as naturally separate that the dominance of one sphere over another strikes him as wrong.[7] Here Walzer adopts, in short, a naturalist position.[8]

Walzer's second normative maxim regards the sort of equality that ought to exist in a just society. The plurality of spheres, he states, should be reflected in an ideal of "complex equality" that takes account of each individual's participation in a variety of distinct distributive contexts. The goal of complex equality is sought through the pursuit of a society characterized by the absence of dominance among spheres. Equality thus exists when the possession of advantages in one sphere does not lead automatically to advantages in other spheres (20). This view of equality is not affected by the existence of monopolies in particular spheres since, Walzer assumes, disproportionate distributions in one sphere will generally be compensated for in other spheres. One who is disadvantaged in a given sphere should therefore not be regarded as suffering from inequality so long as this does not in itself lead to disadvantages in other spheres; and it is to be expected that the same person is likely to enjoy advantages in other spheres. This addendum reveals another crucial naturalist assumption undergirding Walzer's position. He assumes that in a just, dominance-free society, each person will be successful in some spheres and not in others; the overall result will be a pluralistic type of equality ensured by a sort of invisible hand. This perception is grounded in his assessment of human nature; he deems it unlikely that enough people will enjoy advantages in enough spheres to constitute a specially privileged class (20).[9] His conclusion is this: As long as the criteria implicit in our understandings of each individual good are properly distinguished and defended, we will have a broadly equal society. Walzer's equality is one not of people but of spheres.

Walzer's normative treatment of membership is presented against this backdrop. Noting that "the primary good that we distribute to one another is membership in some human community" (31), he raises two fundamental questions of distributive justice. First, do political communities have a right to control who moves to their territory? Second, do such communities have the right to exclude people living within their territory from the good of membership? Employing an argumentative strategy relying heavily on analogy[10] and appeals to common moral meanings among his readership,[11] he sets out to show that political communities have a right, within certain constraints, to deny admission, but at the same time, a duty to be internally inclusive. More specifically, he argues that (1) in the question of territorial admissions (immigration), political communities (states) should be allowed to determine whom they admit in accordance with the present members' shared meanings about membership, subject to limitations imposed by a universal principle of "mutual aid" establishing special obligations to admit some refugees (44–51), and (2) in the question of admissions to political membership (naturalization), *democratic* states are required by another universal principle, that of "political justice" (59–61), to make citizenship available to all adult residents. The resulting formula is this: States have some political leeway as to whom they admit, but once they admit people, they must be prepared to offer them full membership.

Immigration

Walzer formulates his argument about immigration as a discussion of the right of political communities to shape their own populations (52, 61), a right he views as the core of the universally recognized value of self-determination. Although he acknowledges some "external" constraints on this right, his primary interest is in upholding the state's right to establish its own criteria of admission and exclusion. In the end, however, his argument seems more a vindication of the importance of universal considerations of justice in matters of membership than a defense of states' rights. Not only does he greatly limit his claim about the prerogatives of the state through his treatment of mutual aid and political justice, but he also employs additional unacknowledged universalist assumptions regarding political membership in general. In the end it seems clear that Walzer's initial claim—that national political communities are the sole appropriate context for considering questions of distributive justice—does not apply to the case of membership.

The structure through which Walzer defines and examines membership is an important part of his argument. His strategy is to identify what he calls "internal" and "external" principles for assigning membership.[12] He begins by linking the socially distributed good of membership with admission—more specifically, with admission to residence in the territory governed by a given political community. Countries that attract immigrants, "like élite universities . . . have to decide on their own size and character," he proposes (32). This raises the question, What external moral constraints do "we"—those who are already members—act under in our decisions about who to admit? Walzer elects to define would-be immigrants as "strangers," and then goes on to address the question through an argument about duties to strangers. "We"—all people, presumably—recognize a transcultural principle of mutual aid by which strangers are entitled to our assistance when they urgently need it and when it may be provided at a relatively low cost to us. How this admittedly vague principle bears on membership decisions, however, depends further on one's understanding of the nature of political communities.

Walzer clarifies his conception of states through analogies with neighborhoods, families, and clubs. In the process, he reveals some important anthropological assumptions. For example, in contrasting the closed membership of states with the unregulated admissions policies of *neigh-*

borhoods, he argues that the two are mutually interdependent. In addition to being naturally sedentary, human beings require a degree of cultural closure, and if this closure were not provided at the national level, it would be created and enforced at the local level (38). This solution should be avoided, since local mobility is more important to the exercise of individual choice than mobility on a broader scale. Rather, we should concede that "the politics and the culture of a modern democracy probably required the kind of largeness, and also the kind of boundedness, that states provide" (39). States, it seems, provide a sort of natural balance for securing values fundamental to humans, or at least to democrats. The only alternative to a system of closed states other than a world of walled-off neighborhoods — "petty fortresses" — would be a global state populated by "radically deracinated men and women" deprived of what Walzer allows is a generally recognized human right — the right to cultural distinctiveness (39).[13]

For Walzer, the value of the distinctiveness of cultures is what grounds the right of communities to control admissions (at some level). Political communities are analogous to *clubs* in the way in which they exert this right, namely, through fully autonomous decisions regarding whom they admit. Here, it is important to draw out a point that is rendered implicit by Walzer's methodological individualism: This entitlement is in its essence a group right. Walzer is correct in asserting that a right to control immigration does not entail a right to control emigration and that immigration and emigration are "morally asymmetrical" (40). But he does not elaborate on the nature of this asymmetry. In fact, the rights at stake are basically symmetrical, but involve different subjects. The right to control immigration is a right aimed at protecting the self-determination of communities; the right to emigrate is a right aimed at protecting the self-determination of individuals. The purpose of each right is to prevent a certain type of domination: in the first case, the dissolution of group identity through immigrant movements, and in the second case, the despotic control of individual members by the state.

A country's right to control its membership is, Walzer goes on, constrained in practice by relations that are comparable to *family* ties. Thus, contemporary immigration practices tend to incorporate a "kinship principle" recognizing special claims on the part of people who are closely related by blood to members of the political community.[14] This principle applies in general to immediate family of citizens, but Walzer suggests that this category may legitimately be broadened, at least in the case of true nation-states, to include immigrants sharing the nationality of the political community in question. He bases this suggestion on the view that nation-states are the political expression of a national entity morally comparable to a family, and asks rhetorically, "What else are such states for?" (42) Yet this is a highly dubious apology for the practice of states, not least because national affinity is a much more ephemeral and controversial quality than are immediate family ties. There is no reason to assume that simply because Country X is populated by enough Greens to consider itself a Green nation-state, all Greens the world over have an automatic right to be admitted before non-Greens. However, Walzer's illustration for this claim—"Greeks driven from Turkey, Turks from Greece . . . had to be taken in by the states that bore their collective names" (42)—lends support to a different reason for admitting conationals, having to do with the principle of mutual aid. When people are oppressed because of their national identity in a country in which they are not dominant, they have a claim to aid; and countries in which their nationality is dominant are in a unique position to help them. Oppressed Jews, therefore, may have a special claim on Israel, and oppressed Germans on Germany; but might we not wish to recognize as well that an oppressed Russian Jew or a politically persecuted Iranian has a greater claim on admission to Germany than a successfully integrated German American?

Walzer next considers what distinguishes states from their analogues of neighborhood, club, and family. In focusing on the issue of territoriality, he immediately introduces another external moral factor. Individuals, he says, enjoy a "territorial or locational right"; they are entitled to remain in the place where they have made a life (43). Indeed, it is only on the basis of this right that states may justify the right to the territorial jurisdiction that they all claim. With this move, Walzer builds into his premises a key element of his conclusions. If the rights of states do in fact depend on a human right to remain where one has lived, or grown up, or settled, then the sphere of membership in a given state already includes by definition every inhabitant of that state's territory, in a manner unaffected by either individual exercises of will or national characteristics.[15]

The territorial control exerted by closed and distinct states is justifiable, Walzer argues, because it is necessary for effective political self-determination. Yet, this does not establish an absolute moral right to control who enters a state's territory. The principle of mutual aid, coupled with the economies of scale resulting from the organization of states, generates a strong group duty to help needy strangers, and often this may be fulfilled only by taking them in. States bear a particular responsibility to admit refugees, especially those refugees who have entered their territory and (1) were created by the state in question, (2) are actual or ethnic relatives, or (3) are recognized as ideological "relatives" persecuted because of their beliefs. Walzer insists that the external moral requirements of mutual aid "can only modify and not transform" a political community's decisions about whom it will admit (51). But as we have seen, the right of the community to regulate admissions is derived from or limited by additional external moral considerations, including the communal need for closure, the right to cultural diversity, the right to self-determination, and the locational rights of individuals.

Naturalization

Walzer's disquisition continues with a discussion of naturalization. The question he poses in this context is whether all those living within a territory are entitled to full political membership: whether citizenship should go with residence. As noted earlier, Walzer at one point simply assumes this to be the case, but he goes on to provide additional warrants to support his view that the state has a duty to open naturalization to all native-born residents as well as to all immigrants it admits. Here, his argument relies wholly on another external principle he introduces, namely, that of political justice.

Walzer begins his reflections on the question of naturalization—"second admissions"—by examining typical cases in which it is denied. After suggesting that the reason states often admit persons without giving them citizenship is to exploit them economically as "live-in servants" (52), he goes on to analyze two instances of such servitude: Athenian metics and contemporary guestworkers.[16] The political exclusion of metics in ancient Athens, he argues, might have been justifiable since "the dominance of birth and blood over political membership was part of the common understanding of the age" (55). In modern times, however, individual consent has come to be dominant. Current understandings of democracy agree that political power can be exercised legitimately only with the ongoing consent of those living within the territory in which it is enforced. Because it represents the exclusion of residents from their rightful political voice, the political subordination of guestworkers in a democracy is nothing less than despotism.

The existence of guestworkers as a disenfranchised and economically oppressed class violates what Walzer calls the principle of political justice: "The processes of self-determination through which a democratic state shapes its internal life must be open, and equally open, to all those men and women who live within its territory, work in the local economy, and are subject to local law" (60). Although Walzer does not make the scope of this principle clear, he appears to view it as an external principle that applies in a single form to all democracies.[17] As he formulates it, the principle makes a certain normative claim about the nature of democracies, namely, that membership in the spheres of law, politics, and the economy should coincide. Walzer also tacitly accepts here the notion that ethnicity is not relevant to democratic membership; by emphasizing the unfairness of the political exclusion of workers who "resemble citizens in every respect that counts" (59), he discounts the significance of what is usually the most obvious difference between guestworkers and citizens of their host countries.[18]

In the three criteria of eligibility for naturalization contained in Walzer's definition — residence, socioeconomic participation, and legal integration — three types of moral relations are implicit. Residence, Walzer has already suggested, brings with it a prima facie claim to membership: By being born into or settling in a community, one simply becomes a member of the political community, part of the unit of self-determination. Socioeconomic activity, on the other hand, represents a contribution entitling one to the privilege of political membership: Through performing "socially necessary work" (60), one earns a position in the polity.[19] Enmeshment in the legal system, finally, generates a right grounded in what the Germans call *Betroffenheit* — one's subjection to decisions and their enforcement. Because a person is under the authority of the state, he or she ought to have a political voice.[20]

"Immigration," Walzer concludes, "is both a matter of political choice and moral constraint. Naturalization, by contrast, is entirely constrained: every new immigrant, every refugee taken in, every resident and worker must be offered the opportunities of citizenship" (62). It is clear, at least in the case of democracies, that the principle of political justice trumps the rights of states arbitrarily to restrict membership, obliging them to open membership to all legally and economically integrated residents. Yet, here we encounter a crucial ambiguity in Walzer's formulation, for *opening* membership is not the same as *granting* it. The problem that results is twofold: What happens if membership is not accepted? And what happens if it is offered on unreasonable terms?

Walzer the consent theorist is forced to face the possibility that migrant workers and others like them might choose not to become citizens and so to remain resident aliens. One must wonder if Walzer would be satisfied with the thought of a large disenfranchised minority held to have "chosen" its subordinate status, an especially troublesome notion given the difficulties alluded to earlier with the notion of choice in such a context. The extent to which the decision not to belong can be designated as free and binding depends on a number of factors, including above all the manner in which the choice is structured.

Here, the question of fair minimum conditions for the offer of membership arises. On this point, Walzer simply suggests that naturalization for residents should be subject "only to certain constraints of time and qualification" (60). He is unenlightening on the crucial question of what these constraints might be.[21] Presumably they vary from state to state — but within which bounds? Determining whether it is within the purview of states to condition naturalization on, for example, periods of residence over ten years, or on qualifications such as cultural assimilation or the renouncement of all other citizenships, remains a problem. Prospective citizens are to have a choice, but questions persist: How might their choice be fairly structured? What is a fair price for citizenship?

If Walzer does not provide us with adequate answers to these questions, he has contributed a useful framework for addressing them. The power of his approach derives largely from its balanced attention to communal, individual, and universal ethical factors. We have seen how, at the communal level, Walzer highlights the importance of essentially shared meanings and defends a group right to self-determination. We have further noted his basic commitment to individual self-determination and consent. Finally, as I have taken special care in showing, he also demonstrates how universal moral structures and principles provide both the context for and constraints on the distribution of political membership. In addressing the problem of specific criteria for a just naturalization policy, we do well to follow Walzer's example by attending to the requirements of the communal self, the voluntaristic self, and the universal self.

Political Membership and Human Rights

In the theoretical framework suggested by Walzer's work, the balance of communal, voluntarist, and universal elements appropriate to an account of distributive justice will always be determined to a large extent by the specific character of the good involved. As we have seen, Walzer seems to recognize that there is something about the good of membership, or more specifically about the good of full membership or modern citizenship, that requires a greater relative emphasis on universal criteria of distribution than is required in any other sphere. The overall picture of membership norms that he presents reduces the role of communal meanings to a limited sphere of decision making regarding territorial admissions. The scope of individual voluntarism is confined to the question of whether or not one chooses to apply for naturalization. All other membership issues — who receives preference in admissions (the needy and "relatives"), at which level closure is enforced (the state), who has a right to self-determination (political groups and individuals), who has a right to remain in a territory (all residents), who has a say in determining the shape of admissions policies (all residents), who is entitled to eligibility for naturalization (all legally and economically integrated residents), whether cultural homogeneity is an admissible criterion (a qualified no) — are resolved by Walzer with reference to "external," that is, transnational, criteria. In an author who attempts, like John Stuart Mill, to forego relying on the idea of human rights (xv), and whose theory consequently emphasizes particular social meanings and individual consent, such a dependence on supranational norms is conspicuous. There are, however, very good reasons for this exception. These derive, I argue, from the nature and scope of the good of modern political membership.

The Distinctiveness of Modern Political Membership

Citizenship is a Janus-faced status. In its scope, it is inextricably both national and international. On the one hand, citizenship is a state institution, and individual citizenship is a good in many ways similar to other goods distributed by a state. Accordingly, some aspects of citizenship, such as whether one is allowed to vote, or is required to provide military service, or is provided with welfare, are questions that we expect individual political communities to determine, much in the same way that they determine how wealth is redistributed, or how public space is utilized, or how criminals are punished. On the other hand, national citizenship arises only within an international setting, as a category used collectively by states to divide persons among themselves and to determine the sphere of their authority. In this regard, it is a matter of transnational concern, a fact reflected in international agreements on such issues as statelessness and multiple citizenship. In practice, citizenship is, therefore, a global institution, responsive in some respects to national norms, and in others to broader norms grounded in contracts among states or in international customs.

This practice reflects a basic antinomy in the concept of political membership, or at least in the concept of democratic political membership. Even if the idea that a community should have the sole right to determine who belongs to it were accepted, the logically prior question of who should be recognized as part of the community that decides would remain unresolved. Does democracy necessarily presuppose the closure of citizenship (Hailbronner 1989a), or must citizenship itself be democratic (Oberndörfer 1990)? Who should decide who belongs? "Those who are officially already members" is an answer that begs the question, for there is no reason to suppose that the status quo is a morally defensible distribution. A second answer would assign such decisions to the sovereign nation, but this too is a dubious solution. Nations are not naturally separate, clearly defined entities whose members are objectively discernible; and even if they were, it would not resolve the question of whether cultural identity bears sufficient normative weight to determine political membership, particularly when a territory is shared by different national groups (cf. Bader 1995, 217–21). A third answer would recognize authority in matters of membership as accruing to those who together constitute the state through an act of association. Yet, as shown in the previous chapter, there are some problems with the notion of freedom of association in determining who belongs, having mainly to do with the absence of means other than force for resolving cases of disagreement.

What these attempts at a solution share is their recommendation of criteria of belonging that are internal to political communities. The inadequacy of these attempts suggests that, by its very nature, the problem of morally defensible norms for political membership can be resolved only with reference to external criteria of the sort we have been examining. States may appropriately provide the context for the rights of citizens, but only so long as citizenship itself—"the right to have rights"[22]—is distributed according to criteria that go beyond the interests of individual states. In part, this condition holds simply because the context of decisions about citizenship is transnational in a way that other political decisions are not. Mainly, however, this conclusion flows from the character of modern citizenship as membership in a *territorial* political organization. In light of the degree of control modern states possess over the lives of their residents, it is the territorial aspect, not the organizational aspect, that must receive the normative emphasis in democracies: It is the impartial criterion of the *place* where people have made their lives, and not anything that states deem important about them—their personal credentials or ethnic character or allegiances—that ought to determine their eligibility for political membership.

The grounds for this normative emphasis may be clarified through some observations about the nature of political membership. We might agree that appropriate criteria for the distribution of goods such as education, commodities, jobs, or love should reflect social meanings shared at the national level, as Walzer suggests, or even in smaller communities. Political membership is in some ways a good like these others, but it is also unique in a way that has an immediate bearing on principles for its distribution. Through the political sphere, people are able to shape other spheres. As Walzer puts it,

> political power is the regulative agency for social goods generally. It is used to defend the boundaries of all the distributive spheres, including its own, and to enforce the common understandings of what goods are and what they are for . . . we might say, indeed, that

political power is always dominant — at the boundaries, but not within them. The central problem of political life is to maintain that crucial distinction between "at" and "in." (15n)

His point is that through politics, persons are able to protect social goods from encroachment and domination by other goods. In effect, having political membership is akin to being part of a volunteer police force with a special mandate to preserve the autonomy and equality of spheres.

But putting it this way underestimates both the creative role we ascribe to democratic politics and the difficulty of separating political actions from social phenomena. Certainly, political measures may legitimately aim at implementing, and protecting, shared criteria of distributive justice. But sometimes they will go further, altering social meanings or intervening in conflicts between spheres by, for example, instituting racial integration or restructuring church-state relations. At least sometimes, most would agree, these alterations or interventions constitute a just use of power. Politics is, as I claimed earlier, a sphere of agency through which participants collectively exert leverage on the arrangements within which they live.

Beyond its effects on social structures and living conditions, political activity subtly but deeply conditions norms regarding goods and equality. It is hard to deny that the social meanings shared by many Western countries today regarding goods such as, for example, welfare have been greatly shaped by past political decisions. It is not necessary to identify the extent of this role in order to recognize the special significance of the political sphere. Indeed, national identity itself is in large part a political artifact. Because of the unique importance of political power not only in protecting but also in changing and shaping the values of any given territorial political organization, eligibility for political membership requires standards of a different order than those of other spheres. The good of citizenship must be exempted from the sort of complex equality applying to the rest of the spheres, for unless it is distributed on a model of simple individual equality within the territory of a state, some members of society will be ineligible for activities that may bear on the distribution of all other social goods. Since the sphere of political activity is at its heart concerned with social agency, political membership must be distributed to all agents; where it is not, where a monopoly in this sphere is held by the few, a special form of deprivation exists.[23] The very gravity of political membership, the manner in which it transcends the two-dimensional geography of shared goods, is what dictates that it be subject to criteria that go beyond the self-contained social meanings of the state.

What might these criteria be? In a formal sense, in the absence of rules enacted through a global political process, they can only be *norms* for the treatment of persons that are widely held to be universally binding: in short, what we have come to know as human rights. But what, specifically, are human rights, and how do they bear on political membership? These questions go not to the institutionalization of human rights in international and national law, but rather to the normative basis of human rights viewed as a social practice involving what might be called global self-determination (cf. Donnelly 1989, 16–19).

Human Rights to Nondomination and Self-Determination

The hallmark of the human rights perspective is its attempt to make individual conduct, political decisions, and social structures answerable to standards of a certain type. Human rights standards embody principles that subordinate considerations of individual voluntarism or communal identity to values linked to the sphere of humankind in general. In this section, I give substance to the perspective I have argued must form the core of a modern ethics of political membership and support it through an account of transnational justice developed in terms of the prohibition of domination. Human rights, in this account, are understood as rights to nondomination and self-determination that are designed to protect and foster human beings in their various aspects as individuals, as parts of communities, and as members of the human race.

Philosophers, theologians, and political scientists have provided us with many theories regarding the nature of human rights. Often they seize on a central concept that they hold to capture the basis of human rights, a fundamental principle which generates the normative force behind justifiable claims about how people should or should not be treated. The theoretical landscape is occupied by a formidable array of such conceptions of the foundation of human rights. One extremely influential view, for example, is that human *dignity,* conceived either as something innate to humans or as something that they are due, serves as the source of human rights.[24] Another approach, sometimes articulated in conjunction with notions of dignity, justifies human rights as requirements of human *agency*, understood as the capacity of individuals for purposive action.[25] A related perspective views human rights as shaped and secured by the very nature of *rationality*.[26] On a fourth view, human rights are entitlements to those goods that are necessary conditions for *eudaimonia* — human flourishing.[27] Other accounts of the foundations of human rights have emphasized the significance of human *needs*,[28] *existence*,[29] *self-preservation*,[30] and *difference*.[31] As grounds of human rights, these concepts are not necessarily mutually exclusive; in fact, they are often combined, though generally one remains dominant.

What these views all have in common is that they seek to explicate a substantive account of human nature as the basis of claims of human right.[32] The move to rights that they all embrace is an expression of egalitarianism, for at the heart of the notion of rights is the idea that all subjects of a given class — in this case, humans — are *equally* entitled to a given good. Egalitarianism is a universally powerful normative force. But specific arguments in favor of equality are often weakened by the inherently controversial nature of the substantive accounts of human beings on which they are based (cf. Waldron 1987, 162–66). I recommend a pragmatic approach that attempts to avoid this problem by dealing only indirectly with the theoretical grounding of human rights, concentrating instead on the practice through which such rights are actually articulated and recognized. I believe that human rights do entail some idea of human nature, but this nature may be specified only dimly and heuristically, and often — in a fashion reminiscent of classical negative theology — only in terms of what it is not.

The criterion I endorse for determining which human rights we are entitled to is presaged by Walzer in his reflection on the moral significance of domination (xii–xiv).[33] It is my contention that the human experience of domination — a type of injustice involving a violation against human nature (be it understood in terms of dignity or agency or *eudaimonia*) committed through the agency of others[34] — is what in practice gives rise to compelling claims of human right.[35] We may — and do — grant the legitimacy of such claims without a full and perfect understanding of the human nature they evoke.[36] It is easier to tell what represents a (drastic) abuse against some aspect of human nature than it is to specify what human nature ideally requires and when its requirements are not met (cf. Wolgast 1987). This is, I think, a modest epistemological claim, of a sort appropriate to our relation to moral knowledge in a world that increasingly values individual conscience and religious pluralism. Still, modest claim or not, if we are to replace substantive accounts of human nature with the phenomenon of domination as our guiding normative concept, we must spell out what we mean by it.

What is domination? Domination is, first and foremost, a type of moral and political experience. It is not simply the experience of inequality, as Walzer rightly notes.[37] Nor is it simply the experience of unfreedom (cf. Shklar 1986, 1990). It is the experience, directly or mediated through social structures, of harm or deprivation or subordination at the hands of others occupying a position of power (cf. Seidler 1991).[38] The distinguishing feature of this experience is a certain type of social relation in which one party uses its political position to intervene in another party's enjoyment of important goods.[39] Domination is, in short, the essence of tyranny.[40]

Beyond this assessment, it is difficult to generalize about domination precisely because it is a contextual phenomenon that varies somewhat in form according to the particular circumstances that constitute it. In part, whether domination obtains in a given situation depends on what goods are important to the persons involved; it may also depend on the sort of relationship that exists between those who are in a position to exercise power and those who are not. Thus, deprivation of a good such as, say, access to the news media might constitute domination for some and not for others, while restraining freedom of movement, under certain conditions of authority, might be perceived as a justifiable precaution or a fair punishment rather than domination. However, this is not, to say that domination is purely subjective and hence relative, but simply that it is partially contingent. The surest guide to judging the authenticity of instances of domination would be through a well-developed phenomenology of domination; that, however, would considerably exceed the scope of this study. In lieu of this, I offer some provisional observations regarding crucial characteristics of the experience of domination as a ground of rights.

The experience of domination is characterized by a three-part structure. The first part consists of the effects of domination on the person dominated. The victim is exposed to circumstances that prevent the attainment of some important good that would otherwise be enjoyed. It is conceivable that these adverse effects may go unmarked.[41] Usually, however, they will be sensed ever more strongly as time passes. These negative circumstances may be experienced as instigating a loss — of freedom, of funds, or of food. Or they may be experienced as the frustration of one's projects or aspirations, or as a personal debasement, or, most direly, as psychological or physical injury. At this point, however, the effects of domination are not yet distinct from other sorts of misfortunes that affect us.[42]

The second moment in the experience of domination is the establishment of a causal link between the effects on the victim and the agency of others. Where a negative influence on human prospects is revealed to be not arbitrary, but brought about or perpetuated through the actions of others, a subtle alteration occurs: the experience is no longer impersonal. A loss comes to be a deprivation, frustration is transformed into defeat, debasement turns into humiliation, and injury becomes harm. The broken leg accidentally sustained on the soccer field is not, however, morally equivalent to the broken leg inflicted in the torture chamber, and the mere fact that an injury has human origins does not qualify it as an instance of domination.

This transition occurs only with the third component of the experiential structure of domination, in the attribution of culpability to the dominator for the effects borne by the victim. Acts that negatively affect others take on a special character when they are committed in a manner experienced as in violation of moral relationships with those persons. How exactly to determine when one is morally responsible for a given state of affairs is a difficult question that cannot be resolved here.[43] It is a mistake to assume that an intention to harm is a necessary characteristic of domination, for even negligence or acts of omission on the part of those in a position of power may produce a structure of domination. Even so, when the circumstances disadvantaging the victims are intentionally created and explicitly upheld — as for example under apartheid — the experience of domination becomes all the more intense. With the addition of this moral dimension to the other elements of negative effects and human causality, domination assumes its distinctive character. Deprivation becomes robbery, defeat is transformed into sabotage, humiliation turns into persecution, and harms come to be abuses.

The ethical premise of the human rights perspective is quite simply that domination is wrong.[44] To accept this assertion is to accept that it is wrong for human beings to dominate others; or conversely — from the point of view of the prospective victims — that it is right for human beings not to be dominated by others.[45] If we consider moral rights to be, in the most rudimentary sense, justified moral claims,[46] then the step from right to rights in this instance is a small one, and we can state that human beings have a moral right not to be dominated. This formulation provides the generic form of human rights.

To fill out this notion, it is necessary to say a bit more about the character of rights. Analytically, a right, whether moral or legal, is a relational concept presupposing at least six different aspects, including a class of subjects, an object, a class of respondents against whom the right is held, a purpose, an authority, and a social context in which it is held.[47] Hence we may always ask: Who has the right? To what? With respect to whom? Why? On what basis? Within what bounds? Within this framework, specific claims of human right are constructed according to the components of the experience from which they arise. From the three-part structure of domination — victim, causal link, and agent — emerge the subjects, object, and respondents of the right. Other features of the right — that is, the sort of community in which it is held and the agency with reference to which it may be claimed (who, in other words, is obligated to enforce it) — depend on the social and political context in which domination occurs, as well as the hermeneutical context in which domination is interpreted.[48]

Within any catalogue of human rights — including, of course, the UN's Universal Declaration of Human Rights — it is possible to identify and draw distinctions among the forms of domination that serve as the basis for each right. In general, the power of claims of human right, in practice, seems to stand in direct relation to the intensity of the experience of domination from which the claims arise.[49] Evidence of this relation can be seen in the tendency of international actors to commit themselves most bindingly to act against precisely those sorts of relations that bear the strongest stamp of domination — such as genocide or slavery.

Further evidence is found in the inclination among theorists of human rights to distinguish between "basic" human rights and those occupying a lesser priority. "Basic rights" seem as a rule to be those rights pertaining to the strongest forms of domination threatening members of contemporary societies — political "disappearances," state-abetted poverty and hunger, arbitrary arrest and detention, torture, and persecution on grounds of race or gender.[50]

Having said something about the source of human rights, we now turn to the question of their form — that is, of the sort of equality they are to embody. If human rights acquire their normative force negatively, as direct responses to inequalities or differential treatment of a certain character, as *rights* they also, if less directly, embody a positive strategy aimed at creating a certain type of equality. Yet what sort of equality should human rights aim to create? Walzer provides us with one candidate. Eschewing conventional notions of simple individual equality, he proposes a more nuanced and intricate conception: complex equality, a state of affairs characterized by the absence of the dominance of any particular sphere. Yet by defining the egalitarian society in purely structural terms, as a question of relations among social spheres, he goes so far as to divorce equality from actual human beings. In contrast, equality as I define it is characterized by the absence of domination not among spheres of social meaning, but among human beings themselves, in all their various individual and social capacities.

Thus far, I have deliberately spoken only in terms of human nature and goods for human beings generally. An extra step is required to extend my claims specifically to "individuals," and to do so at this point would be to be guilty of premature specificity. Like the concepts of society or the community or the group, the concept of the individual is an abstraction, and indeed many important aspects of human being are not individual in nature — such as language, religion, culture, even our perceptions of shapes and forms.[51] Because our communal forms of human being may also, if in ways different from those we experience as individuals, be subordinated or subjected to domination, it is necessary to view equality in more flexible, diversified terms. National groups, ethnic groups, language groups, and religious groups may all be oppressed and may all have their existence threatened. The victims of such acts are always *people,* of course, but depending on the form of domination, sometimes these people are best understood not as individuals (that is, as distinct and independent human agents), but rather, by way of differentiation, as "persons," that is, group members, people defined as parts of a group that acts or is acted upon as a group, independently of its specific membership.[52] Given the fact that groups may be dominated and harmed qua groups,[53] there is no prima facie basis for saying that the equality sought by human rights should apply only to human beings conceived as individuals.[54] The subject of the right, it makes sense to stipulate, should reflect the anthropological nature of the good at issue. The goal of human rights is, then, a type of equality characterized by the absence of domination of human being in all of its various structures.[55]

To summarize, human rights are entitlements of people (individuals or groups) not to be dominated (in respect to some human good). The epistemic asymmetry of human harms and goods determines that human rights are most strongly justifiable as responses to or defenses against relations of dominance; only in a weaker manner may they be defended as steps toward an egalitarian order in which human beings in their various capacities are empowered to pursue their individual and communal goods.[56] We can thus speak of nondomination as the primary norm of human rights, and self-determination — which, as we have noted, similarly applies to both individuals and groups — as a subsidiary norm. Insofar as a group or class of individuals is denied, through some action or human state of affairs, the opportunity to exercise self-determination, the case can be made that that class or group is being dominated. That domination exists will be all the more clear, however, if it is manifest that such a class or group is being seriously harmed and its survival jeopardized. And when the right to self-determination of one group comes into conflict with the right to nondomination of a minority or other group, the right to nondomination as a rule deserves priority. This ordering of rights bespeaks, I believe, a widely shared moral intuition regarding clashes between autonomy and survival. We now have an idea of the basis and form of the human rights standard that, I have argued, should be recognized to govern considerations of political membership. Our next task is to examine the implications of this standard for the structuring of modern societies.

Political Communities and Rights of Membership

One aim of my argument up to this point has been to redefine the central conflict at issue in many national membership policies such as Germany's. The central source of disagreement in debates over membership is usually formulated as a conflict between the positive rights of the sovereign nation-state and the human rights of residents. But this juxtaposition of two competing moral worlds—one defined by citizenship and the boundaries of the state, the other encompassing all humanity—does not capture the actual shape of the problem. As I have tried to show, in virtue of their very structure, questions of membership occupy a normative context that encompasses and goes beyond the state—namely, the context of human rights. To say this is not simply to discount the claims of states; it is rather to draw such claims into a human rights discourse. It is to say that states may have rights not because they say they do and can back this claim with coercive force, but because as representatives of communities that embody important human goods they may plausibly invoke human rights. The rights of human beings qua individuals have the same general ground and form as the rights of human beings qua political communities—or the rights of human beings qua other sorts of morally important groups. This is not to say that conflicts among these sorts of rights are easy to resolve, but it is to suggest that they do not turn on incommensurable moral commitments.

We may see what difference this claim of commensurability makes by examining how some of the basic issues that arise in membership policies are treated under the human rights perspective I have proposed. First of all, to reiterate, the distinctive position of the political sphere in relation to other spheres gives it a unique potential to become involved in relations of domination; for this reason alone a special interest exists in making political membership as open as possible to all morally important entities within the state. But let us focus for now on individuals. From the standpoint of each constituent of a certain set of individuals (namely, those subject to the authority of the political decisions of a territorial state), not to possess full political membership is to be disadvantaged in one or more phenomenologically significant respects. If the state is democratic, politically excluded individuals are deprived of a valuable aspect of self-determination: a voice, however small, in decision-making processes gravely affecting the conditions under which they make their lives. An exclusion such as this falls afoul of what was de-scribed above as a subsidiary human rights norm. More importantly, re-gardless of the democratic character of a state, excluded or subordinated individuals are subjected to policies that affect nearly every aspect of their lives, yet are set by a collectivity of which they are not a part and which need not consider their well-being.[57] This state of affairs represents a violation of their primary human right, the right to nondomination. The minimum requirement of human rights is, on this analysis, a right to membership applying equally to all members of the group in question. And following the universal practice of states, this group includes not just citizens, but all established residents within the territory.[58]

Now, to say that all those residing in a state are entitled to political membership is to go a bit further than Walzer does in his claim that citizenship should be *open* to residents "subject only to certain con-straints of time and qualification." What limitations may apply to this right? To begin with, a certain temporal qualification inheres in the notion of residence. It is generally accepted that residence takes some time to establish. One reason is phenomenological in character: The experience of settling in a society, of belonging there, of having a stake in the running of the community unfolds over time. Another reason is structural: Generally a period must elapse before political activity from which one has been excluded (or in which one has participated) can exert its effects and thereby ground judgments about domination (or its absence). For these reasons, membership policies may legitimately in-clude in their definition of residence a duration requirement, based on the time it is judged to take to establish that a person is not a transient and that he or she is fully enmeshed in the political and legal system. This requirement, I think, might reasonably be expected not to exceed a few years, although a case for a longer period can be made.[59]

Another prospective limitation on a right to membership invokes the notion of competence. Here the question is whether the individual pos-sesses the abilities required to fulfill the social role embodied in the notion of political membership. An answer to this question hinges on the character of political membership in the respective state. Again, a broad distinction may be made between nondemocratic and democratic countries. Where political membership is more or less a matter of sub-jecthood, that is, of simply being subject to the rights and duties applying to citizens, no special competence would appear to be required. In a democracy, on the other hand, an important component of citizenship is the right and duty of political participation, and this requires a degree of responsibility and foresight commonly attributed only to adults. Consequently, democratic political communities may justifiably distinguish between two classes of members: adults, who in addition to enjoying other rights and duties of citizenship, constitute the pool of political participants, or demos; and children and new residents, both of whom have limited rights and duties for the time being but enjoy the promise of full membership with time.[60] For the class of potential full citizens, it is only the provisional nature of their exclusion, or the relative certainty of their eventual inclusion, that justifies their current subordinate status.

We must now consider how the right of individual residents to political membership relates to the right of the territorial political community to determine its own character. This question has several dimensions. A stable political community—be it a democracy, an oligarchy, or an anarchy—is, it has been observed for centuries, integral to the human good. We can agree on this without invoking a timeless and universal conception of human nature, simply on the basis of the observation that persons deprived of any political membership are more often than not condemned to various forms of hardship, to physical insecurity, and to the frustration of life plans. Political organizations may provide a defense against such forms of domination; beyond this, they may provide the opportunity for a level of self-determination that utilizes economies of scale to extend the possibilities for the well-being of members. There is consequently a basic human right at stake in the survival of political communities, and a subsidiary one in their ability to develop themselves as they see fit.

The order of these rights determines in turn the rights of states in different areas of membership policy. In the question of territorial admissions, for example, what is usually at issue is the subsidiary right of the political community to determine its character and direction by allowing in only the immigrants of its choice. As a right of self-determination, this right will be outweighed in cases in which it may be demonstrated that, for prospective immigrants, a right of nondomination is at stake (for instance in cases involving political or "economic" refugees, or race discrimination). However, when only the migrant's individual right of self-determination stands against the right of the community, then the migrant no longer has a superior claim. And in situations in which migration is of such a scope or nature that the very survival of the political and social order of the state becomes threatened, the state might conceivably invoke the right of the community to nondomination in closing admissions even to individuals threatened by oppression and subordination. Such extreme circumstances, however, are extraordinarily difficult to demonstrate and would require extensive empirical support before becoming morally compelling. For this reason, it is unlikely that the exclusion of individuals in truly dire need could ever be justified in practice.[61] Here — and it is an important point — individuals have a firm epistemic advantage, for they are far more likely than states are to be able to show that a primary human right is at stake in the question of their admission.

In the matter of internal inclusion, a political community's human right to self-determination once again comes up against what I have argued to be a right to nondomination — the human right of residents to political membership. Once again, the primary right should take precedence over the subsidiary one. And here, it is difficult to imagine a situation in which the group right to nondomination would be abrogated by the political inclusion of residents.[62] The only viable scenario of this type would be one involving large numbers of illegal immigrants who had successfully settled in a country. One could arguably make the case that admitting such a population to citizenship would result in the destruction of the social and political order, but this would be very difficult to demonstrate satisfactorily.[63] So long as any reasonable doubt remains as to whether the state is actually threatened by domination, a presumption in favor of the rights to nondomination of noncitizen residents should be upheld. Otherwise, the possibility arises that the domination to which they are subject will be intensified by the experience of unwarranted rejection.

One component of the right to self-determination often claimed by political communities is the right to enforce cultural homogeneity in the interest of maintaining a national cultural identity. As noted earlier, the idea of cultures as even potentially homogeneous units stands on shaky empirical ground. Apart from this, though, it is worth emphasizing that in matters of "culture," the claims of groups that happen to possess control of a territory are not different in kind from the claims of minority cultural groups. Because the goods involved in cultural community (language, shared mores and structures of meaning, religious expression, artistic expression, and so on) are only loosely bound up with those of contemporary political community (political self-determination, security, economic efficiency, redistribution of resources) there is no compelling basis for making political membership dependent on cultural membership. It follows that political inclusion in modern states may not justifiably be made contingent on the adoption of the cultural identity of the majority culture.[64] This would — to invoke Walzer's terms for a distinctly non-Walzerian point — represent the dominance of culture outside its sphere.

In a human rights–based ethics of membership, the interest of national majorities in preserving their cultural identities is overridden by the need of minority cultures for a structure of group rights and protections. Minority groups are far more likely to be undermined and oppressed than are majority cultures. When the right of a dominant cultural group to self-determination comes into conflict with the rights to nondomination of relatively coherent minority communities, then so long as the majority culture is not thereby threatened with domination, the minority cultures possess a legitimate claim to certain types of limited protections, and perhaps even to active support from the state.[65] The topic of group rights is taken up in more detail in the next chapter.

Consent and the Conditions of Naturalization

Our discussion of human rights thus far has tried to reconcile, or at least render commensurable, claims involving humans as universal beings and humans as communal beings. But so far nothing has been said about humans as willing and choosing beings. In particular, we have not yet addressed the question of consent. Is there room for the voluntary self in the account of human rights we have sketched?

The role of consent in the distribution of membership has been a central concern of several contemporary writers on citizenship, most notably Walzer and Peter Schuck and Rogers Smith. Schuck and Smith's book, *Citizenship without Consent* (1985), uses the problem of illegal immigration to examine questions about the fundaments of political membership. In it, they develop a distinction between ascriptive grounds of citizenship, which emphasize parentage or place of birth, and consensual grounds, which emphasize voluntarism and commitment. These two grounds represent the opposing sides of a fundamental moral conflict between "transcendent human rights" and consensualism (41). They then argue that, for historical, political, and moral reasons, the United States should place greater emphasis on consent in its membership policies than it previously has; more specifically, it should predicate the extension of citizenship on "mutual consent": "the consent of the national community as well as that of the putative member" (6). National consent should be expressed in laws adopted by representative government, and individual consent, in the application for naturalization (7).

Acknowledging individual consent is important for membership policies, for denying the possibility of consent would constitute a form of domination. But the logic of Schuck and Smith's position, despite its proviso that the "recognized human rights of aliens" must be respected (6), supports the conclusion that on the basis of aggregate individual choice (not security or communal cohesion), nations should be free to exclude any noncitizens they wish from membership—regardless of their residence in, legal integration under, or contributions to the state. And this exclusion involves a different form of domination. Such a situation would establish the immunity of states to claims for nondomination on the part of long-term resident aliens; in so doing, it would violate these residents' human right to inclusion. For this reason, from the perspective I have proposed, Schuck and Smith's notion of mutual consent is an inadequate basis for an ethical membership policy. Because residents do not have the option to exempt themselves from the coercive territorial authority exercised by a political community, it would be unjust to make the basic conditions for political membership a matter for political decision.

Walzer, in his treatment, focuses on a different aspect of consent. A self-described consent theorist, he asserts that democratic rule requires the ongoing consent of all residents of a state (1983, 58–59). At the same time, he also allows that resident aliens may "choose not to become citizens," that is, choose not to commit themselves to their country of residence, but rather to return home to their country of origin, or to remain as outsiders (60). This latter possibility—that some residents may deliberately close themselves out of the arena of consent and self-governance in the society in which they live — seems to conflict with the spirit of Walzer's commitment to democracy. Still, as long as this choice is made not once and for all (in the manner of Locke's notion of express consent), but in an ongoing fashion, as a consistent commitment to alienage, it may be understood as a justifiable expression of individual autonomy. A problem with this view of consent arises, however, when one considers how such a decision is likely to be formulated and expressed in practice. As the German case clearly shows, failure to naturalize may often signify something considerably less than a free act of consent to a subordinate political status, particularly when it occurs in a subtly coercive atmosphere marked by the official promotion of an "illusion of return."[66] If personal consent is to be given its due, much importance must be assigned to how the choice of political membership is structured.

The specific nature of the choice facing foreign residents generates significant consequences for a human rights–oriented political membership policy. As I have claimed, it would be a form of domination to ascribe the rights and duties of citizenship to immigrant residents independently of their choice. Yet under current conditions in Germany and elsewhere, in the absence of a fully decisive commitment to remain, citizenship is generally not sought. Because of the ever-present possibility of imminent return, the decision to commit oneself to stay is rarely made. As a result, many foreign residents are politically excluded not because they decide for alienage in an act of consent, but by default. In other words, the current structure of the choice of whether or not to naturalize, favors the perpetuation of a disenfranchised foreign resident population.

A naturalization policy that hopes to do justice to the human right to political membership, while at the same time respecting the value of consent, must take the problem of the nature of choice into account and structure the process for granting political rights accordingly. When a resident deliberately turns down an offer of citizenship, this constitutes a stronger expression of consent than when one simply declines to apply for naturalization. For this reason, the element of consent in naturalization policies best takes the form of a power to refuse a status of political membership extended presumptively to all established residents. A presumption in favor of political inclusion would leave untouched each person's freedom not to belong. At the same time it would help guarantee that those uncertain of their ultimate life plans would not be assigned to a marginal, politically subordinate status unless they truly and explicitly desired to be.

A Normative Theory of Political Membership

The theory of political membership I have proposed adopts, with some modification, Michael Walzer's method of grounding judgments about justice in accounts of social meanings regarding the good in question. I have argued that political membership in the modern world is, as Walzer implicitly recognizes, distinctively a universal good — and that consequently, universal criteria apply to the question of how it ought to be attributed. I depart from Walzer in proposing that these universal criteria are best conceived as human rights, organized around a basic principle of nondomination. According to this conception, political communities have a prima facie (second-order) human right to choose whom they admit to residence in their territory; but this right may be outweighed if putative members can show that a first-order human right is at stake in their being admitted. Already established residents, I have further claimed, not only have a right to political membership, but should be granted full — or, in the case of children, potentially full — membership status unless they make a point of refusing it. Moreover, cultural groups also possess human rights that support first-order claims for protections on behalf of oppressed or dominated groups. The interest of a dominant culture in enforcing assimilation, by contrast, invokes a second-order right — that to cultural self-determination — which is outweighed by the first-order interest of minority residents in not being politically excluded.

This normative account of political membership seeks to balance the three political anthropological values of communality, voluntarism, and universality. Beyond this, it seeks to integrate them within an overall framework of human rights, conceived not in terms of static features of persons, but rather with reference to shared problems encountered within a context of power relations. In a manner dictated by the vicissitudes of modern political life, the universal self lies at the heart of this account, embodied in the central contention that people qua human beings are entitled to belong to the political systems to which they are subject. The communal self also has an important role, specifically regarding the rights of people qua political and cultural groups to self-determination and protection from domination. This part of the argument is a recognition that people are not simply *reliant* on groups; in certain morally important ways, people *are* groups. Because we are not merely individuals with cultural memberships, but rather beings to some extent *constituted* by the human groups to which we belong, we have a deep stake in respecting and promoting group rights. Finally, the account presented in this chapter also reserves a place for the voluntary self through its insistence that people qua individual agents be allowed to exercise consent in questions involving changes in their political membership. Of the membership orientations discussed in the preceding chapters, the view I have sketched here is most closely aligned with the universalist commitments of the coexistence and cosmopolitan positions. However, in its suspicion of the reductionism inherent in an exclusive focus on individual rights — and in its corresponding concern for communality — it also has something in common with the culture position.

It can hardly be ignored that an important limit for this theory of political membership is posed by its assumption of a cohesive global structure of state citizenships. For as international political structures evolve, so too must their membership mechanisms, posing again and again the question of appropriate norms for the attribution and distribution of membership. An obvious example is provided by European integration, which is in the process of substantially altering the shape of citizenship in Europe, and with it the status of migrant workers in Germany and in other member states.

Yet, just how much is European integration actually likely to change the basic issues of political membership addressed here? European policymakers are committed in the long run to securing full political rights for migrant workers from member countries in all other member countries. It seems likely that the eventual shape of a politically unified Europe will be a confederation of states with a common market, freedom of movement, and reciprocity of citizenship privileges among states (Jessurun d'Oliveira 1990). Whether or not integration will proceed beyond that to a federal state system with a unified citizenship is questionable.[67] In either case, the European Union will almost certainly continue to maintain boundaries against the rest of the world, exercise sovereignty within its territory, and exclude foreigners from the status of political membership. Regardless of whether there are as many naturalization procedures as there are member states, or a single unified one, non-EU residents will still have to gain access to citizenship in order to obtain political rights.

From the point of view of this study, it is encouraging that such residents will in all likelihood be able to benefit from the continually increasing currency of the human rights discourse in the European Union. And as parties to the EU continue to evolve from nation-states into national groups within a larger political system, it is to be anticipated that the idiom of human rights will be extended more and more to the explicit concerns of groups (cf. Kühnhardt 1994). At the same time, however, the resurgence of nationalist sentiments in EU countries such as Germany and France, in the former Soviet republics, and above all in the remnants of what was once Yugoslavia poses a considerable barrier to the application of human rights standards in the structuring of political membership.

Beyond the developments in Europe, are there signs to indicate that the global system assumed by my argument is already giving way to newer models of political organization? Growing economic interdependence among states, supranational organization, and international migration have all been identified as symptoms of a fundamental challenge to state sovereignty.[68] It does seem clear that states increasingly experience incursions into their affairs by various international actors. It also seems clear that the foundation of state sovereignty — the ideal of nation-state citizenship — has been eroded and to a large extent replaced by a system in which social, economic, political, and national memberships are no longer congruent (see Roche 1992; Soysal 1994; Bauböck 1994). Over time, the distribution of goods within state societies has come to be governed more by universalist considerations of respect for personhood than by traditional national interests. The idea of democracy has attained an unprecedented global popularity, and some have even begun to speak of a world polity (see, e.g., Thomas et al. 1987). The concept of human rights has firmly entrenched itself in policy discussions the world over, and human rights activism at the international level continues apace.

Yet, the institutionalization of human rights as it has evolved internationally demonstrates, paradoxically, the continuing strength of state sovereignty. Within states, even when human rights are cited as the normative basis for a particular policy, this legitimation is taken to presuppose the territorial state as the instrument for and scope of implementation. And in the current world order, all international human rights instruments have been established by and remain dependent upon sovereign states. This set of circumstances is unlikely to change in the foreseeable future. A global political society in which the lands we inhabit are no longer divided among competing sovereigns is not yet in sight. For this reason, we may expect that for some time to come, where we reside, work, and make our lives will remain of central importance for the just distribution of political membership.

Although the overall argument thus far has been developed against a backdrop of concrete political considerations, the ethical theory of political membership I have defended remains at a high level of generality. It remains to be seen what sort of answers it might support in response to specific problems of membership policy such as those we have encountered in the German case. What, on a human rights–based view of membership, are acceptable criteria for the distribution of membership in the German political community? Ought German citizenship to be an exclusive identity, or is dual citizenship a tolerable option? What sorts of groups in German society are entitled to the protection of their cultural identities? In the final chapter these questions are taken up in a renewed discussion of the case of the foreign worker population in Germany.

Chapter Five

Citizenship and Group Rights

I t is wrong for people to dominate others. This claim is the touchstone of the human rights criteria that I have argued should govern our approach to questions of political membership in modern states. Where not clearly consented to, the exclusion of long-term residents from the benefits and protections of full membership constitutes a form of domination. Such residents should be recognized to possess a human right to political inclusion. As a right of nondomination, the right to political inclusion outweighs the competing right of the citizenry to determine its membership according to internal criteria. Consequently, those persons who have established indefinite residence in the territory administered by the state should be regarded as full and equal members, unless they explicitly reject this status. In this chapter, the practical consequences of this theory for contemporary citizenship policies are spelled out by tracing its application to the German case.

It is evident that Germany's substantial migrant worker population is entitled to be incorporated into full and equal membership in the German state. In identifying the requirements of this broad objective in terms of specific policies, particular attention must be devoted to two questions. First, how should this incorporation be accomplished? Second, what political structures are demanded by "full and equal membership"?

The first question addresses the shape of a just naturalization policy for the permanent resident population. As we have seen, under present German law naturalization is by no means formally closed to long-term residents.[1] However, difficult questions continue to surround the matter of the terms on which citizenship should be granted. In what follows the implications of the human rights perspective I have advanced are taken up with regard to the question of a fair price for citizenship. The degree of specificity a political theory can reasonably strive for in making policy prescriptions is, of course, inherently limited. Nonetheless, a morally acceptable German naturalization policy will embrace three general aims: the integration of current long-term residents into the political community, the acceptance of multiple citizenship, and the automatic inclusion of future children of permanent residents.

Naturalization policy, however, addresses only half of the problem. The formal legal status of citizenship cannot by itself secure full and equal membership in the German state for the subordinated migrant workers. In an environment marked by ethnic discrimination, socio-economic inequality, and cultural intolerance, all members are not equal, for in such an atmosphere some members will be unable fully to employ even elementary political rights. If groups such as the migrant workers are truly to be accepted into political membership as equals, some re-structuring of the German civitas is required to accommodate them. Specifically, the extension of individual rights in the political realm may need to be accompanied by the establishment, in the socioeconomic and cultural spheres, of group rights such as affirmative action and protec-tions for language and religion.

In exploring the demands of equal citizenship for Germany's migrant worker communities, I draw on the analysis of subordination in chapter 1 and on the view of equality set forth in chapter 4. The issues addressed in German membership policy are extremely complex and cover a broad range; as a result it is not possible to examine them here as thoroughly as they perhaps deserve. All the same, I attempt to provide a suitably de-tailed account of the sort of priorities for a German membership policy commended by the morality of rights that I have argued undergirds the contemporary practice of citizenship; where appropriate, I also offer observations as to the broader applicability and limits of this theory. The membership structure I envision for Germany includes individual rights as well as two sorts of group rights: collective and corporate. While this mixed arrangement is determined first and foremost by the variety of human rights that are at stake, it is also required for the peaceful func-tioning of the multicultural society Germany has become.

Political Membership for Permanent Residents

A human right to political membership inheres in the nature of modern states. States are, in essence, sovereign territorial organizations. It follows that their membership—formal citizenship—should in principle be attributed to those occupying the territory over which sovereignty is exercised. This inference holds independent of the sort of government employed by states: The landless peasant who ekes out an existence in a traditional theocratic society is just as entitled to citizenship in that society as is the resident of a liberal democratic state. Citizenship in this context refers to the bare bones of political membership—the right to have rights, before these rights are fleshed out.[2] The particular content of citizenship, its benefits and burdens, is determined primarily by the character of the state in which it is held, as Walzer and, for that matter, Aristotle point out. In our traditional theocracy, this content may be meager indeed; in a democracy, on the other hand, citizenship will by definition carry with it membership—or at least potential membership—in the demos, as well as a variety of other rights. In a democracy, who counts is, first and foremost, simply a function of who is there to be counted; this number may be determined by a democratic legislative process only insofar as political decisions are able to control who is admitted to residence in the first place.

If contemporary state membership is in principle territorial, where does this leave the notion of the ethnic nation-state? Acknowledging the primacy of residence for citizenship means firmly displacing the nationalist principle as a norm for political membership on the grounds that membership in a (putative) historical community is not necessarily relevant to the question of who should belong to the contemporary state. This does not mean that nationhood is wholly irrelevant to citizenship. It may be, as Walzer suggests, that a particular national identity, either ethnic or political, may form the core of a state's identity, and may indeed provide a basis for deciding among prospective immigrants, all other things being equal. Such considerations, however, cannot take precedence over the principle of residence in a world in which an appreciable number of nation-states, in the true sense of the term, no longer exists.

The view that citizenship should be confined to members, born or assimilated, of a national group depends on demonstrating that national identity is of fundamental relevance to politics. To make the claim stick, the nationalist would have to show that a law-abiding person who was born and educated in the nationalist's country, fluent in its language, employed and with a secure place of residence, and committed to the institutions of the state but who had a separate national identity some-how lacked a quality morally relevant to full membership. Conceivably, in a traditional society, permanent residents might justifiably be denied full (albeit not partial) membership on grounds having to do with the religious beliefs of the society as a whole.[3] Otherwise, claims for political exclusion may be based only on implausible ontological or biological claims about the political significance of national purity. The danger of such claims is well known.

In chapter 1, I traced the history of German membership in terms of three interrelated groups: the *Kulturnation,* the state society, and the citizenry. Placed in terms of these groups, my argument asserts that the citizenry should be shaped to conform to the entire state society, rather than to the entire nation or to the part of the nation present in the state society. As integrated members of the state society by definition, all long-term residents should be granted citizenship, subject to their approval but irrespective of considerations of cultural assimilation. This principle depends upon the assumption that political membership is by its nature appropriately determined with reference to one's social, economic, legal, and political circumstances — jurisdictionally, so to speak — and not ac-cording to one's ethnic or national identity or based on the expressed preferences of those already holding power. To put this principle into practice would require several changes in German policy, dealing with the spheres of naturalization, multiple citizenship, and the attribution of citizenship, respectively.

Permanent Residence as the Basis for German Citizenship

An overwhelming percentage of the German migrant worker minority have long had their *Lebensmittelpunkt* — their official place of residence and employment — in the Federal Republic, which should, I have ar-gued, qualify them for membership in the German polity. But so long as this status is denied them, they are deprived of the human right to membership in the political organization that exerts authority over them. This denial constitutes a violation of the standard of justice relevant to the distribution of citizenship. A just policy would establish integration into the legal, social, and economic structure of the state society as the basis for political inclusion.

This integration may be presumed to occur with residence established over a period of years and maintained on an indefinite basis (as opposed to a period of residence limited, for example, by a university program). The long-term noncitizen resident in Germany as a rule pays taxes, obeys the law, contributes to the economy, and experiences the effects of local and national politics — including, for example, the burdens of German reunification — in the same measure as German citizens. His or her children are socialized through the same educational process as their German peers. In short, native-born or long-term resident aliens are in all relevant respects the equals of citizens and, given the democratic nature of the state, should share in the civic responsibility of political participation. Adult male residents should, in addition, be prepared to provide military service where it is required of citizens.[4] By the same token, it is incumbent upon the government to establish political membership for long-term residents as the central goal of German naturalization policy.

How should this objective be pursued? Germany's political and legal structure offers several different possibilities. One option is to pass a federal law that extends full civil and political rights to all adult long-term residents, including members of the migrant worker population, without necessitating a change in their citizenship status.[5] The result would be a de facto citizenship for long-term residents alongside a formal or symbolic citizenship reserved for members of the German ethnonation and otherwise devoid of content. Such a course would be unobjectionable from a legal standpoint (Kimminich 1985, 206), and it would remedy many of the problems of political subordination that have been identified here. However, a drawback to such a solution is that maintaining an exclusive symbolic German citizenship creates a fertile source for expressions of chauvinism and cultural discrimination. In any event, it is unlikely this strategy would garner much support in Germany's current political climate, not least because its separation of political rights from citizenship would be perceived as taking the ongoing contemporary devaluation of citizenship to new heights. The difficulties involved in such a course suggest that the objective we have defined would be better sought through other means.

The circumstances peculiar to Germany dictate that to include long-term residents in political membership will likely require several coordinated policy steps. As we have seen, for members of the new German minorities the barriers to citizenship lie primarily in the manner in which the choice of naturalization is structured. Basic requirements such as German language competency, familiarity with German culture, and a knowledge of German political institutions are usually fulfilled, willy-nilly, through long-term residence. Yet naturalization remains effectively blocked by two other requirements, one formal and one de facto. The first is the renunciation of other citizenships demanded by German naturalization officials. The other is the psychological commitment to remain in Germany for life, which is entailed in practice by the decision to naturalize.[6] Together these conditions all but assure that few of those eligible ultimately seek political membership. Both must be addressed if this pattern is to be altered.

Whether or not to adopt a new country and take on a new civic identity is a momentous choice. This choice, already difficult, is not made easier by the efforts of governments to propagate the "illusion of return" among migrants. In the absence of full and definite knowledge of our future preferences and interests, there is an understandable tendency to postpone such a decision. The current German policy penalizes this course by equating it with a decision to reject the option of pursuing German citizenship; this decision is then held to justify exclusion from political membership. In this day and age, few would deny that changes in citizenship status should not be imposed, but rather should reflect the will of the persons affected. Yet the weight of my argument suggests that the German policy would be fairer if it restructured the membership choice of its noncitizen residents by presumptively awarding them citizenship and making the option of nonmembership contingent on a considered and clearly expressed will not to belong. Under such an arrangement, for example, a migrant worker who cherishes the prospect of someday retiring to Turkey or Croatia could postpone a final decision without being deprived of the protections and privileges of political membership. In this case the migrant worker would retain the right to leave Germany for good;[7] statistics show, however, that in the end emigration is unlikely.

Perhaps the most practical way of extending citizenship to the migrant worker population would be to enact a mass naturalization coupled with a right of refusal (see Hoffmann 1990, 167–72). Because the establishment of the new minorities in German society occurred in a unique process that has largely run its course, a onetime measure aimed at this population would go a long way toward resolving the current problem of mass disenfranchisement. In its historical closure, the foreign worker immigration is comparable to the episode of the *Vertriebene,* those Germans forcibly expatriated from other countries following World War II. This similarity raises the prospect of incorporating the foreign worker population through the same method of mass naturalization used in the earlier instance of mass migration, namely article 116 of the German Basic Law, the constitutional provision defining who counts as a German. As a response to historical developments, this article might be revised to include members of the migrant worker minority in its definition of "status Germans," those entitled to all the rights and privileges accorded German citizens.

Alternatively, citizenship might be extended through a new citizenship and naturalization law that would supersede the law of 1913. In such a law, citizenship could be declared to extend to all those who have resided for five years or more in the Federal Republic. Whether in the form of a constitutional amendment or a statute, a mass naturalization would need to include a clause exempting anyone who expressed a will not to be included. For those declining citizenship, the rights currently enjoyed by resident aliens ought to be retained and, where possible, enhanced to include local voting rights. It is unclear which of these various strategies bears the greatest chance of success. Whatever the legal means employed, however, the goal of a just policy will remain the redefinition of German citizenship in such a way as to include those migrants who have established themselves in German society. As we have seen, a mere reliance on naturalization on an individual basis cannot achieve this objective. The migrant worker families have completed their migration; now the borders of German membership must be moved.

Allowance of Multiple Citizenships

Restructuring the choice of citizenship through a provisional mass naturalization would further considerably the political incorporation of the
migrants. But unless this step were accompanied by an acceptance of dual
citizenship, the number of those who felt compelled to exempt themselves from the measure would remain high. The question of whether
multiple citizenships should be tolerated lies at the heart of the disagreements plaguing Germany's debates over naturalization. Is the renunciation of other citizenships a fair price to demand for German political
membership, a price required by the nature of contemporary democratic
citizenship? On the analysis that has been presented here, it is not.

We saw in the discussion of naturalization and dual citizenship in
chapter 2 that policymakers are divided on several basic normative
issues: whether citizenship should be seen as a right or a privilege,
whether it should be attributed by the government or earned in some
way on an individual basis, whether its distribution should reflect individual attachments or state interests, and whether it should be condi-
tional on integration into the state society or on a more thoroughgoing
cultural assimilation. The argument I have presented has in each instance
favored the first answer: Those who have made their lives in Germany
have developed a moral relationship to the state that entitles them to be
awarded German citizenship, without further ado and irrespective of any
other ties they may have, including other citizenships. Political membership, and hence naturalization, cannot in this light justifiably be made
contingent on release from all other citizenships. Multiple citizenships,
already countenanced in a number of other cases by Germany,[8] ought to
be allowed for the migrants as well.

Legally, there are no insurmountable obstacles to this course. Many
countries other than Germany officially allow dual citizenship.[9] No
changes in German law would be required, although by changing its
policy Germany would follow several other countries that have already
withdrawn from the 1963 treaty on reducing multiple citizenships. Some
diplomatic efforts might be required to update international arrangements for reducing conflicts and doubled obligations arising from multiple citizenships; whether significant problems still remain in this area,
however, is questionable.

Implementing a system of active and dormant citizenships would be a highly desirable course, if the necessary agreements could be procured, for this would answer a central objection to dual citizenship — the claim that it allows its possessors double political representation. Under such a system, a dormant citizenship would represent little more than a cultural attachment matched by a right to move to the country in question and be automatically naturalized. Even in the absence of such a system, however, double political representation is often avoided, since the current practice of most countries suspends rights to political participation for citizens who have taken up residence in another state.

Two more troubling objections raised by opponents of dual citizenship are that it leads to dangerously divided loyalties and that it gives rise to an unfairly privileged class. In response to the first point, it is useful to distinguish, following Thomas Hammar, among the political, legal, and sociocultural meanings of citizenship (1989, 84–86). Members of the migrant worker minority, like other naturalized or repatriated Germans, often maintain an interest in their country of origin and may prize its citizenship. This sort of attachment tends, however, to be sociocultural in nature; politically and legally, migrants usually come, over time, to focus entirely on their country of residence.[10] Questioning the loyalty of established immigrants can be an enterprise of dubious legitimacy, as the internment of Japanese Americans during World War II illustrates. In any event, the burden of proof regarding the assertion that national security is compromised by dual citizenship should clearly be on those who would use this claim to prolong the disenfranchised status of the migrant minority.

Concerning the inequality of status between dual citizens and others, it is appropriate to recall the normative basis for attributing political membership: political inclusion is due those who, without it, would be subject to domination in the society in which they make their lives. Equality of political membership implies equal inclusion in those political communities that exert power over our lives. Because people do not always make their lives in only one such community, they may be entitled to more than one membership. Of the migrants in Germany, some legitimately live not only in two cultures but also in two societies; accordingly, they should have some citizenship rights in both contexts (cf. Carens 1989, 40). Of course, these citizenships will not always be of the same sort. Generally, dual citizens will enjoy full rights only in the state in which they reside or maintain "effective citizenship," while elsewhere they may enjoy a sort of dormant citizenship, a status of primarily sociocultural significance. To deny them some status in their second country would leave them vulnerable to domination at the hands of the state, a domination to which other German citizens are not vulnerable.[11] Allowing dual citizenship in such cases is thus a concession to equality, not inequality.

Jus Soli Citizenship for Children of Permanent Residents

A policy linking citizenship to residence and allowing multiple citizenships would lead to the political incorporation of most members of the German migrant worker population. Those persons opting to decline inclusion would do so through a clear act of consent that need not be final. There would, however, remain one class of persons denied the status of citizenship through no choice of their own: the children of those migrants who declined German citizenship. These children would remain what they are today: official members of a foreign community they have in many cases never visited, and official strangers in the only land they know, subject to the domination of the German state.

The most important consideration regarding these children is that they are not in any morally relevant ways different from the children of German citizens. They are socialized by the same system, even if this system relegates them to a subordinate social status. Their inheritance of a different citizenship affords them no advantages in the society that is home to them. At the same time, there is no firm reason to assume that they will ever leave, even if their parents nurture an intention someday to return to their country of origin. The second and third generations of resident aliens are in all significant ways integrated into German society, and they are hence entitled to be included politically in the same manner that German citizens' children are: by birth. This moral context supports the case for adopting some sort of limited jus soli policy granting citizenship to children born within German territory, regardless of other citizenships they may possess. In order to prevent the ascription of citizenship to the children of tourists, diplomats, students, or other nonsettlers, this policy could apply only to the children of long-term residents.[12] Moreover, each child affected would reserve the right to elect which citizenships to retain upon reaching his or her majority.

A jus soli policy might be implemented either via a new Aliens Act or through a revision of the citizenship law of 1913. Its detractors note that such a step would represent a break with German citizenship traditions, but this in itself does not present a compelling reason against it, for the change could readily be justified as a response to altered historical circumstances. In any event, there have long been voices in favor of such a policy within the German political process (see Huber 1987). A jus soli policy, combined with the other policies suggested above, would serve the purpose of integrating the new members of German society into the structure of the state. It is difficult to see how anything short of this combined approach might adequately observe the human rights of all involved and thereby satisfy the ethical criteria appropriate to the distribution of political membership.

Migration and the Establishment of Residence
My central contention that citizenship should be extended to established residents admittedly leaves important questions unanswered in regard to the crucial matter of how residence is established. I have considered a case in which the settled nature of the minority in question is relatively clear, even if it is not officially recognized. This is true in general of the migrant worker minorities in western Europe, and true by definition of all territorial minorities. Elsewhere, however — in Japan, in the Arab oil countries and Israel, in a number of African and Latin American states, and in the United States — ongoing foreign worker programs blur the lines between residence and working visits. Moreover, many states are now host to substantial populations of illegals and refugees of various descriptions for whom it is not clear when a return to the country of origin will be possible. So long as host countries are able to prevail upon these groups to leave in a timely fashion rather than settling, the issue of political inclusion of the migrants is likely to be circumvented, especially if the migrants are accorded economic and social rights during their stay. As their period of residence lengthens, however, these migrant groups, precisely because they are distinct from the class of legal immigrants, sharply focus the problem of settlement and the rights of states to control admissions.

One's claim to belonging increases with residence, irrespective of the circumstances of admission.[13] Much, therefore, rides on who is allowed to enter, and on who is allowed to stay. To what extent is a country entitled to restrict residence either by expelling recent migrants or turning potential ones away? The German example illustrates the problem clearly. Official immigration leading to naturalization in Germany remains open only to ethnic Germans, immediate relatives of citizens or permanent residents, and political refugees. But the number of those who continue to migrate to Germany, either illegally or as refugees who are not awarded political asylum, totals hundreds of thousands each year, even if this figure has dropped substantially since the constitutional amendment in mid-1993 restricting the right of political asylum. The question arises as to whether these new migrants should be permitted to remain, eventually to be incorporated into the polity, or whether they might justifiably be compelled to leave.

This issue has been addressed in Germany primarily in the membership debate surrounding the issue of refugees and political asylum. This discussion has been characterized by an array of responses to a central normative question — namely, how to draw distinctions among different types of would-be migrants (*Unterscheidungsproblematik*). The responses have defined a common discourse regarding who belongs to three main classes of immigrants: those with a right to enter and belong, those with a provisional right to enter and not be expelled, and those with no right to enter or stay. Under current German policy, the first category has been defined to include close relatives of citizens, ethnic Germans, and a narrowly defined class of political refugees; the second contains various other refugees who have been offered temporary shelter on humanitarian grounds or who may not presently be repatriated without substantial risk to life; all others, including so-called economic refugees, fall under the third. Although a detailed ethical assessment of this policy cannot be essayed here,[14] two general observations flowing from my theory of membership are relevant.

First, a human rights perspective urges a different order of priority among migrants than that currently in place. Except in extreme cases, the question of admissions involves a secondary human right on the part of the community, a right of self-determination. In the case of all prospective immigrants who are not refugees — including, for example, the great majority of ethnic Germans — this right of the community stands opposed to a personal right of self-determination, with no clear moral advantage for either side. On the face of things, then, such migrants cannot as a rule support a claim to enter or to stay as a matter of right. All they can reasonably expect is that their interests be taken into account in the formulation of admissions and settlement policy. The state, however, retains the prerogative to gauge its own needs and shape immigration accordingly. Still, in the German case, prudential considerations, especially long-term economic prospects, support the conclusion that introducing a program of controlled immigration — for example a U.S.-style quota system — would be advisable (see Cohn-Bendit 1993, 340–41). Such a program, which might, in theory, justifiably include some preference for ethnic Germans,[15] would provide the government with a tool for coping with inevitable migration pressures, especially if it were coordinated with an overall European immigration policy.[16] However, the scope a discretionary immigration program might take in practice is limited by a crucial antecedent consideration: In regard to admissions, refugees, as persons with, in varying degrees, a right of nondomination at stake, enjoy a normative priority over the community's right to self-determination.[17]

This discussion of legal migration is complicated in practice by the class of migrants — many of them refugees of some sort — who lack permission to enter or reside in the first place. As the number of migrants who live, the world over, in violation of domestic immigration restrictions continues to grow, an important question arises. Are large populations of illegal immigrants — such as the one in the United States — entitled to citizenship once settled, despite the fact that their presence expressly contravenes the will of the community at large as reflected in its laws? I believe that under certain conditions they are so entitled, but a full treatment of this issue would require, among other things, a more thorough treatment of the ethics of immigration restrictions than I am able to give here.[18] As with legal immigration, however, the circumstances of persecution and flight are likely to bear a special moral weight.

This brings us to the second point: the right of refugees to nondomination, except in cases in which their situation is in some part attributable to the actions of the particular state from which they seek assistance, is general in nature and applies to any and all countries that are in a position to help. The frequent assertion that Germany's social fabric and stability have come to be imperiled by the sheer volume of migration is an arguable proposition at best, and, in the absence of persuasive empirical evidence to that effect, no normative basis exists for claiming that refugees may rightfully be expelled. Yet it is hard to deny that Germany, which in recent years has absorbed as many as 60 percent of all migrants coming to Europe, has thus far borne a disproportionate burden of aid with respect to its neighbors. As a community, the European Union presently finds itself in a position of responsibility toward a sizable number of the world's refugees, and fairness demands that this responsibility, which entails both an abundant provision of refuge and a concerted effort to combat the causes of flight, be apportioned equitably among member states (cf. Hailbronner 1995, 12). Ultimately, of course, the refugee problem is global in scope, and must be addressed through cooperative action at the international level (see Castles and Miller 1993).

Refugees and other new migrants aside, there should no longer be any question of a fair price for citizenship in regard to Germany's long-term resident alien minority. Those migrants and their families who were drawn to Germany to work and who ended up settling there have already paid and continue to pay the price. Now, full membership is due them if they want it. Once Germany's migrant minority is inducted into the ranks of citizens, it is to be hoped that the way will be cleared for a successful completion of their integration into German society. In this endeavor, however, many obstacles remain. Formal legal and political equality can be only a first step toward political equality more broadly construed. And as we have seen, many spheres remain in which the new groups in German society must battle against systemic subordination. So long as the migrants continue to face severe political, socioeconomic, and cultural inequalities, they cannot be said to enjoy equal citizenship. We now turn to the question of what such an equality would require.

Equality and Group Rights

The ongoing history of the civil rights movement in the United States provides a telling example of how the search for equality of membership does not end with the acquisition of formal citizenship (see, e.g., Karst 1989, 195–96; Weisbrot 1990; Shklar 1991). For members of the new minorities in Germany, naturalization in itself can provide no guarantee that they will not remain second-class citizens in terms of their socio-economic status, political power, and cultural life. Questions of membership status are appropriately considered in terms of human rights, and above all the human right to nondomination. Thus far we have examined the implications of this argument for the citizenship status of permanent residents who live under the authority of the German state. But I have also argued that domination in matters of membership is not only an individual issue but also may apply to humans as groups. This claim has important implications for a full account of equal citizenship in a democratic order such as Germany's, for it supports the position that Germany's permanent residents must, if they are to be included on a truly just basis, have their social dimensions taken into account. They must be accorded, in short, certain group rights.

The need for group rights is grounded in the particular sorts of domination to which the resident alien minority is susceptible. One sort of domination, that domination enforced through the subordinate political status of the minority, may be largely overcome by extending them citizenship. But resident aliens are also as a group relegated by systemic forces to the bottom of the German socioeconomic structure, even as their labor and taxes help German society maintain its prosperity in the face of its rapidly aging native population. And culturally, the various linguistic and religious immigrant communities are at once subordinated in relation to the dominant German secular-Christian culture and subjected to formidable forces of assimilation. Economically and culturally, the migrant worker population remains a disadvantaged minority, and this must be taken into account in formulating a policy that would offer them full membership in society on morally acceptable terms.

In restructuring society to include the migrants on equal terms, the precise ways in which their minority status should be recognized are best determined by the specific types of domination they face. In discussing the structure of rights implied by the ideal of equal citizenship in Germany, it is useful to invoke the analysis of subordination presented in chapter 1. Although the legal and political disadvantaging of some of the migrants justifies little more than granting them the individual political rights of citizenship, the position in other spheres of some significant populations — most notably the Turks — justifies various sorts of group rights. Specifically, these migrants are entitled in the socioeconomic sphere to some form of affirmative action and in the cultural sphere to certain language and religion rights. Three different models of equality apply to the different spheres of membership: an individual one focused on political expression, a universal one focused on economic circumstances, and a communal one focused on cultural solidarity.[19] Only an approach that respects all three models can, in a balanced manner, attend to the individual, communal, and universal aspects of human beings at stake in the issue of political membership.

The Nature of Group Rights

The notion of group rights is controversial among Western scholars. Historically, group-rights claims, like claims for individual human rights, have arisen as practical responses to specific situations of domination or oppression. As a result, group rights have often attained legal status without a corresponding theoretical justification regarding their moral warrants. The most conspicuous internationally recognized group right is that of peoples to self-determination. The long history of international law pertaining to groups also includes provisions for the protection of minorities ranging from the Treaty of Westphalia of 1648, through a series of agreements adopted in Europe following World War I, to the modern system of minority protections under the UN regime.[20] The present international human rights system formulates minority protections, for the most part, in terms of individual rights,[21] but it also specifies rights that apply explicitly to groups.[22] In addition, it takes up separately the issue of the rights of indigenous communities.[23] At the national level, in the drafting of new constitutions and in jurisprudence, a growing recognition of group rights has been evident the past few decades (Sigler 1983, 201; Sanders 1991). And at the regional level, in 1991 the Council on Security and Cooperation in Europe produced a document on the Rights of National Minorities, in which it revises its definition of the sovereign national state to reflect a new consensus accepting that "issues concerning national minorities . . . do not constitute exclusively an internal affair of the respective State" (Minority Rights Group 1991, 30).

However well established the legal and political rights of groups may be, agreement on their moral foundations remains elusive. Philosophical discussion of group rights tends to take the form of attempts to explain systematically the basis of the moral intuitions reflected in court decisions and policies that vindicate group rights-claims (see, e.g., Garet 1983). Much speculation surrounds the question of the relevance of group membership to questions of right. A measure of consensus exists behind the social-scientific observation that group identity exists in a sort of symbiotic relationship with the phenomenon of cultural discrimination. In addition, many thinkers subscribe in some measure to the view that certain sorts of groups deserve to be fostered because of their significance to the moral constitution of their members.[24] Opinions diverge, however, as soon as debate focuses on the ontological character and status of groups.[25] And disagreement reigns in particular in regard to three central normative questions. First, what specific sorts of groups are entitled to rights, and why? Second, how should these rights be structured? And third, how should conflicts between individual rights and group rights be dealt with? It is necessary to say a word about each of these theoretical issues before proceeding to an examination of the German case.[26]

In the international context, a wide variety of groups contend for recognition as entities morally entitled to exert autonomy over their affairs, to receive preferential treatment, or simply to exist. Some candidates are political groups such as states and "peoples" — a term generally understood to vary slightly in meaning according to its context. Others are cultural entities ranging from dominant national groups to various sorts of minorities: linguistic, religious, ethnic, and indigenous.[27] Many, but not all, of these groups have, or at least claim, a territorial base.

Several sorts of considerations are important for determining which of these groups qualify for group rights.[28] The most important consideration stems from my argument about human rights, nondomination, and equality and involves the *basis* for attributing group rights. The Turkish minority in Germany can present a firm justification for some cultural protections, but the same cannot be said of, say, German immigrants in the United States today.[29] Palestinian citizens of Israel also appear to have a good case for certain group rights; it is more debatable whether the same goes for the white minority in South Africa, or whether some arrangement of individual rights might suffice to protect their interests. As these examples illustrate, the chief variable at issue in assessing the basis of group rights is the nature of the domination the groups face. The strongest form of group right is owed members of groups that are subjected to domination *as groups*. This domination may occur in two ways: Persons may be targeted for harms or deprivations because they are members of a particular group (for example, in racial discrimination), or the structures of the group itself may come under attack (for example, in genocide). In either case the people constituting the group will be entitled by the fact or threat of abusive treatment to invoke a right of nondomination.[30] In addition, a weaker, secondary type of right — a right to self-determination — may be possessed by groups prevented from exercising autonomy on equal terms with other comparable groups.[31]

Some additional criteria bear specifically on the *strength* of claims of group right. One such criterion derives from the manner in which certain types of groups, such as linguistic and cultural communities, take part in constituting our identities as human agents by, for example, prefiguring our understandings of our experience and the world around us.[32] In general, the more constitutive a group is of its members' personal identities and agency, the stronger its claim to being an entity capable of bearing rights. An intuitive recognition of this relationship is reflected in the evident tendency, in both national and international jurisprudence, to view the claims of group right made on behalf of ascriptive groups as stronger than those made for voluntary assemblages. A related criterion particularly relevant to autonomy rights is the extent to which a group exhibits a strongly communal nature. More cohesive sorts of communities, such as indigenous cultures, are much more likely to merit such rights than noncohesive entities such as gender groups; and similarly, groups with a territorial basis generally have stronger claims than ones without such a basis. Another important consideration in such a judgment is often what might be called the degree of cultural contrast between dominant and subordinate groups. This factor is one reason why the rights of aboriginal or indigenous groups are generally seen to be stronger and more pressing than those of other cultural groups less at odds culturally with the surrounding society.

A final criterion has to do with the moral *character* of the group. At times it may be held that groups are not entitled to rights because they possess a morally objectionable structure or, in the case of voluntary groups, purpose. Groups that are committed to values or practices entailing the domination of their own members or of other groups generally fall into this category. For example, if a group is deeply racist, this orientation generally undermines its claims for distinctive protections. On the whole, however, it is extremely difficult to formulate general guidelines regarding the applicability of group rights. The requirements of a fair structure of political membership will always be determined partly by the specifics of each case.

With reference to this set of criteria, Germany's migrant population, though nonterritorial, nonetheless has a strong case for group rights in two ways: as a minority subject as a whole to economic and political domination, and as a collection of several smaller minorities (for example, Turks, Serbs, Croats), each subject to important cultural disadvantages. For groups deemed to have interests that warrant protections through rights, the question arises as to the structure of the rights they should enjoy. Here, the two most important issues are how to conceive of the *subject* of rights and what *shape* to give the rights at issue. In regard to the subject of group rights, it is useful to distinguish further between collective rights and corporate rights. Collective rights take as their subjects persons distinguished as members of collectivities; an example would be affirmative action, in which a certain class of persons is entitled to a special privilege deriving from, and only from, the context of their membership within a distinct disadvantaged population. Corporate rights, by way of contrast, apply directly to groups; hence, rights to special political representation or autonomy accrue only to entire peoples or minorities.[33]

The basic issue at stake in the question of the shape minority rights should take is whether individual rights or some type of group rights should be employed. Opinions vary as to the merits of each formulation.[34] I suggest, however, that individual, collective, and corporate rights are each required by different settings, depending on the type of domination or group interest involved. Moreover, the specific context determines the shape that group rights ought to take.[35] The strongest type of group rights arises in response to domination by other groups, and are hence externally oriented, taking the form either of protections or of special treatment aimed at compensation for past harms. A second set of rights, also external, seeks to establish the autonomy of groups — usually territorial ones — vis-à-vis other groups; as rights of self-determination, these are generally weaker than the first variety.[36] Finally, certain highly communal groups may also have internal rights bearing upon their members. However, these rights are in general not very strong and do not, for example, supersede central individual rights, such as the right to leave the group. Viewed in connection with this schema, the nature of the German migrant minority qualifies it for, and only for, group protections and some forms of special treatment.

Acknowledging the moral legitimacy of rights for groups raises the problem of how to deal with conflicts between the rights of groups and the rights of other groups or individuals. Despite the claims of some that the rights of groups and of individuals are interdependent (see Sanders 1991), in practice conflicts inevitably arise. Such conflicts are extremely difficult to resolve satisfactorily, and there are no theoretical blueprints for the task.[37] Yet, if the rights of individuals and groups have the same ground and are morally commensurable, then a basis exists, at least in principle, for judging their respective weights in given cases. Two especially important considerations are the type of rights involved and their relative urgency. If the right of a cultural group to survival clashes with the rights of individuals to nonessential positive freedoms, the group right is generally to be upheld. A prominent instantiation of this calculus is the case of the Inuits in Canada, whose right to preserve their traditional means of subsistence has rightly been held to justify restrictions on the freedom of movement of Canadian residents to move into Inuit territory.[38] Sometimes, however, the human right of a group to survival will collide with individual rights that are so fundamental as to be inviolable. When the cultural practices of endangered groups violate individual rights to life and physical well-being, to recognition as a person, to freedom of conscience, or to nondiscrimination on the basis of race or gender, in general they should not be protected.[39]

Once claims of group right are recognized as legitimate, many different strategies become available for institutionalizing them.[40] Protections for groups may be established through civil rights measures establishing formal equality before the law or through active antidiscrimination legislation. Other strategies include constitutional provisions of minority rights, "positive discrimination" programs, judicial activism on behalf of disadvantaged groups, regionalist or federalist reorganizations of government, and special voting arrangements.[41] Once again, to a great extent the appropriateness of different strategies will depend on the sort of group interests involved in each case. For this reason a discussion of measures aimed at equalizing treatment of the German minorities is best organized around the categories of subordination identified in chapter 1.

Political, Social, and Cultural Equalities

As we have seen, Germany's migrant minorities face barriers to equal membership in several distinct yet interrelated spheres of common life. In the legal structuring of society — the sphere of *civitas*-building — they have been assigned a subordinate status and excluded from the political process. In the distribution of social and economic benefits — the sphere of state-building — they have as a group been relegated to a position at the bottom of the German societal order. And in cultural relations — the sphere of German nation-building — they have been subjected to pressures to assimilate and penalized in a variety of ways for not being German. Equal membership for the migrants in the German political community will require measures in each of these areas, the shapes of which are best cast in accordance with the type of inequalities involved. Although the situation is highly complex, a rough sketch of the main contours of what might constitute a just solution follows. The type of equality called for in the political and legal sphere is individual, in the social sphere, collective, and in the cultural sphere, corporate.

Legally and politically, most of the inequalities faced by the migrants will be erased once they possess the individual rights accompanying citizenship. In order to secure their legal equality most effectively, the additional measure of some form of antidiscrimination law imposing penalties for discriminatory conduct would be advisable.[42] Such a law could be formulated to apply to groups of migrants as well as to individuals. Apart from this measure, however, there seems to be no call for special group privileges for the migrants in regard to their legal status. And in light of the particular nature of the migrant worker minority, the same can be said for the political sphere as well. If the minority in question were an indigenous group or a territorial entity, some form of local autonomy, federalism, or bloc-vote and veto system might well be called for. But as an immigrant minority distributed throughout Germany and comprising several different ethnic or national groups, the foreign worker population has no appreciable claim to this species of rights of self-determination. Effective political participation for the migrants may be provided simply through inclusion as individuals into the demos. At most, the process of delineating political districts might be expected to take account of ethnic residential patterns in order to ensure that entire cultural minorities are not, in practice, excluded from political representation.

The social and economic inequalities experienced by migrants will not be erased or even much affected by a change in citizenship status. The foreign worker minority is economically and socially subordinated precisely as a group, so its situation is not remedied through an individual rights strategy. Prospective solutions instead need to focus on migrants collectively, as members of a systemically disadvantaged minority. The group-related basis of socioeconomic inequality, in short, dictates that the structure best suited to promoting equality will be a model of compensatory justice emphasizing collective rights to what has euphemistically been called, in India, positive discrimination, and in the United States, affirmative action.[43] To have the greatest effect, such a scheme of rights should focus on the second and subsequent generations and should be established above all in regard to the educational system, for it is here that the migrants' subordinate position is presently most decisively reinforced. In addition to supporting special treatment for minorities in schools and job training, the goal of equality in education may also require some reassigning of students in urban areas where all-immigrant classes would otherwise be the norm.[44] On the same grounds, a policy of preferment should be instituted in hiring and employment — especially for the civil service — and in housing. In general, however, as with the U.S. form of affirmative action, these collective rights should be understood to aim at their own obliteration once the structures of subordination have been dismantled.

While the goal of equality in the political-legal sphere is the eradication of the subordination of individuals, and in the socioeconomic sphere is rectification of unjust discrimination against individuals as members of groups, in the cultural sphere it is the defense of groups per se against domination. The migrants' cultural groups, be they ethnic, linguistic, or religious, merit protection where threatened, simply because of their important constitutive role in the lives of the migrants. At the same time, a pragmatic reason exists for protecting them. Culturally, the largest groupings of migrants are sufficiently distinct from the majority of Germans to make it unlikely that they will quickly be assimilated (Safran 1986, 109). Yet, as long as they continue to be subordinated, the migrants are likely only to exaggerate their ethnic identities and to resist becoming integrated.[45] For this reason alone, Germany's minorities deserve to be respected in their group identities as part of an overall strategy of political inclusion. The nature of cultural communities further determines that this respect should be institutionalized primarily in the form of corporate rights because most of the goods at stake are essentially communal and are hence not reducible to individual goods.[46] In Germany, the two most important cultural rights at issue involve language and religion.[47]

In the matter of language, there can be no question of the sort of territorial linguistic rights asserted, for example, by the Québecois in Canada. As immigrant groups, Germany's settled linguistic minorities can hardly claim to be entitled to any more than the preservation of their respective languages alongside German within the public educational system. This entitlement, however, is enough to ground a right, accruing to each linguistic community of appreciable size, to bilingual education for its children.[48] How this right might be implemented is, of course, open to debate.[49] It would be advisable, however, for the German state to provide materials and training for such instruction, if only to diminish the influence of other national governments in the German school system. The various established linguistic communities might also reasonably expect that care be given to the cultural diversity of Germany's students in the drafting of educational materials, especially historical texts, and that their languages be accepted as second languages for university admissions. Beyond the area of education, these linguistic communities also deserve access as groups to the media, especially radio and television, and to public funding for the arts.

The question of the rights of religious groups is raised by the large Islamic contingent among the migrants in Germany. The nature of Islam, with its strong emphasis on orthopraxy as opposed to orthodoxy, renders the maintenance of an active religious community particularly important for its adherents (Thomä-Venske 1988, 83). For Germany's

Muslims, the protection of their religion hinges on two issues in particular: religious education and the legal status of Islam. On the first issue, disagreement concerns whether instruction in Islam should be offered in public schools or left to private Qur'an courses sponsored by religious associations. A place for religion classes in public schools is guaranteed by the German Basic Law (art. 7, par. 3), and it is difficult to see why the Islamic community should be deemed any less entitled than are Germany's Christian communities to have its religious instruction sponsored by the state. Assuming that agreement on a course of study can be reached, Islamic religion courses should be a prima facie curricular requirement for Muslims, with exemption or—as is the case with Christians—the substitution of an ethics class available upon request. A benefit of this policy is that it would draw students away from the influence of the private Qur'an courses, which often actively pursue reactionary political agendas. At the same time, it would go some distance toward accommodating the concerns of more secularized Muslims. Overall equality for Islam in education, finally, would also require the inclusion of Islamic scholars in the university system.

Legally, Islam has yet to be recognized in Germany as a "body of public law" comparable to the Catholic or Lutheran churches, as has occurred in Austria and Belgium (Abdullah 1985). This important disadvantage must be remedied if Muslims are to have equal membership in German society. The major obstruction to granting Islam this legal status is that Muslim communities, unlike the churches, do not have a hierarchical structure that might provide an effective corporate representative for the group. But there are ways of overcoming this obstacle, for instance by forming an Islamic council bringing together the various elements of the Muslim population, that should be actively sought. If Islam were to possess this status it would mean that there could be public Islamic religious holidays, a federal "church tax" for Muslims, military chaplaincies for imams, official Islamic charity organizations, and state aid for religious activities, private schools, and mosques.

Formal parity might also result in the securing of more controversial rights: for example, the right to slaughter animals without anesthesia, the right not to be proselytized, or the right to public calls to prayer by muezzins. Possibilities like these frighten some who worry about granting recognition to a group they see as fundamentally opposed to the liberal political and social climate in Germany. In response to them it should be made clear that group rights for Islam can be extended only in the context of the overall incorporation of the migrant worker minority into the constitutional order of the Federal Republic. This will necessarily include concessions and adaptations on the part of the Muslim community. It is true that historically Muslim populations have had little experience with existence as a minority culture. Yet there is ample reason to believe that Islam possesses the resources necessary for adjusting successfully to the demands of life in the diaspora.[50]

The various policy measures I have endorsed here are all steps that have been suggested by participants in the German membership debates regarding the migrant population. They are all, to varying degrees, admissible under German law, and they would furthermore be consonant with the relevant international law dealing with citizenship and minorities.[51] Together, the individual, collective, and corporate rights described here constitute the structural conditions necessary for equal membership in the multicultural society that Germany has become. It should be noted that this group-rights strategy does not aim at producing a society in which rigid divisions based on nationality are nurtured or even protected. It is not national cultures but rather class, linguistic, ethnic, and religious memberships, that provide the appropriate frame of reference for responding to concerns regarding equality among groups. This approach promises to foster an environment in which, in the language of consociation theorists, overlapping memberships might generate political crosspressures on individuals that would encourage political moderation and stability, thus aiding the project of integration (Lijphart 1977, 10–12).[52]

The goal for the German multicultural society must be an atmosphere of mutual tolerance, in which no member of society is subordinated either individually or as a member of a minority group. In pursuing this goal, it is to be expected that in the short run the integration of the German migrants will continue to benefit from the maintenance of strong minority communities, so long as these communities are respected and not marginalized.[53] Yet, these communities have already, in an important sense, become "hyphenated" German communities instead of simply Turkish or Yugoslavian or Greek communities, and there is no reason to hinder their further development along these lines. The assimilation that will take place in the Germany of the future must strive to match all parts of the society to the whole, not just minority parts to the dominant part. The result will be nonetheless German. Ultimately it may be that the dominant and minority cultures in Germany will be brought together more by the indiscriminately assimilating forces of modernity than by adaptation to one another. This possibility, however, does not alter the fact that a successful integration can occur only in conjunction with changes in the structure of society designed to secure the equality of political membership that, after all these years, has become the migrants' right.

Notes

Introduction

1 The term, popularized in his day by Locke (1967), has been revived in current debates by Hammar (1985, 1990).

2 Citizenship may be pictured as a protective shell built up around a political community over the years, with suffrage and basic civil and political protections near the core, and other sorts of rights — lesser political rights, socioeconomic rights, cultural rights — making up the outer layers. For those potential members who have overcome the considerable barrier of admission to a country, the outer, softer layers are easily penetrated, but the resistance becomes ever greater as one moves toward the center. The last set of rights are attached to a second major hurdle: naturalization, that is, induction into full membership or citizenship. For the latecomers, the migrants of the last decades, this last hurdle has in many countries come to be all but insurmountable (cf. Hammar 1990, 9–26, especially 17).

3 On the ways in which aliens experience themselves as outsiders, see Elias and Scotson 1965; Korte 1984; and Leggewie 1990, 97–109.

4 Three historical developments in particular help to explain why resident aliens remain excluded in the political sphere. One involves the normative dynamic between ideas of political community and national identity in the formation and organization of modern states. Here the locus classicus is Meinecke 1908; see also Brubaker 1989a and 1992. The second is the gradual filling out of citizenship through the extension of individual rights: basic civil and political rights in the eighteenth and nineteenth centuries, and social and economic rights in the twentieth century. The classic account is Marshall 1964; for critiques of Marshall's Anglocentrism, see Mann 1987 and Turner 1986, 44–49; for a description of how migrant workers missed out on certain rights because they were not "present at the creation" of modern welfare states, see Heisler and Heisler 1990. A third

development has been a gradual shift in emphasis in the structuring of citizenship away from duties and toward protections and entitlements; as a consequence of this shift, migrant workers, who fulfill most of the traditional duties of citizenship, are still not seen as entitled to this status. See Schuck 1989.

5 A political hypothesis for why the extension of rights to long-term foreign residents has stalled at the level of full political and civil rights is that the democratic rationale for inclusion in the social and economic realms no longer wins out against self-interest and conservatism when the basic mechanism of power and policymaking is at stake — that, in effect, a balance exists precisely at the point at which the overall exclusion of foreigners might finally be compromised.

6 In their discussions of citizenship, Jürgen Habermas (1994, 122–28) and, following him, Veit Bader (1995, 213–29, 236) distinguish between moral and ethical aspects of membership debates. Based on Hegel's opposition of *Moralität* and *Sittlichkeit,* this usage is employed to contrast universalistic, liberal arguments with particularistic stances embodying the substantive standards of a specific national community regarding the good life and its legal requirements. The distinction seems to me misbegotten in this context, implying as it does that beliefs about individual human rights and claims about the normative status of groups are not only structurally divergent but also fundamentally different in kind. For an account of morality that integrates universal and particularistic moral claims, see Michael Walzer's exposition of "reiterative universalism" (1990). In my discussion, "ethical" refers simply to "moral" values — be they oriented toward humanity, groups, or individuals — insofar as they are submitted to reasoned reflection.

7 For various formulations of the different meanings of citizenship see Walzer 1989, 216; Leca 1990; Shklar 1991, 3–15; Kymlicka and Norman 1994, 353–54; Gunsteren 1994; and Minogue 1995. The notion of citizenship as a virtue has received a host of classical treatments; for some modern views see Arendt 1958, Walzer 1974, Galston 1991, Ignatieff 1995, MacIntyre 1995, and Pocock 1995.

8 I conceive of this designation as referring not only to the definition of citizenship per se but also to a broad class of ethical issues concerning the construction of community, including nationalism, immigration, separatism, genocide, ethnic cleansing, slavery, suffrage, minority policy, and other related problems.

Chapter One: The Making of Boundaries

1 On the difference between ethnic and national consciousness see Armstrong 1982; and Smith 1986, especially pt. 2.

2 A noteworthy study of the links between religion and German nationalism is Smith 1995.

3 I use "state society" rather than "political society" precisely for the reason that many members of German society are politically excluded. "State" on the other hand encompasses, in addition to political relationships, the complex of social and economic memberships that are shaped by the relation of "people and government" (Walzer 1979, 220) in a given territory.

4 As Armstrong points out, because ethnic groups tend to posit their identity negatively, in opposition to other groups, it is difficult to speak of the essence or character of the group (1982, 4–6). On this problem, see also Barth 1969; Bell and Freeman 1974; Glazer and Moynihan 1976; Van den Berghe 1981; and Bausinger 1986, 141–59.

5 A number of writers refer to this status of membership as a "new" or "social citizenship" (e.g., Barbalet 1988, 59–79; Heisler and Heisler 1990; King and Waldron 1988; Turner 1986). I restrict my usage of "citizenship" to the status of full membership, however, for reasons that will be made clear.

6 See note 3 above.

7 On this phenomenon see Smith 1986, 2 and pt. 2. Benedict Anderson describes three further "paradoxes" of nationalism (1983, 14): (1) its objective modernity (to social scientists) versus its subjective antiquity (to nationalists), (2) its formal universality versus its irremediable particularity in concrete instances, and (3) its philosophical poverty versus its political power.

8 Much of the scholarship on nation-states in general, and on German nationalism in particular, has focused on the contrasting models of state development in France and Germany. The fundamental distinction concerns the voluntary, political basis of the state in France as opposed to the attributive, ethnocultural basis in Germany. The state is held as the foundation of the nation in France; the opposite is the case in Germany. For the seminal work, see Meinecke 1908; see also Kohn 1967, and for a good recent treatment Brubaker 1992. As Brubaker's nuanced analysis shows, the two states' divergent citizenship policies in fact reflect different responses to a shared problem involving the tension between political and ethnocultural models of organization. The interesting question remains the extent to which developments in France caused a reaction against a political development of national consciousness in Germany.

9 For an argument presenting a more complex assessment of particularist and universalist strains in both Herder and Fichte's conceptions of the German nation, see Dumont 1986, 113–32. In similar fashion, Julia Kristeva subjects Herder to a comparison with Montesquieu (1993, 27–33, 53–54).

10 Hegel's philosophy of the state was, as many have noted, intimately linked with the Prussian constitutional monarchy, and Hegel himself was opposed to the dismantling of the Prussian state in order to form a more comprehensive "German" entity. It is nonetheless clear how his thought provided ammunition for

those portraying the Germans as a nation in search of a state. A sample from the *Philosophy of Right:* "A nation does not begin by being a state. The transition from a family, a horde, a clan, a multitude, etc., to political conditions is the realization of the Idea in the form of that nation. Without this form, a nation, as an ethical substance — which is what it is implicitly, lacks the objectivity of possessing in its own eyes and in the eyes of others, a universal and universally valid embodiment in laws, i.e., in determinate thoughts, and as a result it fails to secure recognition from others" (1967, 218–19).

11 See Sheehan 1985, especially 5–8.

12 See Nipperdey 1983, 595–673; Sheehan 1989, 655–711.

13 The treatment of Poles forms a highly instructive chapter in the history of German membership. Ethnic Poles who were German citizens in virtue of their inclusion in the boundaries of the new Reich were isolated and subjected to conditions, particularly in the industrial Ruhr region, that encouraged the defensive development of a separate ethnic identity. This development led the government to adopt strict assimilationist policies toward the Poles, including, for example, a ban on speaking Polish — to which Poles responded by holding "silent assemblies." Polish migrant workers, on the other hand, were excluded to the point of being forced to return to their homeland for several months each year so that they would not qualify for residence status. They were pointedly barred from being able to work or live with the German Poles. Some treatments of this episode are Broszat 1963 and Hagen 1980.

14 This is most arguable in the case of redistribution. A lively debate has surrounded the question of whether it was popular mobilizations or state attempts to co-opt the worker class that played the leading role in the creation of redistributive policies. See, for example, Macpherson 1966.

15 This step occurred following the repatriation of virtually the entire population of foreign workers who were denied *exit* during the war and became forced laborers for the duration. This type of forced membership set a precedent as well, which was taken to an extreme under the slave labor policies of the Nazi war effort. On both of these periods see Bade 1984–85, vol. 2; Herbert 1986; Woydt 1987, 30–51, 60–134.

16 See Walzer's discussion of "countries as national clubs or families" (1983, 40–42), but see also Veit Bader's criticism of Walzer on this point. In practice, "states are not such warm, horizontal *Vergemeinschaftungen* or free and democratic associations, based on consent, but rather cold and vertical institutions, based not on free entry but on enforced membership and physical violence" (1995, 218).

17 Brubaker uses this basic formulation to distinguish between the French and German nation-building processes: he associates the French project with assimilation and the German project with ethnonationalist inclusion (1989a). He also, how-

ever, takes pains to emphasize that both countries have to some extent employed both strategies.

18 There is, however, an additional class of ethnic German immigrants and expellees who form an exception here: once they become residents in Germany, members of this group — called "status Germans" as opposed to citizens — enjoy virtually all of the benefits of citizenship, including the franchise, without the necessity of naturalization. Status Germans possess a statutory right to be naturalized once they satisfy a set of minimal criteria. See Kanstroom 1993, 186–89.

19 For more on civil rights, see section entitled "The Current Problem."

20 During the Gulf War, for example, an Iraqi national could be threatened with expulsion even though he had been resident in Germany for over two decades (*Der Tagesspiegel*, February 2, 1991, 15).

21 The drafting of this law was accompanied by a debate that is fascinating to read in light of current discussions of citizenship policy. All the basic contemporary positions in debates over naturalization policy, voting rights for foreigners, and the "multicultural society," and indeed many of the same specific proposals, surfaced in the course of the deliberations. The Social Democrats, for example, argued for the rights of economic participants in German society to political representation, proposed a right to naturalization for residents after a certain period, and strongly criticized the "racist" assumptions and the supposition of cultural homogeneity they saw as underlying the conservative position in favor of strict jus sanguinis citizenship. See Huber 1987, and the discussion in Hoffmann 1990, 91–103.

22 As early as 1920 the National Socialists proposed that Jews be placed under *Ausländer* law, that they in effect be denaturalized (Fraenkel 1974, 12), that is, demoted from the entitled status of citizenship to the tolerated status of foreigner.

23 This stream of immigrants reached a peak of roughly 400,000 in 1990, prompting measures aimed at stiffening the procedures whereby potential *Aussiedler* demonstrate their Germanness and gain entrance to German territory. See Kanstroom 1993, 164–67.

24 As of the beginning of 1996; the largest subgroup comprises the just over two million Turkish nationals (*Zeitschrift für Ausländerrecht und Ausländerpolitik* 1997 no. 1, 2). Of the remaining foreigners, the substantial number applying for asylum in Germany has given rise to a major set of political concerns that make up an important part of the overall "foreigner question." The liberal political asylum policy extended under article 16 of the German Basic Law was originally a response to the aftermath of World War II, but in the late 1980s it began to attract increasing numbers of so-called economic refugees from less-developed countries. This development led to heated debates between proponents of closed borders and those in favor of introducing immigration policies, and culminated in a constitutional amendment in 1993 severely restricting access to political

asylum. Because the question of asylum presents a distinctive set of problems having more to do with *admissions* than with *membership,* a detailed treatment of it remains outside the scope of this study. See, however, the brief discussion of refugees in chapter 5, as well as Germershausen and Narr 1988; Nuscheler 1988; and Kälin and Moser 1989.

25 Here a word about terminology is necessary since, in discussions about this population, the labels themselves have been highly politicized. Due to its association with forced labor policies under the Nazis, the original German term for the migrants, *"Fremdarbeiter"* (alien workers), was officially replaced with the oxymoronic term *"Gastarbeiter"* (guestworkers), which gained wide currency in the 1970s. This term has since fallen out of favor in many circles because of its pointed implication that the workers are visitors without rights or claims in the host society. A popular replacement has been the more generous phrase *"ausländische Mitbürger"* (foreign co-citizens). This formulation is troublesome both to those who wish to emphasize that the foreign workers are precisely *not* citizens (Galanis 1989, 2) and to those who resent being described as the *"co-*citizens" — presumably those who go along with the wishes of the citizens proper (Dikmen 1990, 60). The more general term *"Ausländer"* (foreigners) applied to the workers and their families is argued by many to be inappropriate because it lumps them together with all other foreign citizens including tourists, when in fact this population comprises mostly *"Inländer"* in the sense of economically integrated, permanent legal residents. Another controversial term is *"Arbeitsimmigranten"* (labor immigrants), which is criticized for suggesting that the migrants have become immigrants in spite of their refusal in most cases to naturalize. In my treatment, I use the more neutral notions "migrant workers" (*Arbeitsmigranten*) and "foreign workers" (*ausländische Arbeitnehmer*). I describe the more encompassing group of these workers and their families as the migrant worker minority or simply as foreign permanent residents.

26 The forming of minorities is in general a complex reciprocal process involving the accentuation and even the promotion of points of difference between the groups in question. For treatments in the German context see Heckmann 1981; Korte 1982; Schulte 1985; Bausinger 1986; Bukow and Llaryora 1988; and Esser and Friedrichs 1990.

27 See, for example, Bade 1983, 1984–85, and 1987; Schlaffke and Voss 1982; Dohse 1985, 135–358; Herbert 1986, 179–236; Woydt 1987, 135–50; Okyayuz 1989; Castles 1989, 60–76; and Schöneberg 1993.

28 See especially Dohse 1985; Herbert 1986; and Woydt 1987.

29 The initial waves of German returnees, expellees, and refugees represented successive instances of (im)migration that have continued on and off for years, reaching a new peak during the opening of the Eastern Bloc and the collapse of

the GDR. Ethnic German migrants from the GDR, other East European countries, and the Soviet Union form a minority that faces many of the same problems of integration as the foreign worker minority. That these groups have an
automatic claim to German citizenship has at once eased their integration and
obscured their minority status. See Hoffmann 1990; Lüttinger 1989; and Otto
1990.

30 On the general types of problems faced by foreign worker populations in European countries, see Bethlenfalvy 1987; Frey and Lubinski 1987; Reuter and
Dodenhoeft 1988; Bischoff and Teubner 1991; and Ireland 1994.

31 Although this framework emerges from a consideration of the German case, it
seems to me that it might also be fruitfully applied to the treatment of minorities
in a range of other countries including the EU nations, the United States, and
Israel. Assessing its usefulness as a basis for comparative study remains, however,
beyond the scope of this study.

32 See, for example, Tajfel 1981.

33 Even though they remain under the discretion of administrators and are hence
not often invoked, the grounds for expulsion under the new Aliens Act of 1991
(arts. 45–47) are disturbingly broad. In addition to those already named, these
grounds include the violation of regulations regarding foreigners, the operation
of an illegal business, endangerment of public health, and in certain cases eligibility for social aid. In addition, unemployment can lead to the refusal to renew
the residence permit, which in effect is equivalent to expulsion.

34 Although the number of naturalizations has slowly risen in the last years, especially in Berlin, it remains the case that a negligible percentage of those migrant
workers eligible for naturalization actually apply. In this category Germany lags
well behind the other western European countries with guestworker populations. See, for example, Brubaker, ed. 1989.

Chapter Two: Membership Debates

1 The correlation between economic hard times and antiforeign sentiment — which
in turn translates readily into exclusionist policies — is widely recognized among
German social scientists. See especially Hoffmann and Even 1984.

2 The reasons for this, I suspect, have much to do with the conceptual gap that
remains between conventional individualistic conceptions of agency and the
crudely mechanistic understanding of collective phenomena still prevalent in
much of the social sciences. Because of this gap persuasive answers to problems
such as that of responsibility for the Holocaust continue to elude us. For interesting approaches to the problem of social agency from several different directions,
see Merleau-Ponty 1962; Lovibond 1983; and Honneth and Joas 1988.

3 Here I am thinking of politics primarily in terms of lawmaking, government, and public discourse. My usage does not conflict, however, with a broader conception of politics that extends, for example, to institutions often considered "private," such as the family. See Fraser 1989 and Benhabib 1992.

4 One may argue that a categorical rejection of any membership status for non-members based on, for example, racial grounds — as under the Nazis — is both irrational and immoral, without at all denying that such a view is norm-guided and indeed makes sense on its own terms.

5 Brubaker (1989b, 3–6) presents an excellent discussion of the nation-state conception of citizenship. In his account, this classic, "vestigial" notion of citizenship combines six partially discordant ideals: "Membership . . . should be egalitarian, sacred, national, democratic, unique, and socially consequential" (3). Various aspects of this ideal are attacked by Foucault (1988) and Waters (1989).

6 Cf. Bauböck 1994: "A comprehensive analysis of citizenship has to take into account three different aspects: (1) the rights and obligations attributed to citizens as members of a polity, (2) the determination of individual membership, and (3) the nature and shape of the polity itself" (vii).

7 That the difference is generally in practice merely one of degree is pointed out by Daniel Kanstroom (1993, 202–204).

8 Klaus Bade, one of the leading German researchers of migration, has proposed a typology that makes some sense of the disagreement over Germany's status as an immigration country (Bade 1990). He distinguishes between the *experience* of immigration as a social and cultural process and a self-conscious *policy* allowing immigration, and characterizes West Germany as, paradoxically, having an "immigration situation" without being a country of immigration (*"Einwanderungs-situation ohne Einwanderungsland"*). Given this distinction the question becomes, To what extent should government policy take account of the changed realities of immigration? As Bade points out, in the *new* immigration countries of western Europe, a policy of expanding and diversifying the citizenry could never take on the formative role it took in *classical* immigration societies such as Australia or the United States. Rather, new countries of immigration may react *formally,* in that they change their orientation to accept new immigrants; or *informally,* in that they persist in denying their status as countries of immigration while at the same time making possible the legal integration of already present immigrants by easing naturalization requirements. The central issue in the debate over immigration policy, then, is whether or not Germany is to develop into an informal new country of immigration.

9 A rather different understanding of the two is that of Günter Endruweit, who understands assimilation as a process in which "the members of a cultural system

essentially conform to the patterns within a different cultural system without internalizing them." Integration may result "when they internalize the new culture, thereby removing themselves from their previous cultural system, and when the target society displays a readiness to accept them" (quoted in Bischoff and Teubner 1991, 99).

10 On this point see Esser (1983, 28–29), who in like fashion describes how various political orientations may *oppose* assimilation or pluralism.

11 On this debate see, for example, Esser 1983; Miksch 1983; Schulte 1990; Leggewie 1990; Geissler 1990, chap. 5; Tsiakalos 1990; Hofmann 1990; Schmid 1990; Hoffmann 1990; Klein 1992; Faul 1993; and Jansen and Baringhorst 1994.

12 Much has been written, for example, regarding the existence of a "guestworker literature." See Klimt 1989.

13 The sometimes violent extension to German soil of Turkish political conflicts, especially those involving the Kurdish Workers Party (PKK), has been cited in support of this view.

14 This was soon after the far right Republikaner party attained stunning successes in votes for the Berlin and Hessian assemblies and for the European Parliament. At this point, the percentage of Germans in favor of reducing the foreign population was measured at 57.8 percent (*ZAR Aktuell*, 1 November 1988, 2).

15 In Europe as a whole, the notion of voting rights for foreigners at the local level has made considerable progress since the early 1970s. Prior to the introduction of reciprocity of local voting rights in the European Union, foreigners enjoyed some form of voting rights in the following countries: Denmark, Ireland, the Netherlands, Portugal, Spain, the U.K. (for Commonwealth and Irish citizens), Finland, Iceland, Norway, Sweden, and in the cantons of Jura and Neuchatel only in Switzerland (Sieveking et al. 1989). The German Democratic Republic introduced — with questionable motives — voting rights for foreigners shortly before German reunification. In the Federal Republic, foreigners have been extended political representation in the form of advisory committees to local governments. These committees, which were established primarily in two waves from 1972 to 1975 and from 1980 to 1981, take a great variety of forms (Federal Commissioner 1988). None of them, however, offers the opportunity to take part in making decisions, and for this reason they have been strongly criticized as a sop for foreigners. Practically the only legal opportunity for foreigners to participate directly in local government is through their appointment to government committees as experts. For a thorough treatment, see Berlin Institute 1987.

16 For more on this point, see Bernsdorff 1986.

17 Opponents of voting rights for foreigners, it should be noted, generally concede that these arguments lose a great deal of their force at the communal level.

18 A 1994 poll showed that among Turkish and Yugoslavian migrants, 83 percent
    and 67 percent respectively held local voting rights to be "important" or "very
    important" (*Informationsdienst zur Ausländerarbeit* 1995 no. 1:12).

19 More specifically, they would tend slightly toward greater support for the Social
    Democrats — a projection readily accounted for by their overrepresentation in the
    working class. This fact is likely an important factor in the determined opposition
    of the Christian Union parties to voting rights for foreigners.

20 They claim that the vote for foreigners may be established without violating the
    German Basic Law or any of the individual state constitutions apart from those of
    Bavaria and the Rhineland Palatinate. See, for example, Bücking 1992, 121.

21 Examples are the freedoms of assembly (art. 8) and association (art. 9), and the
    right to resistance (art. 20, par. 4).

22 Here, it should be noted, a double standard is applied. Those who are born
    German citizens are not required at any time to demonstrate their loyalty to
    the state. Non-Germans who naturalize must, however, perform feats demon-
    strating a certain level of assimilation, and in addition renounce all other national
    loyalties.

23 Exceptions to this rule have traditionally held for cases in which the release from
    citizenship is impossible, arbitrarily refused, or attached to inordinate difficulties
    for the applicant.

24 As of 1985, for example, one of every 600 Turks with ten years' residence in
    Germany had applied for citizenship (Hailbronner 1989a, 70). Since measures
    easing the eligibility requirements for children and residents of at least fifteen
    years were adopted in 1990, the number of applications has increased somewhat,
    especially in Berlin, where a liberal naturalization program has been pursued.

25 These naturalization proposals have been accompanied by other proposals seek-
    ing an improved status for migrants independent of German citizenship. Thus,
    for example, the Greens have suggested adopting a "settlers law," which would
    extend full legal and political equality to residents of five years or more, while the
    government has concentrated on creating greater security for foreigners in the
    sphere of residence and work permits. For a full discussion, see Bernsdorff 1986.

26 See, for example, the Bundestag debate of February 9, 1995 over the SPD/Green
    proposal to accept dual citizenship.

27 According to the Federal Commissioner for the Integration of Foreign Workers
    and Their Family Members, one-third of all discretionary naturalizations in 1993
    involved acceptance of multiple citizenship ("Bundestag debattiert über Staats-
    angehörigkeit," *Zeitschrift für Ausländerrecht und Ausländerpolitik* 1995 no. 2, 96).

28 This view has been most influentially formulated by Dieter Oberndörfer (1990).
    It is echoed in the analyses of Hoffmann (1990), Geissler (1990), Hammar
    (1990), Habermas (1995) and many others writing on this topic.

29 The phrase *"Verfassungspatriotismus"* was coined by Dolf Sternberger (1990). For criticisms of the use of the term by Habermas and other leftist thinkers, see Sutor 1995.

30 On this point Oberndörfer differs from Brubaker over the question of France. Brubaker (1992) sees the developments in France as the establishment of a republican variety of nation (also tempered by ethnonational influences), whereas Oberndörfer (1990) sees the rise of Napoleon as the demise of French republicanism.

31 My analysis has much in common with Jürgen Fijalkowski's (1991b, 243–46). He presents a typology of four basic positions that he calls "regressive ethnonationalism," "nation-state conservatism," "liberal multiculturalism," and "rigorous egalitarianism."

32 Naturally, individual members of these parties vary widely in their views.

33 More specifically it is the Christian Union parties that have implemented this view, in many respects in spite of objections from their coalition partner, the FDP.

Chapter Three: Political Anthropologies

1   It is necessary to distinguish between moral *arguments* and moral *preferences* in regard to membership policy. Nonreflective preferences on the part of voters and policymakers undoubtedly play a major, perhaps decisive role in shaping membership. Here, however, I am interested in arguments, since it is only reasoned claims—including the claim that political membership should be determined according to the individual preferences of full members—that offer the potential for criticism and revision inherent in an ethical view.

2   For example, Vattel, who in most ways conformed to a consent-based approach, was one with the great common-law writer Blackstone in advancing a strict jus sanguinis criterion for political membership (see Whelan 1981, 645–48; Blackstone 1983; Vattel 1805).

3   Machiavelli and Jefferson may both insightfully be understood as republicans, but this alone will not take us far toward understanding their views on membership in sixteenth-century Florence or in the fledgling United States.

4   Rousseau, for example, had no trouble embracing all three in his political philosophy.

5   The three membership images discussed here bear some resemblance to the analogues of the club, the neighborhood, and the family used by Michael Walzer in his discussion of membership (1983, chap. 2). Broadly speaking, the communal self corresponds to the family member, the universal self to the neighbor, and the self-constituting self to the club member. See my discussion of Walzer in chapter 4.

6 Thus, one could argue, as political membership becomes more and more "transnational" (Bauböck 1994), its normative basis becomes increasingly universal in nature.

7 This is a question broached by Charles Beitz in the context of a discussion of "Eligibility, Boundaries, and Nationality" (1979, 105–15). In a manner similar to the treatment here of contract, communal sovereignty, and natural law, Beitz considers freedom of association, common cultural characteristics, and considerations of justice as possible normative grounds for self-determination, before arguing for the last. However, his concern, it should be noted, is with grounds for political separatism, not inclusion, and his argument is framed accordingly.

8 This is the standard term in international documents.

9 This argument might for example be made in connection with the Sorbian minority in eastern Germany, a group that continues to try to preserve its own language and culture.

10 For a list of linguistic, ethnic, racial, religious, and tribal minorities in 124 countries, see Sigler 1983, 205–13.

11 This is John Stuart Mill's argument in *Considerations on Representative Government;* he writes of nations, but the idea is assimilable to my use of culture (1978, chap. 16). See also Beitz 1979, 112–14.

12 The culture position therefore relies on the notion that cultural attachments may be altered at will by individuals. Yael Tamir (1993) has argued that this possibility may serve as the basis for a "liberal nationalism." She seems to me, however, to underestimate the existential problems involved in genuinely switching cultures. Will Kymlicka (1995, 84–93) provides a rather more nuanced discussion of the "difficulty of leaving one's culture"; yet, by framing the issue in terms of individual autonomy and "cultural membership" he nonetheless fails to do justice to the extent to which the agent — the "self" — is *constituted by,* and hence analytically inseparable from, his or her cultural context.

13 In other city-states such as Sparta, citizenship was also further reserved for the landed, nonworking class (Wood 1988).

14 The distinction between citizenship and other statuses was brought home in the area of homicide law, where the court in which a citizen might be tried, as well as his penalty, depended on whether or not his victim was an Athenian (Manville 1990, 10–13; Sinclair 1988).

15 A classic argument in favor of this view is made by Aristotle in book 3, chap. 13 of *Politics* (1941); some other noted proponents include Mill (1978), Schmitt (1970), and Acton (1985).

16 On differences here between admissions and the treatment of residents, see Carens 1987.

17 Although this is not a problem in the (West) German case, the culture and

closure positions' privileging of communal structures of moral authority over universal or individual rights may also lead to a denial of the right of citizens to emigrate.

18 This is not to say that states organized according to the culture view may not respect and even constitutionally recognize the validity of other human rights within their territory. But where this occurs it is with the tacit understanding that the nation determines which rights hold and which do not.

19 An argument advancing the choice position on these grounds is made by Elsa Chaney (1981). Chaney emphasizes that a diversified system of political membership tends to work in favor of economically disadvantaged populations by making it possible for migrant workers to pursue opportunities without being constrained by all-or-nothing citizenship policies. It also allows migrants to maintain formal ties with the countries they have left, which may be important for reasons having to do with property, inheritance, and so on. As her argument notes, many long-term residents are migrant workers who intend eventually to return to their country of origin. On the choice model, this limited involvement in their home country need not rule out limited political representation during their stay.

20 Walzer makes the point that countries, like clubs, have the right to regulate admissions but not to bar withdrawals (1983, 40). See also chapter 4.

21 Riley shows that major contemporary contractarian arguments tend to avoid the philosophical problem of the link between will and political legitimacy. He concludes, rather optimistically, that a Kantian metaphysics of morals can provide the missing link for theories such as those put forward by Walzer, John Rawls, and Robert Paul Wolff.

22 This is a crucial problem with the notion of mutual consent advanced by Schuck and Smith (1985). Another difficulty with their argument has to do with how the consent of a nation is determined. See my discussion of their view in chapter 4.

23 Habermas, whose political theory largely conforms to the coexistence position, notes the element of contingency involved in the constitution of state populations, but in my view fails to take adequate note of its moral significance (1994, 126).

24 An early proponent of this tradition was the Spanish Dominican Francisco de Vitoria, who wrote in 1532 that

> if children of any Spaniard be born [in the New World] and they wish to acquire citizenship, it seems they can not be barred either from citizenship or from the advantages enjoyed by other citizens — I refer to the case where the parents had their domicile there. The proof of this is furnished by the rule of the law of nations. . . . Aye, and if there be any persons who wish to acquire a domicile in some state of the Indians, as by marriage or in virtue of any other fact whereby foreigners are wont to become citizens, they can not be im-

peded any more than others, and consequently they enjoy the privileges of citizens just as others do, provided they also submit to the burdens to which others submit. (1917, 153–54)

25 The shift from a natural law paradigm to one of natural rights was a complicated one; on this topic see Tuck 1979 and Haakonssen 1996.

26 For his part, Kant identified the essential criteria for citizenship as simply individual autonomy and self-sufficiency: "The only qualification required by a citizen (apart, of course, from being an adult male) is that he must be his own master (sui juris), and must have some property (which can include any skill, trade, fine art or science) to support himself" (1991, 78).

27 This observation supposes a world in which citizenship policies are not unified. In a world in which all citizenships were determined on the coexistence model, the question in regard to multiple citizenship would be whether one could be integrated enough in more than one polity to justify multiple political representation.

28 Political borders need not be taken entirely for granted; certainly cases will exist in which they are contested, with good reason. Here, historical arguments will undoubtedly play a central role.

29 Habermas (1995) attempts to counter such criticisms by arguing, first, that the historical connection between cultural community (ethnos) and democratic self-determination (demos) is accidental and not conceptual in nature; and second, that a communitarian conception of citizenship, with its assumption of a self-determining, ethically homogeneous polity, is in any case no longer applicable to modern conditions. Based on these claims, he defends the view that states — and a unified Europe — are morally required to disassociate ethnocultural identities from the universalistic political culture that properly forms the basis of citizenship. In my view, he is rather sanguine about both the theoretical and practical prospects for separating nationalism and republicanism.

30 For arguments distinguishing political participation and other core human rights from secondary rights, see Shue 1980 and Hollenbach 1979.

31 Shue argues for a right to "genuine influence upon the fundamental choices among the social institutions and the social policies that control security and subsistence and, where the person is directly affected, genuine influence upon the operation of institutions and the implementation of policy" (1980, 71). See also Lichtenberg 1981.

32 For several related criticisms of the abstract character of some formulations of human rights, see Waldron 1987, 166–74.

33 The point of my criticism here is that the idea of an *individual* right to *national* citizenship is a logically and practically flawed construction. This does not mean that a more broadly conceived human right to political representation in general may not serve as an effective moral ideal in national political discourse.

Chapter Four: Inequality, Nondomination, and Human Rights

1 As I shall argue in this chapter, the shape of just membership policies may also be affected by the requirements of a commitment to democracy (that is, to a positive role for political members in the governance of the community, as opposed to a status as a mere subject) as well as by contextual factors such as the nature and size of modern states and the extent of global interdependence.

2 I take "harm" here to refer in a general way to damage to personal interests occasioned through human agency. For a discussion of some of the philosophical issues surrounding different varieties of harm, see Feinberg 1980, 45–68.

3 This general claim could perhaps be made about any political theory, as I suggested earlier. As Ian Shapiro notes, "substantive conceptions of the good cannot be avoided in arguments of right and justice" (1986, 304). John Finnis goes further in writing of an "interdependence between the project of describing human affairs by way of theory and the project of evaluating human options with a view, at least remotely, to acting reasonably and well" (1980, 18).

4 See Walzer 1970 and 1977.

5 Here Walzer seeks to distinguish his perspective from that of Bernard Williams (1973). Walzer interprets Williams as deriving criteria of justice from the essential meanings of goods, while he (Walzer) wishes to emphasize the historical and social nature of such meanings (9). I suspect Williams would be reluctant to subscribe to this distinction in connection with his argument.

6 This claim comes as the last in a set of six propositions summarizing Walzer's "theory of goods" (7–10). The first five points are descriptive in nature; the sixth takes the form of an imperative: "When meanings are distinct, distributions must be autonomous" (10).

7 My point here is supported by Walzer's extension of the notion of dominance to the act of reshaping the meanings of social goods (10–11). Meanings may evolve on their own, but it is illicit to change them artificially. This claim, however, raises problems, to which I will return, concerning the role of politics in shaping shared meanings. Walzer, it should also be noted, allows that in some societies—his example is the Indian caste system—the differentiation of shared meanings of social goods may not be very great, in which case the dominance of a single value (e.g., ritual purity) need not be an injustice.

8 That Walzer recognizes his argument as an attempt to derive a political theory from modest claims about human nature is suggested in his introduction. His theory assumes, he writes, "our recognition of one another as human beings, members of the same species. . . . We are very different, and we are also manifestly alike. Now, what (complex) social arrangements follow from the difference and the likeness?" (xii). See also his attempt to develop a pluralist notion of moral

universality distinct from traditional conceptions of a single global morality (1990).

9   In *Thick and Thin* (1994), in the context of distinguishing between the universal, "minimalist," and particular, "maximalist," aspects of his political theory, Walzer continues to insist that his account "does not require or 'rest on' a theory of human nature. But there is a picture of the self, nothing so grand as a theory, that is consistent with 'complex equality'" (x–xi).

10 For example, Walzer at different times compares political communities to universities, families (urban, Western), neighborhoods, and clubs; he also develops comparisons between immigrants and children, and guestworkers and live-in servants.

11 A much-commented-upon feature of Walzer's work is his frequent reference to the beliefs of an unspecified "us." As Walzer explains in *Just and Unjust Wars* (1977, especially xiv–xv, 11–20), his use of the first person plural reflects his belief that his readers share a common moral experience, that they indeed inhabit one moral world. Elsewhere Walzer has made it clear that he believes this experience to be more or less universal (1994a).

12 This use of terms is somewhat problematic insofar as it presumes the finished product of membership policies, the state to which rationales are "internal" and "external." What he means by "external" criteria are criteria that are logically prior to and independent of specific political communities; they are in short, I argue, universal criteria.

13 Cf. Walzer 1994b, 83:"[O]ur common humanity will never make us members of a single universal tribe. The crucial commonality of the human race is particularism."

14 It is significant that in Germany, as we saw earlier, this principle has been recognized to extend to family members of guestworkers regardless of their formal membership in the political community.

15 It should be noted that this implication of Walzer's theory fits well with his overall concern with shared social meanings. It would obviously be difficult to separate the roles of citizens and "denizens" in establishing a community's norms about the distribution of memberships. It would be easier to claim that all residents are implicated in a community's standards for admission and exclusion, thereby tacitly acknowledging the membership of all residents.

16 Walzer's observations on this issue are difficult to apply to today's noncitizen minorities for two reasons. First, his focus on economic reasons leaves out of consideration a not insignificant number of student immigrants. Second, the situation of the guestworker minorities has changed in significant legal and moral respects since the situation in the early 1970s sketched by Walzer. There are many more ways in which guestworkers who have settled in industrial societies are acknowledged as members; yet, their undiminished political exclusion is now

portrayed not as a structural state of affairs, but as a state chosen by them. And it is true; by now, in many countries, guestworkers have become "potential citizens," in however thin a sense.

17 It is perhaps the case that for Walzer, the nature of political justice in regard to citizenship is determined by the meaning of "citizen," which he seems to view as an intrinsically democratic concept. Thus, he argues that in an oligarchy, even citizens are really simply resident aliens (61).

18 The reference to fairness here, it could be argued, enlists yet another external normative criterion in support of Walzer's argument.

19 This notion has been given a theoretical exposition in the work of Georges Sorel (see Vernon 1986). For an account of its contemporary influence see Wihtol de Wenden 1987.

20 For a discussion of the view that "it is men-within-the-normative-structure be- tween whom justice must be done," see Taylor 1985, 294–96.

21 Herman van Gunsteren, in an attempt to compensate for what he sees as the overly global logic of Walzer's position on membership, proposes a list of require- ments for admission to "local" citizenship that includes, in addition to economic self-sufficiency and a general capacity for political judgment, the will and capacity to identify culturally with the society in question. He accepts, however, that what this may mean in practice can not be determined theoretically, and further allows that ample discretion must be practiced in any case (1988, 736–37).

22 The phrase is Hannah Arendt's (1967, 296).

23 In her discussion of the links between statelessness and vulnerability to human rights violations, Arendt provides a powerful argument regarding the unique significance of political membership: "Something much more fundamental than freedom and justice, which are the rights of citizens, is at stake when belonging to the community into which one is born is no longer a matter of course. . . . [The stateless] are deprived, not of the right to freedom, but of the right to action. . . . Man, it turns out, can lose all so-called Rights of Man without losing his essential quality as man, his human dignity. Only the loss of a polity itself expels him from humanity" (1967, 296–97).

24 The view that human rights are legitimate claims in virtue of their requirement by a foundational standard of human dignity is embraced in international docu- ments including the UN's Universal Declaration of Human Rights and, in a more fully articulated form, in the documents of the Catholic social tradition as well as in a great variety of other authors' works. These sources differ in their accounts of the basis of human dignity, identifying it variously as our theological status as children of God, or as our existence as self-actualizing moral beings, or simply as our given human nature. What unites these views is that they hold 1) that human dignity requires that persons be treated in certain sorts of ways and 2) that this

gives rise to entitlements to these sorts of treatment in the form of human rights. It is worth noting here that the reliance on a language of rights is a major reason why human rights have been criticized as a Western notion imposed on the rest of the world (see, e.g., Pollis and Schwab 1979). In response to this complaint, one defender of the dignity view, Jack Donnelly, argues that while the problem of how to protect dignity is universal and a human rights approach is only one strategy — a liberal strategy — among many possible alternatives, given the contemporary global prevalence of liberal political and social institutions and market economies, it is clearly the best strategy available (1989, 17–27).

25   In this view, inspired by the philosophy of Kant, the essence of human being is found in the capacity to act intentionally and rationally. The nature of human beings as actors justifies the claim of each individual to the conditions necessary for human action, which include above all freedom and well-being. As Alan Gewirth develops this argument, it is the human capacity for action that grounds the notions of both dignity and rights (1982, 28–30). A related approach relies upon Kant's categorical imperative (1964) in establishing a basic principle of respect for persons. See, for example, Donagan 1993.

26   This, ultimately, is the thrust of John Rawls's considerably nuanced "constructivist" view of human rights (1993). In his self-consciously modest account, a set of universally applicable rights is required by a "liberal conception of justice" he believes should be acceptable to all well-ordered societies, liberal or not. This conception of justice is in turn the product of a "reasonable procedure" in which rational agents, employing the original position and the veil of ignorance, agree on common principles first in a (liberal) domestic context, then in an international context.

27   In this Aristotelian approach, a full-blown account of human potentialities provides the normative linchpin for explaining what human beings are entitled to. John Finnis, for example, provides a fixed list of philosophically and empirically demonstrable goods that are held to be the "conditions and principles of practical right-mindedness, of good and proper order among men and in individual conduct" (1980, 18, 59–99). The fact that these goods are each required by the end of human flourishing is what makes them human rights and, indeed, duties. This approach thus moves from a universal teleological conception of human well-being to specific claims of right.

28   This strategy, advanced most notably by Christian Bay (1982), understands human rights as justified claims to the satisfaction of human needs, as distinguished from wants.

29   Ronald Garet, in his work on group rights, identifies existence itself — whether structured individually, in groups, or in society — as the essence of human being and the basis of legitimate claims of right. Drawing on Sartre's philosophy, he

claims that existence provides the "utterly primitive goodmaking element" for basic human goods, and thereby requires respect for these goods in the form of rights (1983, especially 1065–75).

30 For David Pacini, self-preservation, the fundamental drive to maintain one's personhood, is the governing motif in the modern individualistic concern with rights, including human rights (1987, 67–82).

31 Jean-François Lyotard argues that human rights depend upon the recognition of the other in oneself, of a "likeness that . . . follows from the difference of each from each," so that to harm one person is to harm the entire human community. This recognition is made possible through the dynamics of language (1993, 136–47).

32 For a somewhat overstated critique of this tendency in moral theory, see Rorty 1993.

33 Cf. Jeffrey Reiman's discussion of "justice as reason's answer to subjugation" (1990, 1–82).

34 For a historical analysis of the effects of injustice understood as systematic violations of "natural morality," see Moore 1978, especially chapters 2 and 3. On the connection between agency and harm, injury and torture, see Scarry 1985.

35 Cf. Judith Shklar's observation that "it is not remembered [in political theory] that the history and present function of rights is the expression of personal outrage at injustice and cruelty" (1986, 24). See also Bryan Turner's attempt to provide a philosophical anthropology that interprets rights as a sympathetic response to the perception of the universality of human frailty: "It is from a collectively held recognition of individual frailty that rights as a system of mutual protection gain their emotive force" (1993, 186).

36 The thesis that the experience of domination is a more important determinant of the legitimacy of human rights claims than substantive theories of human rights helps explain why, in the international institutionalization of human rights, considerable agreement exists on a general list of human rights without a comparable consensus regarding the underlying nature of human beings. Cf. Maritain (1951, 76–107), who, in noting that "men mutually opposed in their theoretical conceptions can come to a merely practical agreement regarding a list of human rights," comments, "This fact merely proves that systems of moral philosophy are the product of intellectual reflection on ethical data that precede and control them and reveal a very complicated type of geology of the conscience, in which the natural work of spontaneous, pre-scientific, and pre-philosophical reason is at every moment conditioned by the acquisitions, the servitudes, the structure and evolution of the social group" (80).

37 Walzer, discussing egalitarianism, writes, "What is at stake is the ability of a group of people to dominate their fellows. It's not the fact that there are rich and poor that generates egalitarian politics but the fact that the rich 'grind the faces of the

poor,' impose their poverty upon them, command their deferential behavior" (xii–xiii).

38 In defining domination, I want to be careful not to imply too much about the sort of agency required on the part of dominators. Those who dominate may do so in a great variety of ways: individually and intentionally, or collectively and tacitly, with greater or lesser degrees of self-consciousness. Those who suffer the deprivations of housing or subsistence enforced through an inequitable economic order, for example, are dominated by a system imposed, maintained, and exploited by others.

39 By "good" I mean here simply something that is beneficial to the person in question. "Important goods" are those goods that bear heavily and perceptibly on the well-being of persons, whether or not they are explicitly recognized to do so. They may include health or mobility or food or housing or a long list of other things; what they are precisely does not bear on my description of domination.

40 There are many authors, especially Marxists and feminists, who provide analyses of domination and the related concepts of oppression, repression, subordination, subjugation, exploitation, discrimination, alienation, victimization, objectification, and exclusion, not to mention opposing concepts such as liberation and emancipation. I eschew speaking of oppression both because the term tends to be applied to diffuse, all-encompassing phenomena and because it often carries structural connotations that undermine a sense of the human agency involved. Exploitation, on the other hand, implies a focused sort of exchange among agents that constitutes only a subclass of the broader category of domination. Subordination and discrimination have been given fixed meanings above (chapter 1). For various distinctions among types of power relations see, for example, Weil 1958; Arendt 1967; Foucault 1979; Bay 1981; Brittan and Maynard 1984; Ramazanoglu 1989; Bartky 1990; Scott 1990; and Young 1990.

41 The question of whether persons may experience domination without being conscious of it is a crucial one. Claims of false consciousness, I would think, would need to be buttressed by a demonstration that what persons are being deprived of is in fact a good that is at some level important to them. Thus, for example, in the example of "happy slaves" one would need to make the case that the good of liberty, of which they were deprived, was in fact of deep importance to them. On the other hand, it is an oft-noted feature of domination that it may tend to induce its victims to believe that they deserve or are even responsible for their own subordination. For an analysis of this process based on Frantz Fanon's phenomenology of "psychic alienation," see Bartky 1990, 22–32.

42 For a discussion of the difference between misfortune and injustice, see Shklar 1990, 51–82.

43 A strong collection of essays on this topic may be found in Fischer 1986. An

interesting "pragmatic" conception of responsibility that explicitly attends to the significance of communal boundaries is developed by Marion Smiley (1992). A persuasive argument for an expansion of conventional notions of responsibility to include more than what persons directly cause and to recognize shared responsibility is provided by May 1992. On the question of collective responsibility, see also Arendt 1987; the essays in May and Hoffman 1991; and Lucas 1993, 75–85.

44 My approach bears some similarities to the "rational intuitionist" understanding of human rights proposed by David Little (1993). Little sees human rights as responses to the transparent wrongness of acts that impose arbitrary suffering. This he illustrates by employing William Gass's "Case of the Obliging Stranger": the wrongness of overbaking a person can be accounted for not by any theoretical considerations, but only by pointing to the circumstances constituting the act — "Well, I put this fellow in an oven, you see. The oven was on, don't you know" (78). Although Little's analysis focuses on torture, he implies that such acts may include a variety of forms of social, political, and cultural domination (86).

45 Although I employ the admittedly deontological language of "right" and "wrong" here, the point does not seem to me to exclude teleological interpretations.

46 This I take to be the core sense of rights as referred to in contemporary moral philosophical discussions. See, for example, Gewirth 1989, 98; Finnis 1980, 205; and Cranston 1989, 19.

47 Cf. the accounts of Ian Shapiro (1986, 14–19) and Alan Gewirth (1978, 65). An indispensable source for distinctions among different sorts of rights is Hohfeld 1919.

48 A helpful jurisprudential source on both the hermeneutics of law and the relation between legal and moral rights is Cover 1983.

49 Support for this observation is provided by the work of the organization Amnesty International, which devotes itself to preventing human rights abuses and aiding their victims. In order to provide itself with the strongest possible moral appeal, Amnesty confines its efforts precisely to the sort of abuses that most clearly bear the character of domination: torture, political persecution, and unlawful imprisonment. The international success of this strategy, one could argue, testifies to the centrality of domination in the structure of human rights.

50 The most influential account of basic rights is Shue 1980. A discussion of several basic rights theories may be found in Donnelly 1989, 37–45.

51 There is an obvious ambiguity involved in speaking simultaneously of *human beings* and *human being* in this context. It should be clear, however, that the connection between the two terms is very close: With *human beings* I mean, quite simply, "people" in general, while with *human being* I am referring to what might correspondingly be called our "peopleness" — that is, that which constitutes us as people. Neither term necessarily connotes individuality.

52   As an example, suppose that a religious group experiences domination in the form of an outright ban within a given political context. My contention is that because religion as a human good is a communal phenomenon, the appropriate human rights claim would take as its subject the religious community itself, not its individual members. An individually held right to religious belief does not necessarily secure the well-being of a religious community, which may require collective protections or even active support in order to survive.

53   On the question of how groups may be harmed, see May 1987, 135–55.

54   The assumption that human rights entail only individual subjects, though rarely supported, is widely shared among liberal theorists. Will Kymlicka, for example, speaks of "traditional human rights standards" (that is, individual rights) as distinct from a supplementary set of "minority rights" (1995, 3–6). In arguing for a single theory of justice encompassing both of these categories, however, Kymlicka implicitly recognizes their common normative basis and structure. For a criticism of the tendency to separate individual rights from respect for cultural groups, see Habermas 1994, 109–16.

55   Here the difficult problem of conflicts between different levels of human beings or human goods arises. What human right prevails when the survival of a group good, say a language, is perceived as in conflict either with another group good, such as the functioning of the national economy, or with individual freedoms? I do not have a general answer to this problem, although I suspect that two important considerations will always be the extent of the domination (is survival or merely self-determination at stake?) and the relative importance of the goods to the people in question (is the moral significance for a minority community of a shared linguistic heritage comparable to the interest of society at large in linguistic homogeneity or to that of individuals in being able to choose in which language they express themselves and are educated?). Cf. Garet's treatment (1983), and, on the Québecois, the essays in Baker 1994, and Kymlicka 1995.

56   Thus, rights formulated as prohibitions against forms of domination such as slavery and torture tend to be stronger than rights formulated positively. As John Finnis shows, this is reflected in international human rights documents, which tend to treat rights of the first sort ("No one shall be . . .") as unqualified and rights of the second sort ("Everyone has the right to . . .") as generally subject to limitations imposed, for example, by the common good (1980, 210–18).

57   I leave aside the question of the extent to which, in nondemocratic states, citizens who have no access to political participation are dominated. It seems to me that this will often be the case. Here, however, I wish to focus on what I take to be a morally relevant difference between being subject to a group's policies as a member and being subject as a nonmember.

58   The case that "people who live in a state for any significant period of time . . . are

morally entitled to citizenship" is made by Joseph Carens (1989, 46). Although his argument is ostensibly based on liberal democratic principles of consent and toleration, these values in fact only qualify his central claim that, over time, immigrants establish a relationship with the society in which they live that makes it simply wrong to exclude them. This stance seems to me consonant with the human rights perspective advanced here. See also Rainer Bauböck's defense of the proposition that "human rights are the cornerstone as well as the most extended application of a transnational conception of citizenship" (1994, 240).

59 The IRS's distinction, for tax purposes, between "temporary" and "indefinite" assignments in another country seems to me to be as good a guideline as any: Residence of over one year is presumed to be indefinite, although this presumption may be overcome; while residence of two years or more is understood as indefinite in any case (1991, 2). But this is a rule of thumb; there is no reason to insist on a single universal period for residence, so long as particular policies respect the underlying notion of integration into the state society. In the case of demands for a period of residence much longer than this, however, the onus should be on demonstrating how a longer period of residence is necessary to secure the integration of the persons in question.

60 Here I follow Robert Dahl's insightful discussion of the problem of inclusion (1989, 119–31). After identifying full democratic inclusion as a "categorical right," he modifies this claim, concluding that "the demos must include all adult members of the association [i.e., those subject to a government and its laws] except transients and persons proved to be mentally defective" (129). I have addressed the problem of transients; as to mentally defective persons, it seems to me that, particularly in the case of those capable of political participation, we should be slow to conclude that they do not possess the political judgment requisite for inclusion in the polity.

61 An argument arriving at similar conclusions is provided by Habermas (1994, 140–42; 1995, 276). For an attempt to grapple with the problem of how to develop criteria for deciding among too many qualified applicants for admission to a state, see Gunsteren 1988, 740–41. His account makes clear the internal link between the modern notion of citizenship and human rights.

62 A persuasive analysis of the difficulties involved in justifying exclusionary policies in the interest of "public order" is provided by Joseph Carens (1992, 28–34). On the philosophical poverty of both liberal and communitarian resources for justifying exclusionary admissions practices, see Booth 1997. The case of Proposition 187 in California furnishes an example of the ethically problematic consequences of excluding residents from the rights of membership.

63 One might argue that admitting a large group of illegal residents to citizenship would impose a financial burden that would derail the national economy, for after

all citizenship is, among other things, a commodity worth a good deal of money in terms of social services and other benefits. But this argument is greatly weakened when one considers that even illegal immigrants are in many countries eligible for social services, that as laborers they often represent an economic boon rather than drain, and that as citizens they pay more taxes.

64 It might be made contingent on the ability to function in the language of the state; the strength of such an argument would depend on whether or not the national language itself acted as a medium of domination. In any event, for the majority of legal long-term residents this minimal criterion would not present a problem.

65 As Walzer notes, sometimes the survival of a cultural group will depend on stronger measures, and when such a group has a territorial base, it may have a legitimate claim to political separation (1983, 43–44).

66 This crucial point is ignored by Annette Baier in her otherwise illuminating "Some Virtues of Resident Alienage" (1992).

67 Raymond Aron has argued that so long as Europe has not become a single integrated megastate, "there are no such animals as 'European citizens'" (1974, 653). Elizabeth Meehan (1993), on the other hand, makes the case that a European citizenship similar to that of the Roman Empire is emerging alongside, or above, the traditional national citizenships of EU members.

68 But see Walker and Mendlovitz 1990 on the imprecision of such concepts as internationalization, globalization, and interdependence.

Chapter Five: Citizenship and Group Rights

1 As a result, the concerns of Walzer and others with whether or not citizenship is *open* are not here relevant.

2 In this thin sense, citizenship arguably includes the right to remain in the state and not be deported, although contexts are readily imaginable where this right would be construed as alienable by the state. On the notion of citizenship as an empty category, see Makarov 1971.

3 Walzer makes a similar point in his discussion of the Athenian *metoikia*. He argues that perhaps in Greek city-states, but certainly in contemporary democracies, there is "no conceptual barrier to the extension of citizenship" (1983, 55).

4 Whether military service should be required, and whether, if so, it may be required of men only are complicated questions I can not go into here, other than to note that the military service requirement remains a point of controversy in Germany.

5 An example of such a strategy is Veit Bader's argument that "democratic citizenship ought to be disentangled from citizenship as state membership" (1995, 224).

He cites as a warrant Habermas's contentions regarding the conceptual indepen-
dence of republicanism and nationalism (1992).

6 The second requirement is partially dependent on the first one: The decision
never to move back to one's country of origin would not be of such moment if
naturalization did not require the forfeiture of one's native citizenship and accompanying rights to, for instance, inheritance and private property.

7 On the international human rights to leave the country and to change one's
nationality (arts. 13 and 15 of the Universal Declaration), see Whelan 1981.

8 See chap. 2, n. 27.

9 For a list of thirty-three such countries, see Rau 1990, 200–204.

10 This process has been fully documented in the case of the Turkish German minority by Ertekin Özcan (1989).

11 An example is the loss of property and inheritance rights that has been incurred by
Turks who have taken up German citizenship. It is interesting to note that, in
recent years, Turkey has hit on a legal stratagem for circumventing restrictions on
dual citizenship for Turks in Germany. Turkish nationals who give up their citizenship in order to become naturalized in Germany may have their former citizenship automatically reinstated at the Turkish consulate. The German government has expressed its intention to close the legal loophole that makes this
practice possible (*Informationsbrief Ausländerrecht* 1995 no. 1:43–44).

12 A similar policy is in place in the U.K. (Hammar 1990).

13 Carens identifies the relevant principle here as "the longer the presence, the
stronger the claim to membership and hence the stronger the claim to citizenship" (1989, 42). Both Carens (38) and Walzer (1983, 58–59) hold that the
terms of the labor contract agreed to by guestworkers eventually cease to justify a
subordinate status for them. I am inclined to agree with them; it is worth noting,
though, that the reasons for this development are not mainly contractual, but
rather dictated by broader criteria of justice.

14 A noteworthy effort in this area is Hans Tremmel's painstaking analysis of Germany's asylum policy from the standpoint of Christian social ethics (1992).

15 Habermas has argued that ethnic-cultural criteria are not appropriate for the
immigration policy of a country — such as, arguably, Germany — whose constitution is premised on universal human rights. Because such states invest their
identity in their political, as opposed to their ethnic, culture, all that they may
rightly require of immigrants is their *political acculturation;* fundamentalists, consequently, may be turned away (1995, 276–79; 1994, 132–42). It seems to me,
however, that even highly liberal democratic cultures are not in practice separable
from particularistic forms of life, and there may hence be pragmatic grounds for
at least slightly favoring prospective immigrants who share in what Habermas
terms the "ethical-cultural" form of life of the community.

16   Some proposals for German and European immigration policies are presented in Apel 1992; Schiffer 1992; Winkler 1992; Cohn-Bendit 1993; Rittstieg 1993; Schmalz-Jacobsen et al. 1993; Weber 1993; and Bunz and Neuenfeld 1994.

17   Distinguishing among different types of refugees is a complicated issue that extends beyond the scope of this study. Nonetheless, we should note that from a normative perspective, the conventional legal distinctions between political refugees, humanitarian refugees, and economic refugees are difficult to sustain due to the interpenetration in practice of political, military, economic, and other factors inducing flight. Ethically, it makes more sense to speak of a continuum of grounds for flight, ranging from focused political persecution to more subtle forms of oppression, including official negligence and economic deprivation. As with the concept of domination, being a refugee is something most readily established in phenomenological terms.

18   For an answer in the negative, see Schuck and Smith 1985.

19   For a very helpful discussion of equality, see Rae et al. 1989. Perhaps the only shortcoming of this treatment is that it does not take full account of corporate as opposed to collective equalities.

20   On the history of minority rights agreements, see Hannum 1989; and Rubin and Laqueur 1989, 125–60.

21   Article 27 of the UN International Covenant on Civil and Political Rights, for example, guarantees that "persons belonging to [ethnic, religious, or linguistic] minorities shall not be denied the right, in community with other members of their group, to enjoy their own culture, to profess and practice their own religion, or to use their own language."

22   In, for example, the International Convention on the Prevention and Punishment of the Crime of Genocide (1948).

23   This issue is taken up primarily in the International Labor Organization's Indigenous and Tribal Populations Convention (1947), and through the activities of the Working Group on Indigenous Populations of the Sub-Commission on Prevention of Discrimination and Protection of Minorities, which has produced a draft of a Universal Declaration on Indigenous Rights (1988).

24   For a collection of views in the debate between "liberal" and "communitarian" political theorists, see Sandel 1984. On the importance of religious communities, see Hauerwas 1981.

25   One classic view, articulated most prominently by Gierke (1957), sees groups as persons possessing a sort of moral subjectivity that entitles them to rights. The idea that groups are entities with an ontological status separable from that of individuals is advanced in different forms by Fiss (1976), Van Dyke (1985), Garet (1983), and the *Volksgruppenrechte* school best exemplified by Veiter (1970). Various formulations of the view that groups consist fundamentally in relations

among their members are to be found in Raz 1986; May 1987; Kymlicka 1989; Nino 1991; and Kukathas 1992. An interesting attempt at marking out a middle ground is made by Hill (1993).

26 There is a superficial sense in which *all* rights are group rights, for rights always apply to some *class* of beneficiaries (with the exception of the genre of transferable rights — rights *in res* — denoting sole possession, e.g., copyrights). However, I use group rights in opposition to the notion of individual rights, with the difference residing in the nature of the class of beneficiaries that is said to enjoy a right.

27 May (1987) also considers the rights-claims of smaller groups such as corporations.

28 Cf. Van Dyke's identification of nine standards for assessing the strength of claims to group rights (1985, 213–15).

29 The Germans may have had a stronger claim in the last century, when there was a movement in support of equal status for the German language with English (Van Dyke 1985, 45).

30 Carens (1990) makes a similar point about the connections between domination, equality, and the morality of differential treatment in the context of a discussion of African Americans. His analysis of how affirmative action is justified by overt and subtle forms of racism is echoed by Walzer in a reconsideration of the theory of complex equality (1993).

31 See the treatment of internal and external rights of autonomy, pp. 165–66. For the development of a similar distinction between negative duties (for example, tolerance, nondiscrimination) of the state toward minorities and positive ones (for example, preservation of language, special political representation), see Cholewinski 1988.

32 For a seminal treatment blending philosophical and psychological analysis, see Merleau-Ponty 1962, especially 434–56. For an account of how ethnicity and social and cultural constraints affect moral development, see Cortese 1990.

33 Cf. Bauböck 1994, 265–91. Also in this regard, Iris Marion Young usefully distinguishes among aggregates, associations, and social groups (1990, 43–48).

34 Theorists such as Gierke (1957), Veiter (1970), Garet (1983), Van Dyke (1985), May (1987), and Freeman (1995) insist that corporate conceptions of the subject of rights are required by situations in which irreducibly communal goods are at stake, while Waldron (1993) more cautiously allows that such a formulation may make sense. The view that group rights may properly be ascribed only to the members of collectivities is advanced by Fiss (1976), Cohen et al. (1977), Raz (1986), and Kymlicka (1989). Critics of group rights who argue that individual rights alone suffice to protect group interests include Glazer (1975), Galston (1980), Van den Berghe (1981), Donnelly (1989), and Nino (1991).

35 Will Kymlicka provides a different typology of "group-differentiated" rights

(1995, 26–33). He includes self-government rights, "polyethnic" rights, and special representation rights.

36   A particular instance of the broad distinction drawn here between rights of autonomy and rights of nondomination may be found in David Little's analysis of religious human rights in terms of "the right of nondiscrimination" and "the right of free exercise" (1995, 4–6).

37   For a skeptical view of this whole enterprise, see Dunn 1988.

38   See Kymlicka's discussion (1989, 137–61, 182–205). Such cases reflect an awareness of the danger, pointed out by Dench (1986, 15) and others, that arises when, as often occurs, a structure of individual rights functions to enforce the dominance of majority groups.

39   Compare the discussions in Sanders 1991, 383–86; and Kymlicka 1995, 152–72. As these authors note, it can at times be difficult to specify what precisely constitutes gender discrimination.

40   Wirsing (1983, 178–82) analyzes a range of such strategies.

41   A broad discussion of legal strategies for addressing the problem of equality among social groups appears in Stopp 1994.

42   Antidiscrimination laws are already on the books in other European countries, including Great Britain and the Netherlands. On the prospects for a German law, see Mager 1992, Just et al. 1993, and Wollenschläger 1994.

43   Affirmative action—the collective rights strategy of linking preferences among otherwise equivalent individuals with membership in particular disadvantaged groups—should not be confused with the corporate rights strategies of fixing minority quotas or granting set-asides, as has unfortunately all too often been the case in debates in the United States. Affirmative action in this narrow sense is merely the least thoroughgoing among a range of possible models for promoting equality. Likewise, positive discrimination should not be confused with reverse discrimination, a rather sloppy misnomer suggesting an equivalency between traditional forms of gender- or race-based oppression and current measures aimed at promoting the status of disadvantaged groups vis-à-vis the broader society. On the controversial topic of affirmative action, see the essays in Cohen et al. 1977.

44   On the situation in German cities, see Bischoff and Teubner 1991, 138. In regard to the difficulties involved in such a policy, the travails of the American experience with desegregation and busing might be instructive. See, for example, Lukas 1985.

45   See Nermin Abadan-Unat on the phenomenon of "re-turkization" as a response to subordination (1985, 16–17).

46   It is for this reason that Kymlicka's (1989) liberal defense of an individual right to cultural membership is ultimately unsatisfactory. A right to belong to a culture—

any culture—cannot substitute for the right of specific cultural groups to exist. The idea that people are not deprived of their rights when their culture is destroyed, so long as they are provided with membership in a surrogate culture, fails to recognize that to remove unwilling subjects from their cultural point of reference is almost certainly to do them serious harm.

47   Some background on these two issues is provided in Rist 1979.

48   This right is perhaps better formulated as a collective right, that is, as the right of each member to be educated in his or her language as well as in German. In either form, it is a right that seems to be a demand agreed upon by immigrants of all political stripes in Germany. For data on Turkish groups, see Özcan 1989, 348.

49   Some of the more reasonable proposals in the German debate involve providing native language instruction beginning in kindergarten, offering five or six hours per week through secondary school of native-language, full-credit courses addressing topics in pupils' native culture, and establishing a full native-language curriculum of no more than two years aimed at preparing new immigrants for German-language classes. For evaluations of varying strategies, see Özcan 1989; Bischoff and Teubner 1991.

50   See especially Khoury 1985. For a favorable assessment of the possibilities for gender equality in Islam, see Hassan 1991.

51   Unesco's Convention against Discrimination in Education (1960), for example, espouses the principle that in the interest of equality, "it is acceptable to classify children by language for purposes of education" (cited in Van Dyke 1985, 21). See also the excerpt from the UN Report on the Protection of Minorities, in Rubin and Laqueur 1989, 157–59.

52   Walzer has recently made a similar point, arguing that "the self is . . . naturally divided. . . . Under conditions of security . . . I will identify myself with more than one tribe. . . . So I can choose to be an American, a Jew, an Easterner, an intellectual, a professor. Imagine a similar multiplication of identities around the world, and the world begins to look like a less dangerous place" (1994b, 82).

53   On this point, see Wilpert 1988b, the various essays in Esser 1983, and Ruth Mandel's reflections on the significance of Turkish headscarves (1989).

References

Abadan-Unat, Nermin. 1985. "Identity Crisis of Turkish Migrants." In *Turkish Workers in Europe*, eds. Ilhan Basgöz and Norman Furniss, 3–22. Bloomington: Indiana University Press.

Abdullah, M. S. 1985. "Islamischer Religionsunterricht in der Bundesrepublik Deutschland." In *Islamische Minderheiten in der Diaspora*, ed. Adel Khoury, 125–161. Mainz: Grünewald.

Acton, John Emerich Edward Dalberg. 1985. *Selected Writings of Lord Acton*. Edited by J. Rufus Fears. Indianapolis: Liberty Classics.

Anderson, Benedict. 1983. *Imagined Communities: Reflections on the Origins and Spread of Nationalism*. London: Verso Editions.

Apel, Günter. 1992. "Gedanken zu einem zuwanderungspolitischen Konzept." *Zeitschrift für Ausländerrecht und Ausländerpolitik* 3:99–107.

Arendt, Hannah. 1958. *The Human Condition*. New York: Doubleday.

———. 1967. *The Origins of Totalitarianism*. New York: Harcourt Brace Jovanovich.

———. 1987. "Collective Responsibility." 1968. In *Amor Mundi*, ed. J. W. Bernauer, 43–50. Dordrecht: Martinus Nijhoff.

Aristotle. 1941. *Politics*. In *The Basic Works of Aristotle*. Edited by Richard McKeon and translated by Benjamin Jowett. New York: Random House.

Armstrong, John. 1982. *Nations before Nationalism*. Chapel Hill: University of North Carolina Press.

Aron, Raymond. 1974. "Is Multinational Citizenship Possible?" *Social Research* 41, no. 4 (winter): 638–656.

Bade, Klaus. 1983. *Vom Auswanderungsland zum Einwanderungsland? Deutschland 1880–1980*. Berlin: Colloquium Verlag.

———. 1994. "Immigration and Social Peace in United Germany." *Daedalus* 123, no. 1 (winter): 85–106.

———, ed. 1984–85. *Auswanderer–Wanderarbeiter–Gastarbeiter: Bevölkerung, Arbeits-*

markt, und Wanderung in Deutschland seit Ende des 19. Jahrhunderts. 2 vols. Ost-fildern: Scripta Mercurae.

———. 1987. *Population, Labour, and Migration in Nineteenth- and Twentieth-century Germany.* New York: Berg.

———. 1990. *Ausländer, Aussiedler, Asyl in der Bundesrepublik Deutschland.* Hannover: Niedersächsische Landeszentrale für Politische Bildung.

Bader, Veit. 1995. "Citizenship and Exclusion: Radical Democracy, Community, and Justice. Or, What Is Wrong with Communitarianism?" *Political Theory* 23, no. 2 (May): 211–246.

Baier, Annette C. 1992. "Some Virtues of Resident Alienage." In *Virtue,* ed. John W. Chapman and William A. Galston, 291–308. New York: New York University Press.

Baker, Judith, ed. 1994. *Group Rights.* Toronto: University of Toronto Press.

Balsdon, J. P. V. D. 1979. *Romans and Aliens.* London: Duckworth.

Barbalet, J. M. 1988. *Citizenship: Rights, Struggle, and Class Inequality.* Milton Keynes, England: Open University Press.

Barth, Frederik. 1969. *Ethnic Groups and Boundaries: The Social Organization of Culture Difference.* Boston: Little, Brown.

Bartky, Sandra Lee. 1990. *Femininity and Domination: Studies in the Phenomenology of Oppression.* New York: Routledge.

Barwig, Klaus, Klaus Lörcher, and Christoph Schumacher, eds. 1987. *Aufenthalt, Niederlassung, Einbürgerung.* Baden-Baden: Nomos.

Barwig, Klaus, and Dietmar Mieth. 1987. *Migration und Menschenwürde: Fakten, Analysen, und ethische Kriterien.* Mainz: Matthias Grünewald Verlag.

Basgöz, Ilhan, and Norman Furniss, eds. 1985. *Turkish Workers in Europe: An Inter-disciplinary Study.* Bloomington: Indiana University Press.

Bauböck, Rainer. 1994. *Transnational Citizenship: Membership and Rights in Interna-tional Migration.* Aldershot, England: Edward Elgar.

Bauer, Otto. 1975. "Die Nationalitätenfrage und die Sozialdemokratie." 1924. In *Werkausgabe,* vol. 1:46–622. Vienna: Europaverlag.

Bausinger, Hermann, ed. 1986. *Ausländer, Inländer: Arbeitsmigration und kulturelle Identität.* Tübingen: University of Tübingen Press.

Bay, Christian. 1981. *Strategies of Political Emancipation.* Notre Dame: University of Notre Dame Press.

———. 1982. "Self-Respect as a Human Right: Thoughts on the Dialectics of Wants and Needs in the Struggle for Human Community." *Human Rights Quarterly* 4 (February): 53–75.

Beiner, Ronald, ed. 1995. *Theorizing Citizenship.* Albany: State University of New York Press.

Beitz, Charles. 1979. *Political Theory and International Relations*. Princeton: Princeton University Press.

Bell, Wendell, and Walter Freeman, eds. 1974. *Ethnicity and Nation-Building*. London: Sage.

Benhabib, Seyla. 1992. *Situating the Self: Gender, Community, and Postmodernism in Contemporary Ethics*. New York: Routledge.

Berlin Commissioner for Foreigners' Affairs. 1989. *Zur Lage der jungen Ausländergeneration*. Berlin: Senatsverwaltung für Gesundheit und Soziales.

———. 1990. *Doppelte Staatsbürgerschaft—ein europäischer Normalfall?* Berlin: Senatsverwaltung für Gesundheit und Soziales.

———. 1994. *Bericht zur Integrations- und Ausländerpolitik*. Berlin: Senatsverwaltung für Gesundheit und Soziales.

Berlin Institute for Comparative Social Research. 1987. *Die Diskriminierung von Ausländern durch Gesetze und Verordnungen im Bereich politischer Beteiligung*. Berlin: Berliner Institut für Vergleichende Sozialforschung.

Bernsdorff, Norbert. 1986. *Probleme der Ausländerintegration in verfassungsrechtlicher Sicht: Eine Untersuchung der 3 wichtigsten Eingliederungskonzepte*. Frankfurt: Lang.

Bethlenfalvy, Peter von, ed. 1987. *Problems Arising from Migratory Movements of Refugees, Migrants, and Ethnic Minorities*. Athens: Programme Européen de Lutte contre la Pauvreté.

Bickel, Alexander. 1975. *The Morality of Consent*. New Haven: Yale University Press.

Bischoff, Detlef, and Werner Teubner. 1991. *Zwischen Einbürgerung und Rückkehr: Ausländerpolitik und Ausländerrecht der Bundesrepublik Deutschland—Eine Einführung*. 2d ed. Berlin: Hitit-Verlag.

Blackstone, Sir William. 1983. *Commentaries on the Laws of England*. 1765–69. Birmingham, England: Legal Classics Library.

Booth, William James. 1997. "Foreigners: Insiders, Outsiders and the Ethics of Membership." *Review of Politics* 59, no. 2 (spring): 259–92.

Brittan, Arthur, and Mary Maynard. 1984. *Sexism, Racism, and Oppression*. Oxford: Blackwell.

Broszat, Martin. 1963. *200 Jahre deutsche Polenpolitik*. Munich: Ehrenwirth.

Brown, Peter, and Henry Shue, eds. 1981. *Boundaries: National Autonomy and Its Limits*. Totowa, N.J.: Rowman and Littlefield.

Brubaker, William Rogers. 1989a. "Einwanderung und Nationalstaat in Frankreich und Deutschland." *Der Staat* 1:1–30.

———. 1989b. "Introduction." In *Immigration and the Politics of Citizenship in Europe and North America*, ed. William Rogers Brubaker, 1–28. Lanham, Md.: University Press of America.

——. 1992. *Citizenship and Nationhood in France and Germany.* Cambridge: Harvard University Press.

——, ed. 1989. *Immigration and the Politics of Citizenship in Europe and North America.* Lanham, Md.: University Press of America.

Bücking, Kai. 1992. *Die Beteiligung von Ausländern an Wahlen zum Deutschen Bundestag, zu den Parlamenten der Länder und den kommunalen Vertretungskörperschaften.* Frankfurt: Lang.

Bukow, Wolf-Dietrich. 1989. *Ausländerwahlrecht: Eine vergleichende Analyse der Politik gegenüber ethnischen Minderheiten in der Bundesrepublik Deutschland und in den Niederlanden.* Cologne: Pahl-Rugenstein.

Bukow, Wolf-Dietrich, and Roberto Llaryora. 1988. *Mitbürger aus der Fremde: Soziogenese ethnischer Minoritäten.* Opladen: Westdeutscher Verlag.

Bunz, Axel, and Caroline Neuenfeld. 1994. "Europäische Asyl- und Zuwanderungspolitik." *Aus Politik und Zeitgeschichte,* no. 48:37–45.

Burke, Edmund. 1987. *Reflections on the Revolution in France.* 1790. Indianapolis: Hackett.

Büsch, Otto, and James Sheehan, eds. 1985. *Die Rolle der Nation in der deutschen Geschichte und Gegenwart.* Berlin: Colloquium Verlag.

Carens, Joseph. 1987. "Aliens and Citizens: The Case for Open Borders." *The Review of Politics* 49, no. 2 (spring): 251–273.

——. 1989. "Membership and Morality: Admission to Citizenship in Liberal Democratic States." In *Immigration and the Politics of Citizenship in Europe and North America,* ed. William Rogers Brubaker, 31–50. Lanham, Md.: University Press of America.

——. 1990. "Difference and Domination: Reflections on the Relation between Pluralism and Equality." In *Majorities and Minorities,* ed. John W. Chapman and Alan Wertheimer, 226–250. New York: New York University Press.

——. 1992. "Migration and Morality: A Liberal Egalitarian Perspective." In *Free Movement: Ethical Issues in the Transnational Migration of People and of Money,* ed. Brian Barry and Robert E. Goodin, 25–47. University Park: Pennsylvania State University Press.

Castles, Stephen. 1989. *Migrant Workers and the Transformation of Western Societies.* Ithaca, N.Y.: Cornell University Press.

Castles, Stephen, and Mark J. Miller. 1993. *The Age of Migration: International Population Movements in the Modern World.* New York: Guilford.

Chaney, Elsa. 1981. "Migrant Workers and National Boundaries: A Cosmopolitan View." In *Boundaries,* ed. Peter Brown and Henry Shue, 37–78. Totowa, N.J.: Rowman and Littlefield.

Cholewinski, Ryszard. 1988. "State Duty toward Ethnic Minorities: Positive or Negative?" *Human Rights Quarterly* 10:344–371.

Cohen, Marshall, Thomas Nagel, and Thomas Scanlon, eds. 1977. *Equality and Preferential Treatment*. Princeton: Princeton University Press.

Cohn-Bendit, Daniel. 1993. *Heimat Babylon: Das Wagnis der multikulturellen Demokratie*. Hamburg: Hoffmann und Campe.

Conze, Werner. 1985. "'Deutschland' und 'deutsche Nation' als historische Begriffe." In *Die Rolle der Nation in der deutschen Geschichte und Gegenwart*, ed. Otto Büsch and James Sheehan, 21–38. Berlin: Colloquium Verlag.

Cortese, Anthony. 1990. *Ethnic Ethics*. Albany: State University of New York Press.

Cover, Robert. 1983. "Foreword: Nomos and Narrative." *Harvard Law Review* 97, no. 4:4–68.

Cranston, Maurice. 1989. "What Are Human Rights?" In *The Human Rights Reader*, ed. Barry Rubin and Walter Laqueur, 17–25. New York: Meridian.

Crawford, James, ed. 1988. *The Rights of Peoples*. Oxford: Clarendon Press.

Cu, Nguyen Trong. 1992. "Zur Situation der Ausländer in den neuen Bundesländern." *Zeitschrift für Ausländerrecht und Ausländerpolitik*, no. 1:20–24.

Dahl, Robert. 1989. *Democracy and Its Critics*. New Haven: Yale University Press.

Dench, Geoff. 1986. *Minorities in the Open Society: Prisoners of Ambivalence*. New York: Routledge and Kegan Paul.

Dikmen, Sinasi. 1990. "Ich bin kein Ausländer." In *Bericht '99* by the Federal Commissioner for the Integration of Foreign Workers and Their Family Members, 59–60. Bonn: Bundesbeauftragte für die Belange der Ausländer.

Doehring, Karl, and Josef Isensee. 1974. *Die staatsrechtliche Stellung der Ausländer in der Bundesrepublik Deutschland*. Berlin: de Gruyter.

Dohse, Knut. 1982. "Ausländerpolitik und betriebliche Ausländerdiskriminierung." Berlin: Internationales Institut für vergleichende Gesellschaftsforschung.

———. 1985. *Ausländische Arbeiter und bürgerlicher Staat: Genese und Funktion von staatlicher Ausländerpolitik und Ausländerrecht, vom Kaiserreich bis zur BRD*. 2nd ed. Berlin: EXpress Edition.

Donagan, Alan. 1993. "Common Morality and Kant's Enlightenment Project." In *Prospects for a Common Morality*, ed. Gene Outka and John P. Reeder Jr., 53–72. Princeton: Princeton University Press.

Donnelly, Jack. 1989. *Universal Human Rights in Theory and Practice*. Ithaca, N.Y.: Cornell University Press.

Dumont, Louis. 1986. *Essays on Individualism*. Chicago: University of Chicago Press.

Dunn, John. 1988. "Rights and Political Conflict." In *Civil Liberties in Conflict*, ed. Larry Gostin, 21–38. New York: Routledge.

Elias, Norbert and John L. Scotson. 1965. *The Established and the Outsiders: A Sociological Enquiry into Community Problems*. London: Macmillan.

Esser, Hartmut, ed. 1983. *Die fremden Mitbürger: Möglichkeiten und Grenzen der Integration von Ausländern*. Düsseldorf: Patmos.

Esser, Hartmut, and Jürgen Friedrichs, eds. 1990. *Generation und Identität: Theoretische und empirische Beiträge zur Migrationssoziologie.* Opladen: Westdeutscher Verlag.

Faul, Erwin. 1993. "Multikulturelle Gesellschaft in Deutschland?" In *Migration und Toleranz,* ed. Peter März, 42–66. Munich: Bayerische Landeszentrale für politische Bildungsarbeit.

Federal Commissioner for the Integration of Foreign Workers and Their Family Members. 1988. *Satzungen für Ausländerbeiräte und Ausländerausschüsse.* Bonn: Bundesbeauftragte für die Belange der Ausländer.

———. 1990. *Bericht '99: Zur Situation der ausländischen Arbeitnehmer und ihrer Familien — Bestandsaufnahme und Perspektiven für die 90er Jahre.* 2d ed. Bonn: Bundesbeauftragte für die Belange der Ausländer.

Federal Minister for Labor and Social Order. 1985. *Ausländerpolitik: Fakten, Rechte, Pflichten, Argumente.* Bonn: Bundesministerium für Arbeit und Sozialordnung.

Feinberg, Joel. 1980. *Rights, Justice, and the Bounds of Liberty: Essays in Social Philosophy.* Princeton: Princeton University Press.

———. 1988. "Liberalism, Community, and Tradition." *Tikkun* 3, no. 3 (May/June): 38–41, 116–120.

Fijalkowski, Jürgen. 1984. "Gastarbeiter als industrielle Reservarmee? Zur Bedeutung der Arbeitsimmigration für die wirtschaftliche und gesellschaftliche Entwicklung der Bundesrepublik Deutschland." *Archiv für Sozialgeschichte* 24:1–90.

———. 1991a. "Awareness of National Identity and Concepts of Citizenship in Germany: Ten Definitions and Theses on Trends of Change, and on the Recent Whirlpool." Unpublished manuscript.

———. 1991b. "Nationale Identität versus multikulturelle Gesellschaft: Entwicklungen der Problemlage und Alternativen in der Orientierung in der politischen Kultur der Bundesrepublik in der 80er Jahren." In *Die Bundesrepublik Deutschland in den 80er Jahren: Innenpolitik — politische Kultur — Aussenpolitik,* ed. Werner Süss. Leverkusen: Leske und Budrich.

Finnis, John. 1980. *Natural Law and Natural Rights.* Oxford: Clarendon Press.

Fischer, John M., ed. 1986. *Moral Responsibility.* Ithaca, N.Y.: Cornell University Press.

Fiss, Owen. 1976. "Groups and the Equal Protection Clause." *Philosophy and Public Affairs* 5:107–177.

Foucault, Michel. 1988. *History of Sexuality.* 1978. Vol. 1. Translated by Robert Hurley. New York: Vintage Books.

Fraenkel, Ernst. 1974. *Der Doppelstaat.* Frankfurt: Europäische Verlag.

Francis, Emerich K. 1983. "Einige grundsätzliche Erwägungen zur Integration von Ausländern." In *Die fremden Mitbürger,* ed. Hartmut Esser, 10–27. Düsseldorf: Patmos.

Franz, Fritz. 1990a. "Staatsangehörigkeit: Deutsch." In *Bericht '99* by the Federal

Commissioner for the Integration of Foreign Workers and Their Family Members, 343–352. Bonn: Bundesbeauftragte für die Belange der Ausländer.

———. 1990b. "Staatsrechtliche Aspekte der Doppelstaatsangehörigkeit in der Bundesrepublik Deutschland." In *Doppelte Staatsbürgerschaft* by the Berlin Commissioner for Foreigners' Affairs, 192–197. Berlin: Senatsverwaltung für Gesundheit und Soziales.

———. 1991. "Anmerkung." *Zeitschrift für Ausländerrecht und Ausländerpolitik,* no. 1:40–43.

Fraser, Nancy. 1989. *Unruly Practices: Power, Discourse, and Gender in Contemporary Social Theory.* Minneapolis: University of Minnesota Press.

Freeman, Michael. 1995. "Are There Collective Human Rights?" In *Politics and Human Rights,* ed. David Beetham, 25–40. Oxford: Blackwell.

Frey, Martin, and Volker Lubinski. 1987. *Probleme infolge hoher Ausländerkonzentration in ausgewählten europäischen Staaten.* Wiesbaden: Bundesinstitut für Bevölkerungsforschung.

Friedrich-Ebert-Stiftung. 1986. *Situation der ausländischen Arbeitnehmer und ihrer Familienangehörigen in der Bundesrepublik Deutschland: Repräsentativuntersuchung '85.* Bonn: Bundesminister für Arbeit und Sozialordnung.

Galanis, Georgios. 1989. *Migranten als Minorität im Spiegel der Presse.* Frankfurt: Lang.

Galston, William A. 1980. *Justice and the Human Good.* Chicago: University of Chicago Press.

———. 1991. *Liberal Purposes: Goods, Virtues, and Duties in the Liberal State.* Cambridge: Cambridge University Press.

Garet, Ronald. 1983. "Communality and Existence: The Rights of Groups." *Southern California Law Review* 54:1001–1075.

Geissler, Heiner. 1990. *Zugluft: Politik in stürmischer Zeit.* Munich: Bertelsmann.

Gellner, Ernest. 1983. *Nations and Nationalism.* Oxford: Blackwell.

Gerholm, Tomas, and Yngve Georg Lithman, eds. 1988. *The New Islamic Presence in Western Europe.* London: Mansell.

Germershausen, Andreas, and Wolf-Dieter Narr. 1988. *Flucht und Asyl: Berichte über Flüchtlingsgruppen.* Berlin: Edition Parabolis.

Gewirth, Alan. 1978. *Reason and Morality.* Chicago: University of Chicago Press.

———. 1982. *Human Rights: Essays on Justifications and Applications.* Chicago: University of Chicago Press.

Gierke, Otto. 1957. *Natural Law and the Theory of Society, 1500 to 1800.* Boston: Beacon Press.

Gilbert, Felix. 1984. *The End of the European Era: 1890 to the Present.* 3rd ed. New York: W. W. Norton.

Glazer, Nathan. 1975. *Affirmative Discrimination: Ethnic Inequality and Public Policy.* New York: Basic Books.

Glazer, Nathan, and Daniel Moynihan. 1976. *Ethnicity*. Cambridge: Cambridge University Press.

Goodin, Robert E. 1988. "What Is So Special about Our Fellow Countrymen?" *Ethics* 98 (July): 663–686.

Gough, J. W. 1978. *The Social Contract*. 2nd ed. Westport, Conn.: Greenwood Press.

Grawert, Rolf. 1973. *Staat und Staatsangehörigkeit*. Berlin: Duncker und Humblot.

———. 1984. "Staatsangehörigkeit und Staatsbürgerschaft." *Der Staat* 23, no. 2:179–204.

Groot, Gerard de. 1989. *Staatsangehörigkeit im Wandel*. Cologne: Carl Heymanns Verlag.

Gunsteren, Herman van. 1988. "Admission to Citizenship." *Ethics* 98 (June): 731–741.

———. 1994. "Four Conceptions of Citizenship." In *The Condition of Citizenship*, ed. Bart van Steenbergen, 36–48. London: Sage.

Haakonssen, Knud. 1996. *Natural Law and Moral Philosophy: From Grotius to the Scottish Enlightenment*. Cambridge: Cambridge University Press.

Habermas, Jürgen. 1987. *Eine Art Schadensabwicklung*. Frankfurt: Suhrkamp.

———. 1992. *Faktizität und Geltung: Beiträge zur Diskurstheorie des Rechts und des demokratischen Rechtsstaats*. Frankfurt: Suhrkamp.

———. 1994. "Struggles for Recognition in the Democratic Constitutional State." In *Multiculturalism: Examining the Politics of Recognition*, by Charles Taylor et al., and translated by Shierry Weber Nicholsen, 107–148. Princeton: Princeton University Press.

———. 1995. "Citizenship and National Identity: Some Reflections on the Future of Europe." In *Theorizing Citizenship*, ed. Ronald Beiner, 255–281. Albany: State University of New York Press.

Hagen, William. 1980. *Germans, Poles, and Jews: The Nationality Conflict in the Prussian East, 1772–1914*. Chicago: University of Chicago Press.

Hailbronner, Kay. 1989a. *Ausländerrecht: Ein Handbuch*. 2d ed. Heidelberg: C. F. Müller.

———. 1989b. "Citizenship and Nationhood in Germany." In *Immigration and the Politics of Citizenship in Europe and North America*, ed. William Rogers Brubaker, 67–80. Lanham, Md.: University Press of America.

———. 1995. "Die europäische Asylrechtsharmonisierung nach dem Vertrag von Maastricht." *Zeitschrift für Ausländerrecht und Ausländerpolitik*, no. 1:3–13.

Hammar, Thomas, ed. 1985. *European Immigration Policy*. Cambridge: Cambridge University Press.

———. 1989. "State, Nation, and Dual Citizenship." In *Immigration and the Politics of Citizenship in Europe and North America*, ed. William Rogers Brubaker, 81–95. Lanham, Md.: University Press of America.

———. 1990. *Democracy and the Nation State: Aliens, Denizens, and Citizens in a World of International Migration.* Aldershot, England: Avebury.

Hannum, Hurst. 1989. "The Limits of Sovereignty and Majority Rule: Minorities, Indigenous Peoples, and the Right to Autonomy." In *New Directions in Human Rights,* ed. Ellen Lutz et al., 3–24. Philadelphia: University of Pennsylvania Press.

Hassan, Riffat. 1991. "Muslim Women and Post-Patriarchal Islam." In *After Patriarchy: Feminist Transformations of the World Religions,* ed. Paula M. Cooey et al., 39–64. Maryknoll, N.Y.: Orbis Books.

Hauerwas, Stanley. 1981. *A Community of Character.* Notre Dame: University of Notre Dame Press.

Heater, Derek. 1990. *Citizenship: The Civic Ideal in World History, Politics, and Education.* New York: Longman.

Heckmann, Friedrich. 1981. *Die Bundesrepublik: Ein Einwanderungsland? Zur Soziologie der Gastarbeiterbevölkerung als Einwandererminorität.* Stuttgart: Klett-Cotta.

Hegel, Georg Wilhelm Friedrich. 1967. *Philosophy of Right.* 1819. Translated by T. M. Knox. Oxford: Oxford University Press.

Heidelberg Manifesto of June 17, 1981. 1986. *Im Schatten der Krise,* ed. Matthias von Hellfeld. Cologne: Pahl-Rugenstein.

Heisler, Martin, and Barbara Schmitter Heisler. 1990. "Citizenship—Old, New, and Changing." In *Dominant National Cultures and Ethnic Identities,* ed. Jürgen Fijalkowski et al., 91–128. Berlin: Freie Universität.

Heldmann, Hans Heinz. 1989. *Verwaltung versus Verfassung.* Frankfurt: Lang.

Hellfeld, Matthias von, ed. 1986. *Im Schatten der Krise: Rechtsextremismus, Neofaschismus und Ausländerfeindlichkeit in der Bundesrepublik.* Cologne: Pahl-Rugenstein.

Herbert, Ulrich. 1986. *Geschichte der Ausländerbeschäftigung in Deutschland.* Bonn: Dietz.

Hill, Greg. 1993. "Citizenship and Ontology in the Liberal State." *Michigan Journal of Political Science* 55 (winter): 67–84.

Hinsley, Francis H. 1986. *Sovereignty.* 2d ed. Cambridge: Cambridge University Press.

Hobsbawm, Eric J. 1990. *Nations and Nationalism since 1780: Programme, Myth, Reality.* Cambridge: Cambridge University Press.

Hoch, Martin. 1994. "Türkische politische Organisationen in der Bundesrepublik Deutschland." *Zeitschrift für Ausländerrecht und Ausländerpolitik,* no. 1:17–22.

Hoffmann, Lutz. 1990. *Die unvollendete Republik: Zwischen Einwanderungsland und deutschen Nationalstaat.* Cologne: Papy Rossa Verlag.

Hoffmann, Lutz, and Herbert Even. 1984. *Soziologie der Ausländerfeindlichkeit.* Weinheim: Bellz.

Hofmann, Gunter. 1990. "Grosses Wort, kleiner Geist." In *Ausländer, Aussiedler, Asyl in der Bundesrepublik Deutschland,* ed. Klaus Bade, 157. Hannover: Niedersächsische Landeszentrale für Politische Bildung.

Hohfeld, Wesley N. 1919. *Fundamental Legal Conceptions*. New Haven: Yale University Press.

Hollenbach, David. 1979. *Claims in Conflict: Retrieving and Renewing the Catholic Human Rights Tradition*. New York: Paulist Press.

Honneth, Axel, and Hans Joas. 1988. *Social Action and Human Nature*. Translated by Raymond Meyer. Cambridge: Cambridge University Press.

Huber, Bertold. 1987. "Die Beratung des Reichs- und Staatsangehörigkeitsgesetzes von 1913 im Deutschen Reichstag." In *Aufenthalt, Niederlassung, Einbürgerung,* eds. Klaus Barwig et al., 181–220. Baden-Baden: Nomos.

Ignatieff, Michael. 1984. *The Needs of Strangers*. London: Chatto and Windus.

———. 1995. "The Myth of Citizenship." In *Theorizing Citizenship,* ed. Ronald Beiner 1995, 53–78. Albany: State University of New York Press.

Internal Revenue Service (IRS). 1991. *Tax Guide for U.S. Citizens and Resident Aliens Abroad* (publication 54). Washington, D.C.: Department of the Treasury.

Ireland, Patrick. 1994. *The Policy Challenge of Ethnic Diversity*. Cambridge: Harvard University Press.

Jansen, Mechtild, and Sigrid Baringhorst, eds. 1994. *Politik der Multikultur: Vergleichende Perspektiven zu Einwanderung und Integration*. Baden-Baden: Nomos.

Jessurun d'Oliveira, Hans. 1990. "Tendenzen im Staatsangehörigkeitsrecht." *Zeitschrift für Ausländerrecht und Ausländerpolitik,* no. 3:114–119.

John, Barbara. 1987. "Ausländerstatus als Integrationshemnis." *Zeitschrift für Ausländerrecht und Ausländerpolitik,* no. 4:147–151.

Just, Wolf-Dieter, ed. 1993. *Politische und rechtliche Schritte gegen die Diskriminierung von ethnischen Minderheiten*. Mülheim: Evangelische Akademie.

Kälin, Walter, and Rupert Moser. 1989. *Migration aus der Dritten Welt: Ursachen und Wirkungen*. Bern: Verlag Paul Haupt.

Kammann, Karin. 1984. *Probleme mehrfacher Staatsangehörigkeit unter besonderer Berücksichtigung des Völkerrechts*. Frankfurt: Lang.

Kanstroom, Daniel. 1993. *"Wer Sind Wir Wieder?* Laws of Asylum, Immigration, and Citizenship in the Struggle for the Soul of the New Germany." *Yale Journal of International Law* 18, no. 1 (winter): 155–214.

Kant, Immanuel. 1964. *Groundwork of the Metaphysics of Morals*. 1785. Translated by H. J. Paton. New York: Harper and Row.

———. 1991. "On the Common Saying: 'This May Be True in Theory, but It Does Not Apply in Practice.'" 1793. In *Kant: Political Writings,* ed. Hans Reiss, 61–92. Cambridge: Cambridge University Press.

Karst, Kenneth. 1989. *Belonging to America: Equal Citizenship and the Constitution*. New Haven: Yale University Press.

Kaskin, Hakki. 1990. "Staatsbürgerschaft im Exil." In *Doppelte Staatsbürgerschaft* by the Berlin Commissioner for Foreigners' Affairs, 43–54. Berlin: Senatsverwaltung für Gesundheit und Soziales.

Khoury, Adel Theodor. 1985. *Islamische Minderheiten in der Diaspora*. Mainz: Grünewald.

Kimminich, Otto. 1985. *Rechtsprobleme der polyethnischen Staatsorganisation*. Mainz: Grünewald.

King, Desmond S., and Jeremy Waldron. 1988. "Citizenship, Social Citizenship, and the Defence of Welfare Provision," *British Journal of Political Science* 18:415–443.

Klein, Arne, ed. 1992. *Die Rede von der multikulturellen Gesellschaft*. Berlin: Kunstamt Kreuzberg.

Klimt, Andrea. 1989. "*Ausländerliteratur:* Minority Literature in the Federal Republic of Germany." *New German Critique*, no. 46 (winter): 71–103.

Koch-Arzberger, Claudia. 1985. *Die schwierige Integration: Die bundesdeutsche Gesellschaft und ihre fünf Millionen Ausländer*. Opladen: Westdeutscher Verlag.

Kocka, Jürgen. 1985. "Probleme der politischen Integration der Deutschen, 1867 bis 1945." In *Die Rolle der Nation in der deutschen Geschichte und Gegenwart*, ed. Otto Büsch and James Sheehan, 118–136. Berlin: Colloquium Verlag.

Kohn, Hans. 1967. *Prelude to Nation-States: The French and German Experience, 1789–1815*. Princeton: Princeton University Press.

Korte, Herman. 1982. *Cultural Identity and Structural Marginalization of Migrant Workers*. Strasbourg: European Science Foundation.

———. 1984. "Die etablierten Deutschen und ihre ausländischen Aussenseiter." In *Macht und Zivilisation: Materialien zu Norbert Elias' Zivilisationstheorie*, ed. Peter Gleichmann et al. Frankfurt: Suhrkamp.

Kristeva, Julia. 1993. *Nations without Nationalism*. Translated by Leon S. Roudiez. New York: Columbia University Press.

Krüger-Potratz, Marianne. 1991. *Anderssein gab es nicht: Ausländer und Minderheiten in der DDR*. Münster: Waxmann Verlag.

Kühne, Peter. 1995. "Europäische gewerkschaftliche Migrationspolitik." *Informationsdienst zur Ausländerarbeit*, no. 1:27–31.

Kühnhardt, Ludger. 1994. "Menschenrechte, Minderheitenschutz, und der Nationalstaat im KSZE-Prozess." *Aus Politik und Zeitgeschichte*, no. 47:11–21.

Kukathas, Chandran. 1992. "Are There Any Cultural Rights?" *Political Theory* 20, no. 1:105–139.

Kymlicka, Will. 1989. *Liberalism, Community, and Culture*. Oxford: Clarendon Press.

———. 1995. *Multicultural Citizenship*. Oxford: Oxford University Press.

Kymlicka, Will, and Wayne Norman. 1994. "Return of the Citizen: A Survey of Recent Work on Citizenship Theory." *Ethics* 104 (January): 352–381.

Leca, Jean. 1990. "Individualism and Citizenship." In *Individualism: Theories and Methods*, ed. Pierre Birnbaum and Jean Leca, 141–189. Oxford: Clarendon Press.

Leggewie, Claus. 1990. *Multi Kulti: Spielregeln für die Vielvölkerrepublik*. Berlin: Rotbuch.

Lepsius, M. Rainer. 1985. "The Nation and Nationalism in Germany." *Social Research* 52, no. 1 (spring): 45–64.

Lichtenberg, Judith. 1981. "National Boundaries and Moral Boundaries: A Cosmopolitan View." In *Boundaries,* ed. Peter Brown and Henry Shue, 79–100. Totowa, N.J.: Rowman and Littlefield.

Lijphart, Arend. 1977. *Democracy in Plural Societies*. New Haven: Yale University Press.

Little, David. 1993. "The Nature and Basis of Human Rights." In *Prospects for a Common Morality,* ed. Gene Outka and John P. Reeder Jr., 73–92. Princeton: Princeton University Press.

——. 1995. "Studying 'Religious Human Rights': Methodological Foundations." Unpublished manuscript.

Locke, John. 1967. *Two Treatises of Government*. 1690. Edited by Peter Laslett. New York: Cambridge University Press.

Lovibond, Sabina. 1983. *Realism and Imagination in Ethics*. Minneapolis: University of Minnesota Press.

Lucas, J. R. 1993. *Responsibility*. Oxford: Clarendon Press.

Lukas, J. Anthony. 1985. *Common Ground*. New York: Vintage.

Lüttinger, Paul. 1989. *Integration der Vertriebenen*. Frankfurt: Campus.

Lyotard, Jean-François. 1993. "The Other's Rights." In *On Human Rights,* ed. Steven Shute and Susan Hurley, 135–147. Princeton: Princeton University Press.

MacIntyre, Alasdair. 1984. *After Virtue: A Study in Moral Theory*. 2d ed. Notre Dame: University of Notre Dame Press.

——. 1995. "Is Patriotism a Virtue?" In *Theorizing Citizenship,* ed. Ronald Beiner, 209–228. Albany: State University of New York Press.

Macpherson, C. B. 1966. *The Real World of Democracy*. Oxford: Clarendon Press.

Mager, Ute. 1992. "Möglichkeiten und Grenzen rechtlicher Massnahmen gegen die Diskriminierung von Ausländern." *Zeitschrift für Ausländerrecht und Ausländerpolitik,* no. 4:170–174.

Makarov, Alexander N. 1971. *Deutsches Staatsangehörigkeitsrecht: Kommentar.* 2d ed. Frankfurt: Metzner.

Mandel, Ruth. 1989. "Turkish Headscarves and the 'Foreigner Problem': Constructing Difference through Emblems of Identity." *New German Critique,* no. 46 (winter): 27–46.

Mann, Michael. 1987. "Ruling Class Strategies and Citizenship." *Sociology* 21, no. 3 (August): 339–354.

Manville, Philip Brook. 1990. *The Origins of Citizenship in Ancient Athens*. Princeton: Princeton University Press.

Maritain, Jacques. 1951. *Man and the State*. Chicago: University of Chicago Press.

Marshall, T. H. 1964. "Citizenship and Social Class." In *Class, Citizenship, and Social Development*. Garden City, N.J.: Doubleday.

May, Larry. 1987. *The Morality of Groups*. Notre Dame: University of Notre Dame Press.

———. 1992. *Sharing Responsibility*. Chicago: University of Chicago Press.

May, Larry, and Stacey Hoffman, eds. 1991. *Collective Responsibility: Five Decades of Debate in Theoretical and Applied Ethics*. Savage, Md.: Rowman and Littlefield.

Meehan, Elizabeth. 1993. *Citizenship and the European Community*. London: Sage.

Meier-Braun, Karl-Heinz, and Yüksal Pazarkaya, eds. 1983. *Die Türken: Berichte und Information zum besseren Verständnis der Türken in Deutschland*. Frankfurt: Ullstein.

Meinecke, Friedrich. 1908. *Weltbürgertum und Nationalstaat: Studien zur Genesis des deutschen Nationalstaates*. Munich: Oldenbourg.

Merleau-Ponty, Maurice. 1962. *Phenomenology of Perception*. Translated by Colin Smith. London: Routledge and Kegan Paul.

Merten, Klaus. 1986. *Das Bild der Ausländer in der deutschen Presse*. Frankfurt: Dagyeli.

Miksch, Jürgen, ed. 1983. *Multikulturelles Zusammenleben: Theologische Erfahrungen*. Frankfurt: Lembeck.

Mill, John Stuart. 1978. *Considerations on Representative Government*. 1861. Indianapolis: Bobbs-Merrill.

Minogue, Kenneth. 1995. "Two Concepts of Citizenship." In *Citizenship East and West*, eds. André Liebich et al., 9–22. New York: Kegan Paul International.

Minority Rights Group. 1991. *Minorities and Autonomy in Western Europe*. London: Minority Rights Group.

Moore, Barrington Jr. 1978. *Injustice: The Social Bases of Obedience and Revolt*. New York: Macmillan.

Neumann, Johannes, ed. 1987. *Toleranz und Repression: Zur Lage religiöser Minderheiten in modernen Gesellschaften*. Frankfurt: Campus.

Nino, Carlos Santiago. 1991. *The Ethics of Human Rights*. Oxford: Clarendon Press.

Nipperdey, Thomas. 1983. *Deutsche Geschichte 1800–1866: Bürgerwelt und starker Staat*. Munich: Beck.

Nuscheler, Franz. 1988. *Migration-Flucht-Asyl*. Tübingen: University of Tübingen Press.

Oberndörfer, Dieter. 1990. "Freizügigkeit als Chance für Europa: Europa als neuer Nationalstaat oder als offene Republik." In *Bericht '99* by the Federal Commissioner for the Integration of Foreign Workers and Their Family Members, 301–306. Bonn: Bundesbeauftragte für die Belange der Ausländer.

Okyayuz, Mehmet. 1989. *Entwicklung und Funktion staatlicher Ausländerpolitik in der Bundesrepublik Deutschland*. Berlin: Verlag für Wissenschaft und Bildung.

Oldfield, Adrian. 1990. *Citizenship and Community: Civic Republicanism and the Modern World*. London: Routledge.

Otto, Karl A., ed. 1990. *Westwärts — Heimwärts? Aussiedlerpolitik zwischen "Deutschtumelei" und "Verfassungsauftrag."* Bielefeld: AJZ.

Outka, Gene, and John P. Reeder Jr., eds. 1993. *Prospects for a Common Morality*. Princeton: Princeton University Press.

Özcan, Ertekin. 1989. *Türkische Immigrantenorganisationen in der Bundesrepublik Deutschland*. Berlin: Hitit-Verlag.

Pacini, David. 1987. *The Cunning of Modern Religious Thought*. Philadelphia: Fortress.

Passerin d'Entreves, Alessandro. 1970. *Natural Law*. 2d ed. London: Hutchinson's University Library.

Philpott, Daniel. 1995. "In Defense of Self-Determination." *Ethics* 105, no. 2:352–385.

Pitsela, Angelika. 1986. *Straffälligkeit und Viktimisierung ausländischer Minderheiten in der BRD*. Freiburg: Max-Planck-Institut für Ausländisches und Internationales Strafrecht.

Pocock, J. G. A. 1975. *The Machiavellian Moment*. Princeton: Princeton University Press.

———. 1995. "The Ideal of Citizenship since Classical Times." In *Theorizing Citizenship*, ed. Ronald Beiner, 29–52. Albany: State University of New York Press.

Pollis, Adamantia, and Peter Schwab. 1979. *Human Rights: Cultural and Ideological Perspectives*. New York: Praeger.

Pöschl, Angelika, and Peter Schmuck. 1984. *Die Rückkehr — Ende einer Illusion: Türkische Gastarbeiterfamilien in der Bundesrepublik Deutschland und das Problem ihrer Rückkehr in die Türkei*. Munich: Deutsches Jugendinstitut.

Puskeppeleit, Jürgen, and Dietrich Thränhardt. 1990. *Vom betreuten Ausländer zum gleichberechtigten Bürger*. Freiburg im Breisgau: Lambertus-Verlag.

Quaritsch, Helmut. 1981. *Einwanderungsland Bundesrepublik Deutschland? Aktuelle Reformfragen des Ausländerrechtes*. Munich: Carl Friedrich von Siemens Stiftung.

Radtke, Frank-Olaf. 1993. "Multikulturalismus — Ein Gegengift gegen Ausländerfeindlichkeit und Rassismus?" In *Zwischen Nationalstaat und multikultureller Gesellschaft*, ed. Manfred Hessler, 91–104. Berlin: Hitit-Verlag.

Rae, Douglas, Douglas Yates, Jennifer Hochschild, Joseph Morone, and Carol Fessler. 1989. *Equalities*. 2d ed. New Haven: Yale University Press.

Ramazanoglu, Caroline. 1989. *Feminism and the Contradictions of Oppression*. London: Routledge.

Rau, Hans. 1990. "Doppelte Staatsangehörigkeit — ein Einbürgerungshindernis?" In *Doppelte Staatsbürgerschaft* by the Berlin Commissioner for Foreigners' Affairs, 198–206. Berlin: Senatsverwaltung für Gesundheit und Soziales.

Rawls, John. 1993. "The Law of Peoples." In *On Human Rights*, ed. Steven Shute and Susan Hurley, 41–82. New York: Basic Books.

Raz, Joseph. 1986. *The Morality of Freedom*. Oxford: Clarendon Press.

Reiman, Jeffrey. 1990. *Justice and Modern Moral Philosophy*. New Haven: Yale University Press.

Reuter, Lutz-Rainer, and Martin Dodenhoeft. 1988. *Arbeitsmigration und gesellschaftliche Entwicklung*. Wiesbaden: Steiner-Verlag.

Riley, Patrick. 1982. *Will and Political Legitimacy*. Cambridge: Harvard University Press.

Rist, Ray. 1978. *Guestworkers in Germany: The Prospects for Pluralism*. New York: Praeger.

Rittstieg, Helmut. 1981. *Wahlrecht für Ausländer: Verfassungsfragen der Teilnahme von Ausländern an den Wahlen in den Wohngemeinde*. Königstein: Athenäum.

———. 1988. "Wanderarbeiter und Demokratie: Zum kommunalen Wahlrecht ausländischer Arbeitnehmer." *Information zum Ausländerrecht*, no. 3:65–67.

———. 1990. "Doppelte Staatsangehörigkeit im Volkerrecht." In *Doppelte Staatsbürgerschaft* by the Berlin Commissioner for Foreigners' Affairs, 131–140. Berlin: Senatsverwaltung für Gesundheit und Soziales.

———. 1993. "Einwanderung als gesellschaftliche Herausforderung." *Informationsbrief Ausländerrecht*, no. 4:117–121.

Roche, Maurice. 1992. *Rethinking Citizenship: Welfare, Ideology, and Change in Modern Society*. Cambridge, England: Polity Press.

Rokkan, Stein. 1975. "Dimensions of State Formation and Nation-Building: A Possible Paradigm for Research on Variations within Europe." In *The Formation of National States in Western Europe*, ed. Charles Tilly, 562–600. Princeton: Princeton University Press.

Rorty, Richard. 1993. "Human Rights, Rationality, and Sentimentality." In *On Human Rights*, ed. Steven Shute and Susan Hurley, 111–134. New York: Basic Books.

Rousseau, Jean-Jacques. 1947. *The Social Contract*. Edited by Ernest Barker. New York: Oxford University Press.

Rubin, Barry, and Walter Laqueur, eds. 1989. *The Human Rights Reader*. New York: Meridian.

Safran, William. 1986. "Islamization in Western Europe: Political Consequences and Historical Parallels." In *From Foreign Workers to Settlers? Transnational Migration and the Emergence of New Minorities*. Annals of the American Academy of Political and Social Sciences. Beverly Hills, Calif.: Sage.

Sandel, Michael, ed. 1984. *Liberalism and Its Critics*. New York: New York University Press.

Sanders, Douglas. 1991. "Collective Rights." *Human Rights Quarterly* 13:368–386.

Scarry, Elaine. 1985. *The Body in Pain: The Making and Unmaking of the World*. Oxford: Oxford University Press.

Schäfer, Hermann. 1985. *Betriebliche Ausländerdiskriminierung und gewerkschaftliche Antidiskriminierungspolitik*. Berlin: EXpress Edition.

Schiffer, Eckart. 1992. "Wie stellt sich Europa zur Einwanderung?" *Zeitschrift für Ausländerrecht und Ausländerpolitik*, no. 3:107–111.

Schlaffke, Winfried, and Rüdiger Voss, eds. 1982. *Vom Gastarbeiter zum Mitarbeiter: Ursachen, Folgen, und Konsequenzen der Ausländerbeschäftigung in Deutschland*. Cologne: Informedia Verlags.

Schmalz-Jacobsen, Cornelia Holger Hinte, and Georgios Tsapanos. 1993. *Einwanderung — und dann? Perspektiven einer neuen Ausländerpolitik*. Munich: Knaur.

Schmid, Thomas. 1990. "Multikulturelle Gesellschaft: Grosser linker Ringelpiez mit Anfassen." In *Ausländer, Aussiedler, Asyl in der Bundesrepublik Deutschland*, ed. Klaus Bade, 156–157. Hannover: Niedersächsische Landeszentrale für Politische Bildung.

Schmitt, Carl. 1970. *Verfassungslehre*. 5th ed. Berlin: Duncker und Humblot.

Schöneberg, Ulrike. 1993. *Gestern Gastarbeiter, morgen Minderheit*. Frankfurt: Lang.

Schuck, Peter. 1989. "Membership in the Liberal Polity: The Devaluation of American Citizenship." In *Immigration and the Politics of Citizenship in Europe and North America*, ed. William Rogers Brubaker, 51–65. Lanham, Md.: University Press of America.

Schuck, Peter, and Rogers Smith. 1985. *Citizenship without Consent: Illegal Aliens in the American Polity*. New Haven: Yale University Press.

Schulte, Axel, ed. 1985. *Ausländer in der Bundesrepublik: Integration, Marginalisierung, Identität*. Frankfurt: Materialis-Verlag.

———. 1990. "Multikulturelle Gesellschaft: Chance, Ideologie, oder Bedrohung." *Aus Politik und Zeitgeschichte*, no. 23–24 (June 1): 3–15.

Scott, James C. 1990. *Domination and the Arts of Resistance: Hidden Transcripts*. New Haven: Yale University Press.

Scruton, Roger. 1992. "The First Person Plural." In *The Worth of Nations*, ed. Claudio Véliz, 82–95. Boston: Boston University Press.

Seidler, Victor J. 1991. *The Moral Limits of Modernity: Love, Inequality, and Oppression*. London: Macmillan.

Sen, Faruk, and Gerhard Jahn. 1985. *Wahlrecht für Ausländer: Stand und Entwicklung in Europa*. Frankfurt: Dagyeli.

Shapiro, Ian. 1986. *The Evolution of Rights in Liberal Theory*. Cambridge: Cambridge University Press.

Sheehan, James. 1985. "The Problem of the Nation in German History." In *Die Rolle der Nation in der deutschen Geschichte und Gegenwart*, ed. Otto Büsch and James Sheehan, 3–20. Berlin: Colloquium Verlag.

———. 1989. *German History 1770–1866*. Oxford: Clarendon Press.

Sherwin-White, A. N. 1973. *The Roman Citizenship*. Oxford: Oxford University Press.

Shklar, Judith. 1969. *Men and Citizens: A Study of Rousseau's Social Theory*. Cambridge: Harvard University Press.

———. 1986. "Injustice, Injury, and Inequality: An Introduction." In *Justice and Equality Here and Now*, ed. Frank S. Lucash, 13–33. Ithaca, N.Y.: Cornell University Press.

———. 1990. *The Faces of Injustice*. New Haven: Yale University Press.

———. 1991. *American Citizenship: The Quest for Inclusion*. Cambridge: Harvard University Press.

Shue, Henry. 1980. *Basic Rights: Subsistence, Affluence, and U.S. Foreign Policy*. Princeton: Princeton University Press.

Shute, Steven, and Susan Hurley, eds. 1993. *On Human Rights*. New York: Basic Books.

Sieveking, Klaus, Klaus Barwig, Klaus Lörcher, and Christoph Schumacher. 1989. *Das Kommunalwahlrecht für Ausländer*. Baden-Baden: Nomos.

Sievering, Ulrich, ed. 1981. *Integration oder Partizipation? Ausländerwahlrecht in der BRD zwischen rechtlichen Möglichkeiten und politischer Notwendigkeit*. Frankfurt: Haag und Herchen.

Sigler, Jay. 1983. *Minority Rights: A Comparative Analysis*. Westport, Conn.: Greenwood Press.

Sinclair, R. K. 1988. *Democracy and Participation in Athens*. Cambridge: Cambridge University Press.

Smiley, Marion. 1992. *Moral Responsibility and the Boundaries of Community: Power and Accountability from a Pragmatic Point of View*. Chicago: University of Chicago Press.

Smith, Anthony D. 1986. *The Ethnic Origins of Nations*. Oxford: Blackwell.

Smith, Helmut W. 1995. *German Nationalism and Religious Conflict*. Princeton: Princeton University Press.

Soysal, Yasemin N. 1994. *Limits of Citizenship: Migrants and Postnational Membership in Europe*. Chicago: University of Chicago Press.

Sternberger, Dolf. 1990. *Verfassungspatriotismus*. Frankfurt: Suhrkamp.

Stöcker, Hans A. 1989. "Nationales Selbstbestimmungsrecht und Ausländerwahlrecht." *Der Staat* 28, no. 1:70–90.

Stopp, Alexander. 1994. *Die Behandlung ethnischer Minderheiten als Gleichheitsproblem*. Baden-Baden: Nomos.

Stöss, Richard. 1989. *Die extreme Rechte in der Bundesrepublik: Entwicklung — Ursachen — Gegenmassnahmen*. Opladen: Westdeutscher Verlag.

Struck, Manfred, ed. 1982. *Ausländer — Unsere Sündenböcke? Ausländerfeindlichkeit und Rechtsextremismus*. Bonn: Friedrich-Ebert-Stiftung.

Sutor, Bernhard. 1995. "Nationalbewusstsein und universale politische Ethik." *Aus Politik und Zeitgeschichte*, no. 10:3–13.

Tajfel, Henri. 1981. *Human Groups and Social Categories: Studies in Social Psychology.* Cambridge: Cambridge University Press.

Tamir, Yael. 1993. *Liberal Nationalism.* Princeton: Princeton University Press.

Taylor, Charles. 1985. "The Nature and Scope of Distributive Justice." In *Philosophy and the Human Sciences,* 289–317. Cambridge: Cambridge University Press.

Thomas, George M., John W. Meyer, Francisco O. Ramirez, and John Boli, ed. 1987. *Institutional Structure: Constituting State, Society, and the Individual.* Beverly Hills, Calif.: Sage.

Thomä-Venske, Hans. 1988. "The Religious Life of Muslims in Berlin." In *The New Islamic Presence in Western Europe,* ed. Tomas Gerholm and Yngve Georg Lithman, 78–87. London: Mansell.

Thränhardt, Dietrich, ed. 1986. *Ausländerpolitik und Ausländerintegration in Belgien, den Niederlanden, und der Bundesrepublik Deutschland.* Düsseldorf: Landeszentrale für Politische Bildung.

Tilly, Charles, ed. 1975a. *The Formation of National States in Western Europe.* Princeton: Princeton University Press.

――. 1975b. "Reflections on the History of European State-Making." In *The Formation of National States in Western Europe,* ed. Charles Tilly, 3–83. Princeton: Princeton University Press.

Tremmel, Hans. 1992. *Grundrecht Asyl: Die Antwort der christlichen Sozialethik.* Freiburg: Herder.

Troeltsch, Ernst. 1925. "Die deutsche Idee von der Freiheit." In *Deutscher Geist und Westeuropa,* 80–107. Tübingen: University of Tübingen Press.

Tsiakolos, Georgios. 1990. "Multikulturelle Gesellschaft: Bedrohung oder Hoffnung?" In *Ausländer, Aussiedler, Asyl in der Bundesrepublik Deutschland,* ed. Klaus Bade, 151. Hannover: Niedersachsische Landeszentrale für Politische Bildung.

Tuck, Richard. 1979. *Natural Rights Theories: Their Origin and Development.* Cambridge: Cambridge University Press.

Turner, Bryan S. 1986. *Citizenship and Capitalism: The Debate over Reformism.* London: Allen and Unwin.

――. 1993. "Outline of the Theory of Human Rights." In *Citizenship and Social Theory,* ed. Bryan S. Turner, 162–190. London: Sage Publications.

Turpin, Dominique. 1987. "An EC Policy for Foreigners?" In *Ausländerrecht und Ausländerpolitik in Europa,* ed. Manfred Zuleeg, 69–100. Baden-Baden: Nomos.

Van den Berghe, Pierre. 1981. *The Ethnic Phenomenon.* New York: Elsevier.

Van Dyke, Vernon. 1985. *Human Rights, Ethnicity, and Discrimination.* Westport, Conn.: Greenwood Press.

Vattel, Emerich de. 1805. *The Law of Nations.* Northampton, England: S. and E. Butler.

Veiter, Theodor. 1970. *System eines internationalen Volksgruppenrechts.* Vienna: Braumüller.

Vernon, Richard. 1986. *Citizenship and Order: Studies in French Political Thought.* Toronto: University of Toronto Press.

Vitoria, Francisco de. 1917. *De Indis Relectio Prior.* Translated by Ernest Nys. Washington, D.C.: The Carnegie Institution.

Waldron, Jeremy. 1987. *Nonsense upon Stilts: Bentham, Burke, and Marx on the Rights of Man.* New York: Methuen.

———. 1993. "Can Communal Rights Be Human Rights?" In *Liberal Rights: Collected Papers,* 339–369. Cambridge: Cambridge University Press.

Walker, R. B. J., and Saul H. Mendlovitz, eds. 1990. *Contending Sovereignties: Redefining Political Values.* Boulder, Colo.: Lynne Rienner Publishers.

Walzer, Michael. 1970. *Obligations: Essays on Disobedience, War, and Citizenship.* Cambridge: Harvard University Press.

———. 1974. "Civility and Civic Virtue in Contemporary America." *Social Research* 41, no. 4 (winter): 593–611.

———. 1977. *Just and Unjust Wars.* New York: Basic Books.

———. 1979. "The Moral Standing of States: A Response to Four Critics." In *A Philosophy and Public Affairs Reader.* Princeton: Princeton University Press.

———. 1983. *Spheres of Justice: A Defense of Pluralism and Equality.* New York: Basic Books.

———. 1989. "Citizenship." In *Political Innovation and Conceptual Change,* ed. Terence Ball et al., 211–219. Cambridge: Cambridge University Press.

———. 1990. "Nation and Universe." In *The Tanner Lectures on Human Values,* ed. Grethe B. Peterson, 509–556. Salt Lake City: University of Utah Press.

———. 1993. "Exclusion, Injustice, and the Democratic State." *Dissent* (winter): 55–64.

———. 1994a. "Shared Meanings in a Poly-Ethnic Democratic Setting: A Response." *Journal of Religious Ethics* 22, no. 2 (winter): 401–405.

———. 1994b. *Thick and Thin: Moral Argument at Home and Abroad.* Notre Dame: University of Notre Dame Press.

Waters, Malcolm. 1989. "Citizenship and the Constitution of Structured Social Inequality." *International Journal of Comparative Sociology* 30, no. 3–4:159–180.

Weber, Albrecht. 1993. "Einwanderungs- und Asylpolitik nach Maastricht." *Zeitschrift für Ausländerrecht und Ausländerpolitik,* no. 1:11–18.

Weil, Simone. 1958. *Oppression and Liberty.* Translated by Arthur Wills and John Petrie. London: Routledge and Kegan Paul.

Weisbrot, Robert. 1990. *Freedom Bound: A History of America's Civil Rights Movement.* New York: W. W. Norton.

Whelan, Frederick. 1981. "Citizenship and the Right to Leave." *American Political Science Review* 75:636–653.

Wichmann, Birgit. 1989. *Demokratisch gewählte Ausländerbeiräte: Untersuchungen am Beispiel Göttingen und Kassel.* Felsberg: Migro.

Wihtol de Wenden, Catherine. 1987. *Citoyenneté, Nationalité, et Immigration.* Paris: Arcantere.

Williams, Bernard. 1973. "The Idea of Equality." In *Problems of the Self: Philosophical Papers 1956–1972.* Cambridge: Cambridge University Press.

Wilpert, Czarina, ed. 1988a. *Entering the Working World: Following the Descendants of Europe's Immigrant Labor Force.* Aldershot, England: Gower.

———. 1988b. "Religion and Ethnicity: Orientations, Perceptions, and Strategies among Turkish Alevi and Sunni Migrants in Berlin." In *The New Islamic Presence in Western Europe,* ed. Tomas Gerholm and Yngve Georg Lithman, 88–106. London: Mansell.

Winkler, Beate, ed. 1992. *Zukunftsangst Einwanderung.* Munich: Beck.

Wirsing, Robert. 1983. *The Protection of Ethnic Minorities.* Westport, Conn.: Greenwood Press.

Wolgast, Elizabeth H. 1987. "Why Justice Isn't an Ideal." In *The Grammar of Justice,* 125–146. Ithaca, N.Y.: Cornell University Press.

Wolin, Sheldon. 1961. *Politics and Vision: Continuity and Innovation in Western Political Thought.* London: Harrap.

Wollenschläger, Michael. 1994. "Rechtsfragen eines Konzeptes gegen Ausländerdiskriminierung." *Zeitschrift für Ausländerrecht und Ausländerpolitik,* no. 1:10–16.

Wood, Ellen Meiksins. 1988. *Peasant-Citizen and Slave: The Foundations of Athenian Democracy.* London: Verso.

Woydt, Johann. 1987. *Ausländische Arbeitskräfte in Deutschland: Vom Kaiserreich bis zur Bundesrepublik.* Heilbronn: Distel.

Young, Iris Marion. 1990. *Justice and the Politics of Difference.* Princeton: Princeton University Press.

Zuleeg, Manfred, ed. 1987. *Ausländerrecht und Ausländerpolitik in Europa.* Baden-Baden: Nomos.

France, 11–12, 145, 175 n.8, 176 n.17
Free Democratic Party (FDP), 42–43,
    50, 54–55, 58
French Revolution, 12, 101

Geissler, Heiner, 50
Gellner, Ernest, 85
German Basic Law, 25–26, 30, 153, 170;
    and local voting rights, 62–64
German Federation of Trade and Labor
    Unions (DGB), 43
Gierke, Otto, 86, 198 n.25
Goethe, Johann Wolfgang von, 12
Greens, the, 42–43, 58, 64
Group rights, ix, 115–16, 161–71; col-
    lective, 148, 168; corporate, 148, 165;
    internal, 166; moral foundations of,
    162–65; and religious freedom, 194
    n.52; subject of, 199 n.34; versus indi-
    vidual rights, 166, 199 n.26. See also
    Human rights
Groups: as constitutive of identity and
    agency, 164; moral character of, 164–
    65; ontological status of, 71, 73, 85–
    87, 198 n.25
"Guestworkers," 1, 4, 31, 46; compared
    to metics, 90, 122; German policy to-
    ward, 41–45, 54–58; integration of,
    47–50; terminology regarding, 178
    n.25. See also Foreign workers

Habermas, Jürgen, 72, 185 n.23, 186
    n.29, 197 n.15
Hammar, Thomas, 155
Hegel, Georg Wilhelm Friedrich, 13, 97,
    110, 175 n.10
Heidelberg Manifesto, 73, 86
Herder, Johann Gottfried von, 12, 84
Historikerstreit, 16
Hobsbawm, Eric, 85

Hoffmann, Lutz, 14, 53
Holocaust, 32, 179 n.2
Holy Roman Empire, 11
Homogeneity, cultural, 125
Hooker, Richard, 84
Human rights, 101, 129–30, 136, 145–
    46; applied to groups, 134–35; "ba-
    sic," 134; conflicts involving, 194 n.55;
    defined, 135; human nature as basis
    for, 130, 189 n.24; individualist bias
    regarding, 194 n.54; and political rep-
    resentation, 75–76; positive versus
    negative, 194 n.56; as rights to non-
    domination and self-determination,
    115, 129–35. See also Group rights;
    Political membership: as human
    right

Ignatieff, Michael, 85
Immigration: Germany as country of,
    45–47, 180 n.8; Habermas on, 197
    n.15; illegal immigration, 159, 195
    n.63; Walzer on, 119–22
Inequality, 112–13
Inländer: distinguished from Ausländer,
    10, 21, 22–27; rights of, 23–24. See
    also Ausländer
Integration versus assimilation, 47–50,
    180 n.9
Inuits, 167
Isay, Ernst, 23
Islam, 169–71

Japanese Americans, internment of,
    155
Jefferson, Thomas, 95
Jews, 33, 177 n.22; exclusion from Ger-
    man civil service, 24
Junker class, 17
Jus gentium, 101

William A. Barbieri Jr. is Assistant Professor of Social Ethics at the
Catholic University of America.

Library of Congress Cataloging-in-Publication Data
Barbieri, William A.
Ethics of citizenship : immigration and group rights in Germany /
William A. Barbieri, Jr.
p.   cm.
Includes bibliographical references and index.
ISBN 0-8223-2057-6 (cloth : alk. paper). — ISBN 0-8223-2071-1
(pbk. : alk. paper)
1. Alien labor — Germany — Social conditions.   2. Immigrants —
Germany — Social conditions.   3. Political rights — Germany.
I. Title.
HD8458.A2B28   1998
323.3'291 — dc21   97-40979   CIP